T0068267

Praise for *The*

"It is a measure of [Sokolove's] achievement—and his subjects' own wisdom about their experiences—that Darryl Strawberry's melodramatic saga does not dominate this volume; it is simply another strand in this choral narrative. *The Ticket Out* does for baseball what the 1994 movie *Hoop Dreams* did for basketball."
— Michiko Kakutani, *The New York Times*

"More than the sad saga of Darryl Strawberry, *The Ticket Out* examines and explodes an American myth: that athletic skill offers a magic shortcut to happiness and success. Mike Sokolove is a journalist who finds in sports a window to deeper, more important things. His affectionate but clear-eyed story reaffirms that character (not talent) is destiny, and that even the most amazingly gifted athlete remains a product of his community, his family, and most important, himself."
— Mark Bowden, author of *Black Hawk Down*

"When people say sports are more than just games and deeper than entertainment, they have smart, heartfelt books like [*The Ticket Out*] to back them up . . . It's a moving book that makes you love baseball and mistrust it at the same time."
— Eric Neel, ESPN.com

"*The Ticket Out* is an emotional detective story about baseball, moving and thought-provoking. It is a first-rate book for anyone who seeks to understand the serious human narrative we mistakenly call a game."
— Sally Jenkins, coauthor with Lance Armstrong of *It's Not About the Bike* and *Every Second Counts*

"The city of Los Angeles is one of Sokolove's most fascinating characters . . . Sokolove is masterful at exploring the chemistry of Crenshaw High School."
— *The Atlanta Journal-Constitution*

"Superb investigative interviewing provides a fascinating narrative as to how athletes growing up in that environment view sports and their futures."
— *The Los Angeles Daily News*

"Passionate, heartbreaking, yet sympathetic . . . This is the most insightful account written so far about the roots of Strawberry's troubled life."

—*Publishers Weekly*

"A story of promise wasted and dreams deferred . . . a narrative defined by its compassionate, clear-eyed tone."

—*Entertainment Weekly*

"A sad, powerful, thoughtful, totally engrossing work that's as much sociology treatise as sports book."

—*The Chicago Tribune Special Baseball Issue*

"A sad but fascinating story."

—*San Jose Mercury News*

"[Sokolove's] plainspoken, journalistic writing style steers clear of the fussy prose and scene-setting that dogs other baseball books. Even if it had nothing to do with the game, even if Sokolove had just followed the varied trajectories of nine random friends from the Crenshaw yearbook, *The Ticket Out* would still make a fine survey of poverty and race in America."

—*The Onion*

"A worthwhile read and Sokolove is a top-notch reporter."

—*The Daily News* (New York)

"A stunning work of journalism . . . In many ways, this book is classic new journalism as defined by Tom Wolfe . . . It's simply journalism at its best: illuminating a topic to give you a deeper understanding of the main characters and the subject. And as any purist will tell you, to understand baseball is to understand life itself."

—*Rocky Mountain News*

"Sokolove crafts these stories with a casual but insightful grace that will send shivers up the spine of any baseball fan but still touch a reader who's never heard of Ted Williams. *The Ticket Out* is one of the saddest books you'll never want to put down."

—*The Washingtonian Magazine Online*

"An absorbing look at the 1979 Crenshaw High School team."

"Sokolove has managed the extraordinary feat of writing an inspirational sports book that is neither sentimental nor didactic."

"The best baseball books transcend baseball. *Moneyball* by Michael Lewis, for example . . . *The Ticket Out* is such a book. It's as heartbreaking as the game . . ."

"Michael Sokolove carefully examines the American Dream through sport."

"*The Ticket Out* is a well-written historical account of the 1979 Crenshaw High School baseball team and its players . . . The book is factually based without losing the reader's interest . . . it's certainly worth any baseball fan's time."

"Sokolove's narrative isn't limited simply to a historical retrospective and rote where-are-they-now recitations."

"The understanding or sympathy readers derive about Strawberry's life is only part of this story. There are 17 other 'Boys of Crenshaw,' and this book's where-are-they-now aspect is very engaging . . . It's a boys-to-men baseball detective story, with few players whose names you will recognize, but several you will not soon forget."

"Each [player] had an interesting story, and Sokolove weaves it all together compellingly . . . In an era of many good baseball books, this is one of the better ones."

Also by Michael Sokolove

Hustle: The Myth, Life, and Lies of Pete Rose

The Ticket Out

Darryl Strawberry
and the Boys of Crenshaw

MICHAEL SOKOLOVE

SIMON & SCHUSTER PAPERBACKS

NEW YORK   LONDON   TORONTO   SYDNEY

SIMON & SCHUSTER PAPERBACKS
Rockefeller Center
1230 Avenue of the Americas
New York, NY 10020

First Simon & Schuster paperback edition 2006

Portions of this book were first published in an article in *The New York Times Magazine*
entitled "An American Tragedy" by Michael Sokolove, dated April 15, 2001.

For information regarding special discounts for bulk purchases,
please contact Simon & Schuster Special Sales at 1-800-456-6798
or business@simonandschuster.com

Original hardcover design by Charles Kreloff

Manufactured in the United States of America

1   3   5   7   9   10   8   6   4   2

The Library of Congress cataloged the original hardcover edition as follows:
Sokolove, Michael Y.
The ticket out : Darryl Strawberry and the boys of Crenshaw / Michael Sokolove.
        p.   cm.
Includes bibliographical references and index.
1. Strawberry, Darryl.   2. Baseball players—United States—Biography.
3. Crenshaw High School (Los Angeles, Calif.)—Baseball.
4. Youth league baseball—California—Los Angeles. I. Title.
GV865.S87S65 2004
796.357'092—dc22
[B]
2004041745
ISBN-13: 978-0-7432-2673-8
ISBN-10: 0-7432-2673-9
ISBN-13: 978-0-7432-7885-0 (Pbk)
ISBN-10: 0-7432-7885-2 (Pbk)

For my parents

Contents

CONTENTS

Author's Note

This book evolved from a profile of Darryl Strawberry that I wrote for *The New York Times Magazine* in 2001. Even after I had completed that story, I wanted to know more, not so much about Darryl, but about where he came from and what produced this tragic American icon. And I wanted to explore our sports obsession—America's; my own—through Darryl Strawberry and his 1979 Crenshaw High baseball team, which I knew to be a collection of amazingly talented young ballplayers.

What became of the rest of them? Were the less celebrated ones, those who weren't showered with all that fame and adulation, better off in the end? For all of them, how did their lives turn out after the applause died?

This book is their story, the story of the Boys of Crenshaw. It is also the story of my own journey, a quest to get sports right in my own head.

As a boy, I was virtually inhabited by sports. It is what I did, what I thought about, who I was. If I had a baseball game to play on a spring afternoon, I sat in class all day long staring out the window and up at the sky—on high alert against some rain cloud that might float into the picture and wash out my game. In the winter, my friends and I shoveled snow off the outdoor basketball courts and played in gloves. We could think of nothing better to do. I *still* think there was nothing better to do.

When we weren't playing sports, we were watching it, endlessly: back-to-back college football games on Saturday afternoons, with a dose of *Wide World of Sports*—and frequent breaks to burst outside and reenact what we had just seen.

I gobbled up the sports pages and read the stories as little morality plays. The players who worked the hardest reaped the rewards. Sports, for sure, rewarded character. It *built* character. This is what we were told, and what we were eager to believe.

The sports pages, then and now, included a kind of separate story line for black athletes. Sports for them was redemptive. It was a savior, the way out of a bad situation. All of this buttressed a powerful myth, sports as salvation, perhaps the *only* salvation.

Plenty of black athletes bought into this, or just played along, testifying in print that without sports they would surely be on the streets, maybe in jail, perhaps dead.

I wanted to get beyond the myths that we so comfortably embrace, beyond this well-worn narrative. Sports does, indeed, uplift. But it also distracts, disappoints, and holds out false hope.

I was, briefly, what one might call a real sportswriter, a beat writer who covered a big-league baseball team for one season. I carry a lot of memories from that year, most of them sweet ones, foremost among them the pure pleasure of sitting in the ballparks of the National League night after night and taking in more than 150 baseball games.

But I also saw things that made me wonder if sports really built character, or attacked it like some insidious virus.

I have written about many other subjects besides sports: life in inner-city America; a presidential campaign; the Internet stock bubble; eco-terrorism. But I keep coming back to sports, dipping in and out, trying to find the good, trying to reconcile what I see through my adult eyes with what I believed as a boy.

This book, for me, is a way to go back to the beginning. I wanted to recapture baseball as this group of boys experienced it: fresh, and full of possibility. And I wanted to know them as they are now, to learn how it all came out.

The Ticket Out

Prologue

On a warm afternoon in the spring of 1979, fifteen boys knelt in a semicircle on a baseball diamond that had been picked clean of pebbles, then obsessively raked and dragged to minimize bad hops. The grass had been watered and nurtured to a green lushness. Four hundred feet away in dead center field, and 315 feet down the lines, a high chain-link fence served both to define the outfield boundaries and to wall off school property from the streets of Los Angeles.

This was the beginning of a new baseball season at Crenshaw High School, and the boys wanted, immediately, to have bats in their hands. They wanted to take their mighty cuts, to run under fly balls, to make bullet throws and hear the fine splat of baseballs smacking into freshly oiled leather. They had groomed this field themselves, made it the finest damned diamond in all of inner-city L.A., and they were ready to play on it.

Brooks Hurst, the streetwise white man at the center of this black semicircle, pointed toward the gates in the outfield fences, which were locked against girlfriends, buddies, cousins, gang members, and all other forms of distraction and disorder. This is our world, he told them. Our turf. Just us and baseball.

Menace and temptation outside the gates could destroy this team for sure, but a powerful, countervailing influence bound these boys and carried them onto the Crenshaw High diamond: The neighborhood had baseball in its blood. It had fathers and grandfathers who had played the game on rock-filled fields and parched pastures in the rural South, and in some cases were still playing it on the L.A. sandlots. The boys had grown up with a notion that baseball could somehow set things right—a vague, unexpressed but persistent hope that even if life was rigged, baseball might be fair.

Thedo Jones, the father of a Crenshaw player, had moved from Marshall, Texas, on the Louisiana border, to Los Angeles, specifically to be where Major League Baseball was played—in the city of the Dodgers, the franchise that had employed the great Jackie Robinson. Mr. Jones was among that generation of black men you saw wherever the Dodgers played—quiet men in Dodgers caps who nursed a beer, kept a scorecard, and stayed locked in silent, prayerful homage to the team that had broken baseball's color line in its Brooklyn incarnation. Thedo had four boys, and from the time they were little, his way of greeting any of their friends who walked into his living room was to clear away the furniture, hand them a bat, and say, "Let me see your swing, boy."

On this first day of baseball practice, Thedo's son Carl, the Crenshaw catcher, was kneeling smack in the middle of the semicircle. He was maybe the happiest of all that a new season had dawned. Carl lived in his dirty baseball gear, lived to play ball. He was already chewing his tobacco. At least half the Crenshaw team chewed, but Carl alone had the distinction of both chewing and not brushing his teeth.

Carl's mitt was stuffed under his belt, up against his lower back, as it always was when he wasn't catching—as if he otherwise couldn't keep it close enough. During games, when a Crenshaw pitcher tried to get too cute and nibble at the plate with breaking balls, Carl would rip off his mask, march to the mound, and say the same thing every time: "Punk, throw a fastball!"

Never was the next pitch not a fastball.

Kneeling next to Carl Jones was Cordie Dillard, a plumber's son who called himself "the original varsity player." What did that mean? It was impossible to say, but somehow it fit him. *Cordie Dillard, the original varsity player.* He was a combination of an ultra-cool guy, a smooth man with the ladies, and a ballplayer's ballplayer. Cordie insisted on playing three days after his father's death on the day before the funeral—and hit two home runs.

Big Marvin McWhorter, by the time he finished at Crenshaw, had read Ted Williams's *The Science of Hitting* four times and committed long passages to memory. He saved his change and made long trips to batting cages in the city of Downey, ten swings for a quarter.

"Marvin," his teammates would tease him. "Is that all you like to do—hit?"

"Yep," he would answer.

Marvin was nestled right next to his best friend George Cook, with whom he had a standing date every Saturday morning. George and Marvin. The two of them would sit side by side on the overstuffed sofa in Marvin's living room and stare at the television, transfixed by Mel Allen's *This Week in Baseball.* George liked the clever middle infielders—Dave Cash, Joe Morgan, and especially the Angels' Bobby Grich, whose name he incessantly chirped and somehow shortened. *Bbby Grch, Bbby Grch,* he'd repeat as he stepped into the batter's box. Marvin favored big fellas like himself—Willie McCovey, Jim Rice, Greg "Bull" Luzinski—men constructed to crush baseballs.

The identical twins Darryl and Derwin McNealy were rail-thin whippets, so indistinguishable that they were addressed, always, as Twin. Their mother, who until they were a year old wrote their names in Magic Marker on their butts, moved them from the Bay Area to Los Angeles when they were eight years old, "because that's where the ballplaying was, and I figured that's where they needed to be to get noticed."

The twins were inseparable but sometimes at each other. One day around the batting cage, they got into it and one said to the other, "You ugly." The other replied, "No, you ugly!" They began to fight, one got the other on the ground and roughed him up pretty good, and the rest of the Crenshaw players laughed for weeks over the fact that they had no idea which twin got his ass whupped—or which one was uglier.

Some of the players fidgeted while Brooks Hurst laid down the rules for the season. They were eager to get going, or just by nature not comfortable with someone talking at them. But Reggie Dymally looked straight on at his coach; he didn't nudge anybody or make whispered jokes with teammates. Reggie was the most focused player on the team, and through his daily regimen of push-ups and sit-ups, he was also the strongest. Not everybody was buddies with Reggie—he wasn't an easy guy to know—but they all respected him.

On either side of Reggie were two of the other quiet players: Fernando Becker, the lone Hispanic on the team; and Nelson Whiting, a gifted musician and the most talented of any of them off the field.

Standing, not kneeling, with his baseball glove on top of his head like a hat was Chris Brown. Chris was a hardhead who did not like to listen; he was also the team's flat-out genetic freak, a born ballplayer right out of the womb who twice won football's national Punt, Pass & Kick competition. (Being a naturally gifted player and a hardhead were not unrelated.)

The Crenshaw players loved to toss around baseball clichés, and one they always applied to Chris was that he could wake up in the middle of the night, rub the sleep out of his eyes, and hit a home run. He probably could have, along with just about any other athletic feat you could imagine. If someone had put a pair of skates on Chris when he was little, he'd have been an all-star in the National Hockey League. If you'd given him a pool cue, he'd have been Minnesota Fats, or maybe South Central Chris.

The other one standing up in this clot of young ballplayers was Chris's great rival, Darryl Strawberry. At Crenshaw, Chris was the sturdily built, sure-handed third baseman; Darryl was the lean, graceful right fielder. Chris was widely considered the better player, but in no way could he compete for attention with Darryl, whose combination of talent and vulnerability—not to mention the resonant name itself: *Strawberry*—made adults battle for him like a trophy.

No one ever could take their eyes off Darryl Strawberry. He might hit one of those majestic, game-breaking home runs that lifted off his bat like a space shot. Or he might, without warning or provocation, break down and cry.

At eleven years old, Darryl Strawberry bolted one park-league team to join another when a rival coach offered him unlimited postgame chicken and sodas. By the time he reached Crenshaw, Darryl was much as the public would later come to know him—beautiful, delicate, gifted, flawed, doomed.

These were the Boys of Crenshaw. The greatest collection of high school baseball talent in history. Nearly an entire roster drafted into pro ball. Two future Major League All-Stars.

They were headed that spring to the city championship game, held annually at the mecca, Dodger Stadium—and beyond that, they knew for sure, to fame, glory, and fortune. They were pure ballplayers, believers in the game, investors in America's Pastime. They loved baseball with a piercing intensity, and whenever that love was not returned, it hurt like physical pain.

CHAPTER ONE

Paradise

In the tiny backyard of the Strawberry house at 6034 Seventh Avenue, a grapefruit tree produced an abundant harvest each spring. Darryl and his four siblings—two brothers, two sisters—would pluck the fruit off the tree, peel the dimpled skin back, and slurp it down right there in the yard. Then they would run back out on the street or to the nearby park and resume playing ball, juice still dripping from their faces.

Their house, in the middle of a block lined with tall palm trees, looked like tens of thousands of other dwellings in inner-city Los Angeles: a stucco-faced bungalow with three bedrooms, a small kitchen and eating area, and a patch of green in front and back. (The smallest of these types of houses came prefabricated from an outfit called Pacific Ready-Cut Homes, and were sometimes referred to as "democratic bungalows.")

Most of the Strawberrys' neighbors also had at least one fruit tree in the yard—grapefruit, fig, avocado, orange—along with some shrubs and at least a modest patch of flowers. This was typical of just about any neighborhood in Los Angeles; the city was developed, above all, around the ideal that it should stand as a bucolic alternative to New York and the other old cities back East—that it must never become just another teeming metropolis. And what better way to make this point than to give even the poorest residents at least a sliver of paradise?

"The poor live in single cottages, with dividing fences and flowers in the frontyard, and oftentimes vegetables in the backyard," Dana Bartlett reported in *The Better City*, which was published in 1907. Bartlett observed that Los Angeles had some "slum people," but "no slums in the sense of vicious, congested districts."

The Strawberrys had come up from Mississippi. The Dillards, a whole family of plumbers back in Oklahoma—fathers and sons, cousins, in-laws—migrated en masse to start life and business anew in Southern California. The Browns made the pilgrimage from Mississippi, the Whitings from Texas, the McWhorters from Alabama.

With just two exceptions, the families of the Boys of Crenshaw all came from down South, post–World War II. In Los Angeles they lived in single-family houses, rented in most cases. They drove cars and had driveways. Most kept a little garden plot to grow vegetables and greens.

The sense of roominess in Los Angeles, all the attention given over to flora and natural beauty, was not a ruse, not precisely. Much about Los Angeles really was superior to the crowded cities of the East and Midwest, and still is. Even now, the common reaction of a first-time visitor to L.A.'s inner city is to look around at the greenery, the rosebushes, the purple-flowering jacaranda and statuesque birds of paradise, and say: This is South Central?

But there was also something undeniably slippery about the landscape; the whole L.A. experience seemed a violation of some truth-in-packaging law. Historian Carey McWilliams seized on this in *Southern California: An Island on the Land*, a 1946 book still considered a standard text on the development of Los Angeles. McWilliams wrote of the "extraordinary green of the lawns and hillsides," while adding, "It was the kind of green that seemed as though it might rub off on your hands; a theatrical green, a green that was not quite real."

It is not easy to keep in mind how young a city Los Angeles still is, with its current tangle of freeways, its nearly four million residents, and its dense concentrations of wealth, glamour, and power. Its history begins in 1781, five years after the American Revolution, when forty-four pioneers ventured north from the San Diego area, at the direction of California's Spanish governor, to establish a settlement on the banks of what is now called the Los Angeles River.

The land was exotic—"a desert that faces an ocean," McWilliams called it—as well as impractical. For its first century and beyond, Los Angeles would have two great needs: water and people. These were, of course, related; the city could only grow as it found new sources of drinking water.

When California passed to Mexican control in 1821, the population of the city was only about 1,200. It was still entirely Spanish and Mexican in character, with the gentry consisting of the big landholders, or *rancheros,* whose names still grace many of Los Angeles's major thoroughfares.

California came under U.S. control in 1848, after the Mexican-American War, and two years later became the thirty-first state. The 1850 census counted 8,239 residents of Los Angeles, and the city was still a couple of decades away from establishing police and fire departments, or building a city hall and library.

A series of real estate deals—or "land grabs," as they have often been described—brought much-needed water. Under the direction of city water superintendent William Mulholland, snow melt from the Sierra Nevada was captured from the Owens Valley, some 230 miles to the northeast, and sent flowing toward Los Angeles via aqueduct beginning in 1913.

The job of populating the new city was as blunt an undertaking as the land grabs. Railroad, real estate, and other business interests aggressively marketed the region's natural beauty and healthful living, selling Southern California as the once-in-a-lifetime chance to remake oneself in a new land—creating what came to be known as the California Dream.

The Dream was certainly all true in its particulars. Southern California was lovely, new, different. In what other American city could you eat grapefruit right off the tree? You sure couldn't do that in New York or Philadelphia, or anywhere in the vast midsection of the nation from where California attracted so many of its new arrivals.

But right from the start, the dream was hyped way beyond reality, sometimes comically so.

"California is our own; and it is the first tropical land which our race has thoroughly mastered and made itself at home in," journalist and public relations man Charles Nordhoff wrote in *California: For Health, Pleasure and Residence—A Book for Travellers and Settlers.*

Commissioned by the Union Pacific Railroad and published in 1872, Nordhoff's book was an early articulation of the California Dream and a naked sales pitch to entice people to the sparsely populated land. "There, and there only, on this planet," he wrote of Southern California, "the traveller and resident may enjoy the delights of the tropics, without their penalties; a mild climate, not enervating, but healthful and health restoring; a wonderfully and variously productive soil, without tropical malaria; the grandest scenery, with perfect security and comfort in travelling arrangements; strange customs, but neither lawlessness nor semi-barbarism."

Nordhoff and other promotional writers served to "domesticate the image of Southern California," according to Kevin Starr, the leading historian of the state. They sought to convince would-be settlers that the land was inhabitable, and further, that it afforded an unimagined ease—allowing a farmer from the East, for example, to reinvent himself as "a middle-class horticulturalist."

As the California Dream was refined and expanded over the next half century, the public came to imagine the state as a 365-day-a-year vacation and spa—with bathing and boating on the coast, and golf, hiking, and polo inland. California represented the seamless integration of work and play, the promise that life need not be so crushing. Surfing was invented in Southern California, and so was the new popular trend of suntanning. ("A new phenomenon, the deliberate suntan, became a badge of beauty and health," Starr wrote.)

An early settler in Southern California, Horace Bell, noted in his diaries that he found a land of "mixed essences"—Mexicans, Indians, and Spaniards who were various shades of brown, red, and white. What today we would call multicultural. But a lesser-known element of the dream was the selling of the new land as a racially pure haven: Southern California as an Anglo wonderland, the city of Los Angeles as a refuge for a class of über-whites, a fresh start for those smart enough and motivated enough to flee the immigrant-infested cities of the East.

"New York receives a constant supply of the rudest, least civilized European populations," Nordhoff wrote, "that of the immigrants landed at Castle Garden, the neediest, the least thrifty and energetic, and the most vicious remain in New York, while the ablest and most valuable fly rapidly westward."

Nordhoff and other like-minded writers helped establish an intellectual foundation for hatred and bias, and this peculiar strain of racism was not confined to journalists for hire. Much of the new city's elite, including its academic elite, believed in and propagated these theories.

Joseph Pomeroy Widney, a former dean of the medical school at the University of Southern California, published *Race Life of the Aryan Peoples* in 1907, in which he argued that the people of Southern California, enhanced by their exposure to the sun and toughened by their conquering and taming of the frontier, constituted a new superrace. He called this blessed tribe the *Engle* people, a variation of Anglo. He urged the city's business leaders to be "the first captains in the race war."

Robert Millikan, a former president of the California Institute of Technology in Pasadena and the winner of the Nobel Prize in Physics in 1923, was another proponent of the philosophy (such as it was) that Southern California stood as a bulwark of racial purity. He argued that Southern California was "as England [was] two hundred years ago, the Westernmost outpost of Nordic civilization."

The Los Angeles historian Mike Davis has written that the city in the early part of the twentieth century "distinguished itself as a national, even world center of Aryan revival in contrast to the immigrant dominated industrial cities of the East."

The hypocrisy and ludicrousness of this, in a region filled with brown-skinned people—and with major streets named for Francisco

Sepulveda, Andres Pico, and other *rancheros*—was somehow overlooked. Millikan even urged that Los Angeles rebuff Italians and other ethnic Europeans who might want to resettle from the cities back East, as the city had the "exceptional opportunity" to be "twice as Anglo-Saxon" as any other great U.S. city.

The architecture and emerging lifestyle of Los Angeles, meanwhile, were nothing if not Mediterranean. As Davis, the historian, wrote: "Southern California, in other words, was [to be] a Mediterranean land without any pesty Mediterranean immigrants to cause discontent."

* * *

It is doubtful that anyone of any class or color, who emigrated in any decade, would say that Charles Nordhoff's California—the tropical land that was restorative and never "enervating," that had "strange customs" but no lawlessness—is what they discovered upon arrival. But this vision of paradise was especially far from the Southern California of the Boys of Crenshaw.

Blacks began arriving in the L.A. area early in the twentieth century, in trickles at first. They came for the same reasons as other migrants: a fresh start, a conviction that they would find something better than what they left behind.

Some were lured by the chamber of commerce–packaged dream, the booster copy produced by Nordhoff and his heirs. (Although not, of course, by the tracts recommending California as an Aryan refuge.) Many others were attracted by entreaties from relatives who had already moved there, newcomers to California who sold the state with the zeal of religious converts.

In 1920, Mallie McGriff Robinson, the daughter of freed slaves, was living as a tenant on a plantation in rural Georgia with her five children. Her philandering husband had moved out. A woman of energy, ambition, and, by the norms of her time, an advanced education—sixth grade—she was not content to raise her children where they had no prospects for bettering their lives.

On May 21, 1920, she loaded her possessions and her family into a buggy and headed for the train station in Cairo, Georgia, near the Florida state line. The youngest of her children, just eighteen months old, was Jack—Jackie Robinson—the future baseball star, soon to become a child of Southern California.

In his 1997 biography of Jackie Robinson, Arnold Rampersad recounts how the Robinsons came to point themselves west. The story is in many ways the classic tale of westward migration: California as the bailout from a hopeless situation, the land of rebirth and renewal.

"A way out for Mallie came with a visit to Grady County by Burton Thomas, her half brother, who had emigrated to Southern California," Rampersad wrote. "Elegantly garbed and exuding an air of settled prosperity, Burton expounded to one and all on the wonders of the West. 'If you want to get closer to heaven,' he liked to brag, 'visit California.' "

That first small wave of blacks who came to Los Angeles did find greater opportunity than they had left behind. With the city still thinly settled, people with skills and energy were desperately needed, and initiative could pay off regardless of your skin color. One black man at the turn of the century worked his way up from ranch hand to real estate speculator and was said to be worth $1 million. Blacks earned far better wages than they could down South. Their neighborhoods were planted, just like those of the white folks, with tall palms, cypress and pepper trees, and all sorts of other flora imported from Europe and South America.

Mallie Robinson settled her family in Pasadena, just north of Los Angeles. On the day she arrived, she wrote to relatives back in Georgia that seeing California for the first time was "the most beautiful sight of my whole life."

She got work as a domestic—working hard, nights and days—and was rewarded for it, ultimately owning not only her own home but two others on her street.

Her son Jackie starred in five sports at racially integrated Pasadena High, becoming the greatest athlete ever at a school with a long history of sports excellence. But even as he brought championships and glory to his town, he had to stand outside the fence at the municipal pool while his teammates splashed in water he wasn't allowed to enter. At many Los Angeles–area public pools, blacks were barred from swimming on all but one day of the year—the day before the pool was drained.

The city of Pasadena had no black cops and no black city employees of any kind, not even a janitor. Several incidents during Jackie Robinson's youth left him feeling harassed by the Pasadena police. The barely concealed anger that the nation's baseball fans would see when he reached the big leagues was first seared into him in Southern California, by what Davis has called "the psychotic dynamics of racism in the land of sunshine."

The end of World War I in 1918 actually made life worse for L.A.'s black residents. Tens of thousands of returning veterans needed work, and blacks, whose labor had been prized, were the first to be sent off the job. This, combined with an influx of white migrants from the South, made L.A. begin to feel uncomfortably like Alabama. The coastal towns made their beaches whites-only. A private bus company put out a flyer urging that blacks not be allowed to ride "so your wife and daughter are not compelled to stand up while Negro men and women sit down."

The population of Los Angeles doubled in the 1920s, from 577,000 to nearly 1.25 million residents. Hughes Aircraft and other aircraft manufacturers set up headquarters in the region, which combined with the proximity of engineers at the California Institute of Technology to make L.A. the nation's aviation capital. But only in boom times were nonwhites hired for those good factory jobs.

A pattern took hold, which persists to this day, of blacks in Los Angeles getting shunted to the bottom rung as other newly arrived ethnic groups stepped over them. "Even the seeming inapproachable shoe-shining field was competed for by Greeks," noted researchers from the Federal Writers Project when they conducted interviews in the L.A. ghetto in the 1930s. "Trained English butlers succeeded them as valets and butlers. . . . In 1922, the employment situation was alleviated somewhat, especially for those who sought domestic employment. A larger percentage of Southern whites coming to live in Los Angeles preferred

Negro servants, resulting in an increase in domestic jobs, such as cooks, laundresses and private maids."

In Hollywood, blacks were part of the background, obtainable on short notice and at bargain rates. Their place in the movies paralleled their status in real life: useful when called upon, but otherwise easily ignored. "Negroes have been employed in the motion picture industry for a number of years," the Federal Writers Project reported. "The major portion of these have been and still are employed as extras to create atmosphere in jungle, South Seas island and South American scenes as natives, warriors, etc." Lon Chaney, the silent film star, used two hundred black extras in the 1926 movie *Road to Mandalay,* and praised their utility and adaptability: "You can pull any one of them out of the mob and they can act. It is only a matter of makeup and costume to create anything from a Chinaman to an Eskimo. They require no interpreters and are always available in large number."

In the early 1930s, Los Angeles County began deporting tens of thousands of Mexican nationals who came to be known as *repatriados.* The gentry continued to anglicize the area, to try to make L.A. a white man's land and, to the extent possible, make it seem like it had always been so. In 1932 alone, an estimated 11,000 *repatriados* were sent south by the trainload and truckload, carting with them, according to one account, half-opened suitcases, children, dogs, cats, and goats. The deportations, which Starr called "ethnic cleansing," were hardly a good omen for future nonwhite arrivals.

Blacks began arriving in Southern California in large numbers from the South in the years around World War II. No one had suggested they come west to recline or even to farm the fertile soil; they came as part of a huge black migration that coincided with the need for assembly-line workers in the aircraft and defense industries.

As part of this great migration, the Southern Pacific Railroad began importing huge numbers from the South—400 arrivals a day at the peak; 12,000 new black migrants just in June 1943; at least 100,000 up from the South between 1940 and 1950. Nearly all of them crammed into Watts and a couple of adjacent neighborhoods east of Main Street. Los Angeles sprawled like no other U.S. city, with wide expanses of undeveloped land

and virtual wildernesses spread out across some five hundred square miles. Most blacks lived in a five-square-mile enclave on the east side.

Whites had started to move out of the city center and up onto the hillsides by the 1920s, including the new communities of Hollywood and Bel Air. But blacks stayed put in the basins, because by this time 95 percent of all housing stock in the Los Angeles area was subject to deed restrictions and covenants prohibiting sale or lease to black families. Emerging communities in the San Fernando Valley enacted similar restrictions, assuring that blacks would be hemmed in on all sides.

The new black migrants were citizens, but except for that it can't be said they had any greater standing than the *repatriados*. After World War II ended and the labor market again swelled with returning veterans, the old pattern was repeated: Blacks were thrown out of work or relegated to lower-status jobs, and even returning black GIs found that their combat had not won them opportunity or rights. Peace and prosperity, the comfort felt by the wider white society, had the opposite effect on blacks in L.A.: The less they were needed, the more discrimination they felt.

A middle-aged black worker from that era told author Keith Collins: "One day I was well on my way to being an airline mechanic and the next day I was well on my way to becoming a custodian in the tool shop. In a very short period I went from a position which required expert knowledge in the use of tools to a position which required only that I knew how to properly clean and display them. I felt as if my manhood had been deposed. I felt cheated or tricked and did not know how to fight back."

Hatred and racial bias don't lend themselves to measurement and comparison. Where was it worse, in Chicago, Detroit, or Los Angeles? Was the Jim Crow South, or even slavery, in some ways better than the mix of poverty and rootlessness of the Northern cities? It is impossible to say. What matters is how it *felt*, how it was received. And for many newly arrived black citizens, racism as practiced in Los Angeles felt trickier than what they had experienced elsewhere—in some way crueler, perhaps because it was so unexpected to encounter this dark underside on so beautiful a landscape. In the South, racism was something you were born to, a permanent and inevitable state of affairs. In L.A., it felt more like a blindside punch to the jaw.

Chester Himes, a postwar black novelist who moved to Los Angeles at age thirty-one, wrote in his autobiography: "I had lived in the South, I had fallen down an elevator shaft, I had been kicked out of college, I had served seven and one half years in prison, I had survived the humiliating last five years of the Depression in Cleveland, and still I was entire, complete, functional. . . . But under the mental corrosion of race prejudice in Los Angeles I had become bitter and saturated with hate."

*   *   *

Blacks never stopped migrating to L.A. They came in good times and bad, when jobs were plentiful and when they weren't. They came for the climate. The perceived glamour. The knowledge that life where they were living was fixed and the hope that out west, it might be transformed.

They came, in other words, for the same old reason: The California Dream.

By the time the members of that 1979 Crenshaw High team were born, in the early 1960s, on-the-books discrimination was starting to disappear. Civil rights legislation over the next decade would erase most of the rest of it.

But L.A. was still a tease. Unlike in the hopeless South, a black man or woman in Los Angeles could see the dream of a better life; it had a shape, it lived in the next neighborhood over, or maybe two neighborhoods over. But the Dream demanded a higher rent. It meant banking, say, 20 percent of your weekly salary for a whole year, and hoping no emergencies came up in the meantime. And even if you moved fast, the Dream moved faster. If by chance you got close enough to grab ahold of it, you stood a good chance of falling into some kind of hole just as you made your final reach.

The parents of the McNealy twins tell the classic L.A. story: They worked as if on a treadmill, running hard without making much forward progress.

"I worked nine A.M. to midnight some days, doing hair," Dorothy

McNealy says. "I had a shop on Fairfax, it was called D's and Things. I had clothes, accessories, everything. And then I had a couple other shops after that one. But you know how it is. You work and you work and you work, and you think something is going to come of it, but it doesn't. You just workin', after a while, to keep up with the bills."

Her husband, Napoleon, says: "The boys raised themselves up playing ball. I didn't get to see them play but maybe just once. I was too busy working. I was into construction, carpentry, I was trying to be an entrepreneur. I had a little janitorial service I was trying to build up.

"At one time, we were able to move to Inglewood. But you know, every time you move, you gotta pay a little more security, a little more rent, and it's hard to keep up. You're happy when you get into a better situation, but in a way it's more pressure on you. And then, sometimes, your health kind of catches up with you from all that stress and strain—it wears you down."

The Boys of Crenshaw were not raised in Charles Nordhoff's L.A.— the land of ease—but in the L.A. of novelist Walter Mosley, where the men are exhausted and embittered but also, in a distinctly California way, ever hopeful. "California was like heaven for the southern Negro," Mosley's character Easy Rawlins observes in *Devil in a Blue Dress*. "People told stories of how you could eat fruit right off the trees and get enough work to retire one day. The stories were true for the most part but the truth wasn't like the dream. Life was still hard in L.A. and if you worked hard every day you still found yourself on the bottom."

Easy later observes: "The poorest man has a car in Los Angeles; he might not have a roof over his head but he has a car. And he knows where he's going, too. In Houston and Galveston, and way down in Louisiana, life was a little more aimless. People worked a little job but they couldn't make any real money no matter what they did. But in Los Angeles you could make a hundred dollars in a week if you pushed. The promise of getting rich pushed people to work two jobs in the week and do a little plumbing on the weekend. There's no time to walk down the street or make a bar-b-q when somebody's going to pay you real money to haul refrigerators."

This was the city inhabited by the Boys of Crenshaw. Generations of people perpetually winded from running hard to chase something they couldn't quite catch. A whole culture that felt duped, lured west under false pretenses. Their parents, a half-generation younger than Jackie Robinson, had experienced his Southern California—only without his personal resources, his ability to emerge triumphant.

CHAPTER TWO

Go West, Then Keep On Going

Their families lived the California Dream turned upside down. Less leisure, not more. No time to go to the beach even if they did let you on it. And definitely no polo. Work—usually, but not always, *honest* work—defined a man's existence.

"My dad gave me a ball, a glove, and a bat. I was in the second grade, and a lot of kids were just getting baseball gloves, too," remembers Nelson Whiting, who would become the left fielder on the 1979 Crenshaw team. "We went down to the park and organized our own games. We used to take flour from our moms' cupboards and use it to draw the first- and third-base lines. But when I got into organized ball, my grandfather, he was the one who came and watched my games. My father, he was into all kinds of other mess.

"For a while, he was selling TVs right off the street corner, only they weren't really TVs—they were full of rocks. It looked like a TV. It weighed the same as a TV, but you couldn't watch it. It was just a box of rocks. You can't do that kind of hustle forever and get away with it for long, so I guess that's a big reason he went back down to Texas."

Chris Brown's father worked at a cement company, double shifts and weekends. His mother was a churchgoing woman who kept a spotless home, the type who seemed to spend all day in rubber gloves with a bucket of hot, soapy water swinging behind her. If Chris had three games in a day, he had three laundered and pressed uniforms set out on his bed.

When Chris was just starting school, his parents' marriage fractured and his father left home. One thing his father left behind was baseball: Chris knew that his dad had been the best player in the state of Mississippi—he was aware of this for as long as he can remember. And he knew that his father had stopped playing to take a job and be the man of the house; that, too, was part of family lore. But Chris just had to intuit that his father resented the whole thing—the premature end of his childhood, the lost opportunity to play baseball.

His father played softball for the cement company team. And Chris would go to those games. "And I would watch him pulverize the ball," he says. "I mean just *pulverize* it."

Big Marvin McWhorter's father worked for the Department of Airports, at LAX. He was a janitor who would go to work at three in the afternoon and get home at midnight—and then he would get up in the morning and climb into his landscaping truck and hustle up work doing yards. And then he always had another job, some kind of weekend gig. So that was three regular jobs, and while Marvin couldn't always keep count, he's pretty sure there were times he had a fourth job.

Friday evenings were for father and son, at least for an hour or so.

"We'd play catch in the driveway," Marvin says. "It was like a ritual. Growing up, that was the common link between me and my dad. My dad was in the home, but he was a functioning alcoholic. His only outlet was drinking, and I can remember that there was some physical abuse after he'd been drinking—nothing major, but it occurred, and that's one reason why I never wanted to drink, because I didn't want to be like that. The only time we really got along was when we talked baseball or had a catch. So we started having our catches when I was really young.

"He'd throw the ball to me real hard, I mean *hard*. My father was a big man, like six-foot-five, 250 pounds, not much fat. Just country, he was a big country man. He was from Cecil, Alabama. He never lifted weights. So when he threw the ball like that, it burned your hand. And my mother would be in the kitchen yelling out the window: *Don't throw the ball so hard!* And I remember having tears in my eyes but thinking: I'm not going to quit. Because it's fun; but at the same time, the ball hurts. But that's probably how I became a first baseman, from handling whatever throws he gave me."

But later on, father and son fought over baseball. His father had one leg shorter than the other from a tree that fell on it when he was a kid, and he walked with a noticeable limp. Maybe he resented Marvin's ballplaying for that reason, or just figured that a strapping teenager should be working rather than playing a child's game.

Many days, Marvin would be on his way out the front door carrying his baseball mitt, with his spikes thrown over his shoulder, when his father would shout out after him. Get in the truck, he'd say, and help me do some yards. He told Marvin straight out: There's no money for you in baseball. You'll never make a living at it.

Marvin wouldn't even answer his father back. He'd just keep on walking.

*   *   *

Nearly from the start, soon after getting their first mitts, they saw themselves as part of some larger universe of baseball. Baseball was their defined path and their vision of the future, not a choice but a destiny. So much of the rest of life was fleeting. Darryl Strawberry's father got into a terrible row at home one night with his wife; Darryl and his two brothers got involved, physically, against their father; Henry Strawberry walked out of the house and onto the streets of L.A., and *poof,* just like that, a two-parent household was reduced to one. A lot of the boys were in the habit of saying that they *stayed* at a certain address: They stayed with their mama and brothers and sisters on Fifty-second Street, near Vermont. They stayed with their grandmother on Slauson. They stayed over near the Harbor Freeway. To *stay* somewhere implied that you might soon be leaving. It implied that life as you knew it was in a state of flux, subject to change without notice.

But baseball wasn't like that at all. In a strange way, it was more like the South—orderly, slow to change, defined by everyone staying in their proper place. The very first time he set foot on a baseball field, Chris Brown walked out to third base and claimed it as his own—a simple and possibly random act that loomed larger with each new level of baseball success. How could he have known his position right from the start? How could he, a seven-year-old boy, have flipped forward so many pages into the story of his own life? It was like third base was waiting for him—and third base, having been in the same spot for more than a century, wasn't going anywhere just because a kid from the ghetto stood next to it. Third base was solid ground; it didn't shift under you.

The Boys of Crenshaw moved instantly from *playing* baseball to imagining it as a gateway to a richer life. They were pros from an early age, self-identified and then cultivated in a hothouse by family members and other adults who saw their talent and passion and, not too far down the road, their income potential. George Cook, a slightly built infielder with a big-leaguer's footwork around second base, envisioned this for himself: a ranch with horses that stretched over hundreds of acres, running from the cramped house where he lived with his mother and ten siblings all the way to Crenshaw High. He knew it was stupid—a ranch and horses smack in the middle of South Central—but for years he couldn't get the picture out of his head.

The McNealy twins played hours and hours of "strikeout" against a schoolhouse wall, drawing a strike zone square with chalk and taking turns pitching to each other. When they got tired of that, they threw baseballs sky high and ran under them, endlessly imitating Willie Mays's back-to-the-plate catch in the 1954 World Series, the most famous catch in baseball history. In inner-city L.A., each park had its own youth baseball program, and the twins started playing at Denker Park, which is where they remember being "discovered" and establishing their joint identity as stars on the rise. Dorothy McNealy had moved her boys to L.A. to get them noticed, and sure enough, it worked: By the time they were twelve, everybody in the inner-city L.A. sports set knew about Darryl and Derwin McNealy. The twins. If you got one, you had the other. "Connected at the hip, except they ain't Siamese," the Crenshaw boys would later say.

It was at Denker that Cordie Dillard switched his position from outfield to second base at the urging of an older brother. Baseball was what Cordie considered his "main focus," where he wanted to go pro. His brother advised him what position to play, telling him: "Cordie, with the way you hit for power, if you can learn second base, that's a straight ticket to the pros."

That sounded good to Cordie: straight out of L.A., right into getting paid to play baseball.

Carl Jones, at Denker Park, first made his reputation for grit and utter fearlessness, impressing no one more than his baseball-loving father. "Carl was never afraid of no pitch, never afraid of a ball, not once," Thedo Jones says. "He would want to play and stand up there with a bat no matter how big the pitcher was, or how fast he was throwing it in there. You want to know about a fearless person, that was Carl. When I noticed that about him, I knew his future in baseball was unlimited."

Long before they reached Crenshaw, many of the future high school teammates knew each other—or at least knew *of* each other. George Cook had heard of Chris Brown for years before he met him, even though they played at parks miles apart. Chris was just a kid, but he had a citywide reputation.

Chris, on the other hand, had heard of no one but himself. He didn't need to keep track of any other players. He felt like he was the big man on the block from the time he was little. He never even heard of Darryl Strawberry until he was twelve or thirteen—but he just naturally figured, by the time he did hear that name, that Darryl was already quite well aware of who *he* was.

Rivalries developed, fierce and sometimes even physical. None of the Crenshaw players was raised to turn the other cheek. Most were disciplined physically at home—with a belt, if necessary.

Marvin McWhorter got beatings from parents, aunts, uncles, grandmothers—occasionally, if he was deemed to have embarrassed the family, he got them tag-team, with one relative standing and waiting for a turn. As the oldest of thirty-eight cousins, Marvin was also expected to go out on the street and exact retribution, beat someone up, if anyone roughed up his younger kin. And more than once he got a beating for not carrying *that* out.

The whole scene—in their houses, on the streets, in the schoolyard, on the playing field—was intensely physical. It came from anger and frustration, mixed into a neighborhood of rock-ribbed, socially conservative Christian folk who believed that the evils of the day—gangs, drugs, crime—could not take up residence in a child who was properly and physically disciplined.

Nelson Whiting first encountered Darryl Strawberry at an all-star game at a park with one of the better ballfields, Helen Keller Park. The game ended in a brawl. Darryl Strawberry was pitching for the opposing team. "I was like, wow, this is a large kid," Nelson recalls thinking. "I'm a left-handed hitter, and he's left-handed, so I'm bailing out on his curveballs and then he's throwing me fastballs that I can't even see."

Darryl Strawberry hit a batter in that game—probably not on purpose, but the incident set off a raucous fistfight. "There were fights at games," Nelson says. "It didn't happen all the time, but it happened. It didn't seem like a big deal, to tell you the truth. There was a lot of fighting everywhere."

*   *   *

Previous generations of black Angelenos had lived in a much more confined geographical space. But as overt housing restrictions eased through the 1950s and 1960s, blacks began to move into parts of the city where previously they couldn't stay for more than twenty-four hours unless they were someone's maid or butler. People who had come out of the South and gone about as far west as they could imagine, now wanted to keep on going west—out of Watts; across the former dividing line of Main Street; out of the steamy basins; and up onto the hills in search of better houses, cooler breezes, and maybe even a little view. This was a journey rarely accomplished, at least not in full, but that was the goal.

The ultimate success was to lead the outward migration from the Eastside—to be among the first to claim virgin land. "If you wanted to get ahead, you moved west," says Sid Thompson, a former principal at Crenshaw High and later the superintendent of the whole Los Angeles school system. "And if you could get into one of the neighborhoods that had just turned over from all white, then you were really something to be able to pull that off."

As in all big cities, the flight from the ghetto was a case study in social Darwinism. Those with the most money, education, and motivation got out first and farthest. Class identity, as much as race identity, became a defining feature of life in black Los Angeles. "Everyone wanted to get away from the poorer element," explains Lorraine Bradley, an administrator in the L.A. schools and the daughter of Tom Bradley, the city's first black mayor. "Keep in mind that nearly all of us, in relative terms, were poor. But the least poor among us pointed ourselves west.

"And you can define poor in different ways. When I talk about the wealthier people, I include churchgoing folks who believed in education and hard work. Even if they didn't have middle-class money, they had what you might call middle-class values. The further south and east you went in Los Angeles, the less of that people had."

Lorraine Bradley's father, the police commissioner before becoming mayor, was the prototype of the westward-looking black man. In 1934, the family that employed his mother as a domestic allowed him to use their address to register for school, so instead of attending all-black Jefferson High School—which offered a vocational curriculum—Tom Bradley enrolled at mostly white Polytechnic High School, where he was able to take academic courses and earn a scholarship to UCLA. Fifteen years later, with the help of a white "straw" buyer, Bradley and his young family integrated the previously all-white community of Leimert Park.

Over time, the Eastside became poorer, more isolated, and angrier. The Watts riots in 1965, set off by the most prosaic of triggers—the arrest of a black man for drunken driving by a white officer, followed by unfounded rumors of police brutality—took a horrific toll: Six days of unrest, 34 dead, 3,952 arrested, $40 million in property damage. Newspaper accounts said that "Negro mobs" derided white cops and reporters, chanting "White devils, what are you doing here?" That was a reflection of rage, obviously, but also of extreme insularity—they didn't normally see any white folks in Watts, and not many middle-class blacks, either.

Crenshaw High was set squarely on a new dividing line. The neighborhoods to its east were populated by working poor people who had managed to get just a couple of miles east of Main before bogging down. Right on top of Crenshaw were owner-occupied homes, nothing fancy, with nicely kept lawns, planted gardens, and decent cars in the driveways. Inside these homes were black folks with prospects, people who maybe hadn't fully made it but were pointed in the right direction.

Looming above the high school, and just to the west, were the hillside neighborhoods of View Park and Baldwin Hills, sometimes called "the black Beverly Hills," where an elite of lawyers, doctors, and entertainers made their homes. These homes had luxury cars in their garages. They had verandas that afforded panoramas of the city, the sea, and the mountains, some of the most dramatic views in all of greater Los Angeles.

The black folks who lived in these homes commanded high ground and had no need or inclination to descend from it. They would not even come down the hill to shop at a perfectly nice shopping mall at the bottom, anchored by a Mays department store, that carried the name Baldwin Hills Plaza. They went west to shop.

Crenshaw High opened in 1968 with a stated ideal that was both high-minded and hopelessly naive: It was to draw from all of these neighborhoods, and even a couple of white ones, too. It would be diverse by race and class, a model school. But it was never that, not even on its first day.

Sid Thompson was the school's second principal. A compactly built, no-nonsense man from the tiny Caribbean island of Beque, he took charge after the first principal was judged to have lost control. "My first day in there," Thompson says, "I see this tenth grader walking down the hall smoking a big stogie and I said to him, 'Son, who the hell are you and what is that in your mouth?' Then I yanked it out of there."

Thompson insisted that his gym teachers have students march in cadence, military style, to instill a sense of discipline. Thompson once dropped a student with one punch when the kid lunged at him as he tried to intervene in a hallway rumble. "Caught him square in the jaw," says Brooks Hurst, the baseball coach. "A short left hook. Perfect."

But despite the best efforts of Thompson and others, the school spiraled down. "White folks could afford to experiment with the counterculture; for black folks, it was disastrous," says Lorraine Bradley. "Drugs were everywhere. Gangbangers were everywhere. So many of the men had come home from Vietnam as damaged goods. It was just a bad, bad time. The schools reflected the streets."

By 1979, Crenshaw High School was being called Fort Crenshaw. Violence was common in the corridors and school grounds. The fights were sometimes gang and drug related, but not always. "They were about girls, or whatever young boys wanted to challenge each other about," Brooks Hurst says.

One day, several lowriders—the big, customized American cars popularized on the West Coast—pulled up near the Crenshaw outdoor basketball courts. Gang members in the cars rolled dozens of bowling balls at groups of students milling about, which was taken as some sort of calling card. Several days later the lowriders returned and the young men in them aimed shotguns at the playground, just for the sport of seeing everyone scatter.

Athletes generally were exempt from gang intimidation. "We were on our own island," George Cook says. "The bullies didn't mess with us. It was like—you mess with the players and you're messing with the bragging rights of the school. It was strange, when you think about it. They wanted the school to be known for something good, but at the same time they were tearing the place down."

A kind way to describe the situation at Crenshaw would be to say that the school had taken on the culture of the neighborhoods a couple of miles east. In fact, the school sometimes just seemed like a failed social experiment. And that was inevitable from the moment the very families who might have uplifted Crenshaw High decided instead to shun it.

Under a system of permits that allowed children to attend schools other than the one directly in their neighborhoods, the L.A. school system was like a giant board game—with parents generally sending their kids *west.* But you normally could only move one square at a time, or two at the most. A great many parents who lived in the Crenshaw district sent their kids west to Palisades, University, or Westchester high schools, which were integrated and more academic. Virtually none of the well-heeled black parents from exclusive Baldwin Hills and View Park sent their children down the hill to Crenshaw. (They wouldn't shop at the bottom of the hill, so they certainly weren't going to send their kids to school down there.)

"The people in the hills did not relate to the people in the flatlands," explains Paul Hudson, president of the city's oldest black-owned bank, Broadway Bank, founded by his grandfather. "They saw themselves as different. They sent their kids to private school or worked the public school system to get them west."

Many of the students who did enroll at Crenshaw High, including the majority of the baseball players, had also used permits to move west. They did so in order to avoid attending even rougher schools nearer to them, and by the unwritten rules of the game, Crenshaw was as far west as they could get. That was how the board game worked: Everyone moved more or less in lockstep with the same people they started with.

"When Crenshaw opened you knew what that was going to mean," Lorraine Bradley says. "There was no way that the people who lived up on that hill—Baldwin Hills and View Park—were going to send their children to mingle with another class of child, with the newly migrated who hadn't quite figured it out yet. The parents who sent their kids to Crenshaw and the kids themselves were thrilled to be there. They were going to rub elbows with this higher class of black folks, and maybe some of what they had would rub off. And maybe it would have. But that higher class of black folks wasn't there because they didn't give it a chance. If the folks on the hill had given it a shot, they might have affected a better attitude at that school, but they didn't—they fled west."

Sid Thompson adds, "Crenshaw immediately was almost all black, and a certain kind of black—struggling working class and underclass. On the rare occasions we did get a student from Baldwin Hills or View Park, the kid was an athlete, or a wannabe athlete."

Some years, Crenshaw didn't have enough academic stars to fill a calculus or advanced literature section. But it always had ballplayers; there was never any shortage of them. And to those ballplayers, the way to lift off into a better life rather than just to slide a neighborhood or two over seemed perfectly obvious: pro ball. That was the way to trick the system. What good was it to move twenty blocks to the west? Forty blocks? Most of their families had already tried that. You found the same problems you thought you'd left behind, or they soon enough found you. Or even worse, you got behind on the rent and had to go right back to where you started.

To boys who showed some talent on the ballfield, sports seemed a hell of a lot more powerful, held out a lot more promise, than the daily struggle being waged by their parents.

White Americans hear black kids talking like they might become pro athletes, and they tend to think: *How stupid.* The dream of making a buck playing ball seems like pure fantasy, about as likely as winning the lottery. In 1979, about 500,000 boys played high school baseball. More than 5 million under the age of eighteen played on an organized team. About 1,000 men played big-league baseball, and each year only a small percentage of those slots turned over.

But what is not understood is how immediate the dream of pro sports feels in a place like Crenshaw—and, in fact, how reality-based it is compared to the alternative.

The Boys of Crenshaw knew that former running back Wendell Tyler, then with the Los Angeles Rams, and Marques Johnson of the NBA Milwaukee Bucks were Crenshaw High graduates. They knew that Willie Crawford, the ex-L.A. Dodger, had grown up nearby and, more recently, so had Ozzie Smith and Eddie Murray, who in 1979 were just starting their Hall of Fame baseball careers. They knew that Ellis Valentine, a 1972 Crenshaw graduate, played right field for the Montreal Expos.

Some of the Crenshaw players had older brothers, cousins, or uncles who had played college football or basketball, or minor-league baseball. But they didn't personally know any black doctors or lawyers or the children of any black doctors or lawyers. And they had a pretty good idea that these folks were not crossing the street to come into contact with them—they were, in fact, running in the other direction.

* * *

Nelson Whiting wore braces and "talked proper," and when some of his teammates first met him they figured he must be from Baldwin Hills or View Park. He wasn't. Later, they called him "the scholar" because they suspected when he wasn't hanging out he must be at the library. "I've lost track of Nelson, but I figure he must be a professor somewhere," George Cook says of his old teammate. "Nelson, man, he was different."

When this is repeated to Nelson Whiting, he laughs and laughs. "They called me the scholar? I never knew that. I had a little common sense. But I don't think that made me any damn scholar."

In various ways, the Crenshaw players all took careful and constant note of race and class—of where they stacked up against teammates, classmates, other schools, and other neighborhoods. They were like little urban sociologists, making observations and filing them in memory. Their eagerness sometimes led to erroneous conclusions, but more often than not they were dead-on.

Traveling to play teams in the San Fernando Valley, L.A.'s vast suburb-within-a-city, held a particular fascination. Before one game, the whole Crenshaw team took note of the opposition's star pitcher, future major-leaguer Bret Saberhagen, wearing shorts and coasting around on a skateboard; he was like another species. The Valley kids had three sets of uniforms: one home, one away, and one . . . well, they never did figure out what that third uniform was for. Maybe just for showing off.

The Crenshaw boys liked to run their hands along the Valley infields, some of which were made from specially formulated crushed brick, producing ground balls that rolled as true as putts. From watching TV, they already had a pretty good idea of where they stood in the world—and what they did not have. Not two parents like all those perfect TV families. Not the safe surroundings to lean a bicycle up against a white picket fence while running inside for a hearty bowl of soup. What kind of damn fool would do that? The bike would be gone in a flash.

Their trips to the Valley provided the same information as TV did, but in a hands-on way: Feeling the infield dirt, they knew viscerally that no matter how many pebbles they sifted away, their diamond at Crenshaw would never be as perfect. They suspected that players in the Valley corked their bats—took the tops off their aluminum bats, stuffed them with Super Balls, then resealed them. They had no evidence whatsoever to back this up, just a gut feeling that people born to advantage might cheat to gain even greater advantage.

Reggie Dymally always noticed that the baseballs they used at Crenshaw and other inner-city schools were dirty, while the white kids in the suburbs played with clean ones. When Reggie played on teams that traveled to some of the wealthier areas, those shiny new baseballs rolled right up to the visiting dugout during pregame practice, sometimes coming to rest right at his feet. Reggie stole some of these balls. So did his friends. They would stick a couple in the sneakers they had taken off before pulling on their spikes, then after the game they'd walk off with them. Sometimes, they lifted a baseball bat or two. Soon enough they'd have twenty balls and a couple of decent bats to work out with. Sure, it was wrong, but who could afford to buy equipment? Reggie sure couldn't.

Another thing Reggie noticed was that his textbooks at Crenshaw were old, and they usually showed evidence of having come from other schools. Inside the front cover it would say *Property of Fairfax High*, or property of some other school to the west. (All of L.A. wanted to get west, but the old books migrated east.) Reggie would think to himself: "Why am I reading a book that's six years old and all torn up, and over at Fairfax, I'm assuming, they have new books?"

Like most of the other Crenshaw players, Reggie qualified for free breakfast tickets that entitled him to a hot meal before class: burritos, cheese toast, sausages. Anything packed with calories to fill up an empty stomach. He would put a couple of sausages inside the cheese toast and gobble it all down on the way to his first class.

Chris Brown, too, dug into his free food with a combination of hunger and defiant pride. He didn't care who saw him walk down the line and gobble up a coffee cake or a burrito. "We were all in the same damn boat, poorer than dirt, only some people tried to pretend they weren't," Chris says now. "The hell with them. Pretty much everybody on that team had breakfast tickets except probably Cordie and the Joneses, and we were all hungry enough to use them."

Big Marvin McWhorter came west to Crenshaw, and as rough as the school could be, it was better than what he left behind. Crenshaw gave him one foot out of the ghetto. Marvin lived in an entirely different neighborhood, near the Joneses, where they all should have attended Washington High. But the gang activity at Washington was constant, and Marvin had already gotten himself into a little trouble. He wasn't a talker, but he had a way of convincing other people to do stuff. Marvin was usually the biggest guy on the scene, so if some kind of trouble did break out, all eyes immediately fell on him.

His mother gave him two choices: an all-boys Catholic school or Crenshaw, if she could get him a permit. After he enrolled at Crenshaw, he found that "it was different, no doubt. You had some kids coming to school, and they dressed kind of nice. It was a little step up for me, and I knew it."

But Marvin also knew that Crenshaw had been rejected by others who considered it a step *down*, all those higher-class parents who would not send their children to be educated at Fort Crenshaw. "You played against Westchester, Palisades, and there were black kids on the field who you knew lived around the corner from Crenshaw, that gave a little more *oomph*. You had some incentive. You wanted to stomp them, to tell you the truth."

Chris Brown also made the choice to attend Crenshaw, in large part because it played in the city's Western League and therefore, in his mind, against teams that played *white* baseball. It was a career move. "I was supposed to go to Manual Arts," he says, "but I was close to the Crenshaw line, so I asked my mom to go and get a permit. Compared to the other schools I could have gone to, it was an improvement. Anywhere east, you didn't want to be. Crenshaw had the uppity cute black girls and the guys, to a certain extent, were considered a cut above.

"Plus, a big thing for me was that Crenshaw played against white schools—Crenshaw was the only black school in the Western League—and I always wanted to go to a school where you played against white guys. When you played against black guys, all you saw was fastballs. That's what black guys did—just challenged you with fastballs, and if you could hit a fastball, it wasn't a challenge after a while, and you didn't learn shit about hitting.

"But when you were playing against Venice and Westchester and Palisades, and these guys start dropping a curveball on your ass, and if you haven't seen it before, you're in trouble. It's not that they're pitching around you, but they're showing you the style of pitching that you're gonna have to face down the road."

Darryl Strawberry was one of the handful of players who lived near the school and needed no permit. His mother, raising three boys and two girls alone after her husband left, did not have a lot of money, but a solid job at Pacific Bell provided enough to keep the house going. The family, though—and Darryl especially—struggled in ways beyond money. Darryl's two brothers had played for Brooks Hurst at Crenshaw, so Hurst encountered him for the first time a couple of years before he was high school age; Hurst had stopped by to pick up Michael, and Darryl was sitting on the front step of the house, eating a candy bar.

From that first moment, he struck the coach as a sad boy. "It was hard to get joy out of Darryl," he says. "It was hard for him to be truly happy. Maybe that's something that I could have helped address. If I coached now, I would be different in a lot of ways. I know more, I'm more educated about things that people go through. But back then, I was young myself, and a little hot. But my passion for the kids, my love of the game, I think they saw that."

* * *

Of course they saw it. How could anyone not notice Brooks Hurst's love of baseball, his determination to teach the game and see it played right? But his players perceived other qualities, too, ones they were all too familiar with: Coach Hurst was complicated, restless, angry about something, combustible. They didn't know the source of these bottled-up feelings, but they could tell he had them and they respected him for it. Respected him all the more.

They sometimes called Hurst "the White Shadow," a reference to a TV show of that era about a white coach of an all-black basketball team. But Hurst was instantly recognizable from their own experience—a man who seemed to be boiling deep inside, struggling to keep a lid on himself just like everyone else they knew. Sometimes he was angry at them, other times at himself. Or the world. It wasn't easy to know.

It was well understood that you did not fuck with Coach Hurst. Not because you didn't know what might happen, but because you *did*. Oh, you could sometimes backtalk him a little bit, and Hurst would make you run—he'd just stand there, arms folded, eyes hidden behind reflective sunglasses, and watch until you nearly dropped from exhaustion.

And that was just if you had gotten a little too mouthy. No one went beyond that and threatened Hurst in any kind of physical way. Some real hardcore kids suited up for him over the years, young men still on the fence between playing baseball or playing for the Crips or the Bloods, but even they did not cross that line. If they couldn't handle his rules, they just walked off.

The experience of teaching and coaching at Crenshaw tended to toughen a person up. Earlier in the 1979 school year, an ex-student was stabbed just before a home football game. Brooks Hurst gave him mouth-to-mouth resuscitation as the kid lay dying in his arms, at first without recognizing that the kid had once played for him.

"Gregory?" Hurst finally said.

"Yeah, Coach, it's me," the kid answered.

Paramedics arrived and whisked him off to the hospital, where he was dead on arrival.

(The referees called the captains of the two teams to the fifty-yard line. They flipped the coin to determine who would kick and who would receive. The teams took the field, the whistle blew, and the contest was played to completion.)

Hurst stands about six-foot-three and even now walks with the lithe, easy gait of an athlete. In 1979 he was thirty-two years old, a gym teacher and a coach, but hardly typical in either regard. He was an accomplished cook and a skilled gardener. The rumor at the school was he had a black belt in kung fu. He could converse on politics, history, and Eastern religions.

He grew up working class to the bone, the son of a fisherman who worked off the docks at Venice Beach, and became a star baseball player at Venice High. After four years of college at Cal State Northridge, Hurst signed as a first baseman with the St. Louis Cardinals organization and set off into minor-league baseball, playing the 1968 season in Cedar Rapids, Iowa, and the following year in Lewiston, Idaho. It was a souring experience. "The whole thing, right to the way it ended, was pretty much a big nightmare," he says.

Pro baseball is larded with tradition, superstition, and a code of etiquette all its own. Hurst entered as a college boy, and therefore was instantly suspect and never did fit in. (Just reading a book in some baseball settings makes you an oddball.) In Lewiston, he was sitting in a restaurant bar one night eating—"I wasn't even drinking"—when his manager walked in, looked at him, then walked right out.

Ballplayers are not supposed to drink at the same bars as their coaches and managers, but Hurst was there first and had no idea it was an establishment his manager frequented. "The next day I come to the ballpark and he is beet red and screaming in my face, saying, 'Do you think Mickey Mantle eats with Casey Stengel? Do you?' And I'm just standing there thinking, this is crazy. All I did was sit down and order a hamburger."

A few weeks later, Hurst was throwing batting practice before a game to his roommate as his manager stood nearby talking to a visiting executive from the Cardinals front office. "Am I keeping my weight back?" his roommate asked.

"Try to keep your hands back a little longer," Hurst advised.

His manager went off again. He told Hurst to stick to playing and quit acting like a coach. "But we talk baseball," Hurst said. "Isn't that okay?"

Hurst, hitting well over .300, found himself benched in favor of a newly signed first baseman. Not long after that, he was cut. The manager came up to him before a game and said, "Sometimes things don't turn out right, and things didn't go right between us. Other organizations are looking at you. You've got a lot of potential, and you should get another chance somewhere, but I've gotta release you."

Hurst didn't accept the apology. "I just looked at him and I was sick. I said, 'Coach, you really sort of blew it. What I really feel like doing is grabbing your fucking neck, and ripping it apart. But I'm just gonna get out of here and I never want to see you again.' I got in my car, went home, made my reservation, and within an hour I was driving to the airport in Lewiston. To get there you had to go by the ballpark, and right there, my car stalls. The game was in progress, so there I am, trying to push my car up a hill, while I'm looking right down into right field. So that's what happened. I always felt kind of empty about it.

"I sincerely thought I could make it at that level and beyond. I could hit. I could field. I could really play. I came home, proceeded to get my girlfriend pregnant, and then went out and got a teaching job. I could have given it another shot and signed somewhere else. That's my nature. But I just kind of went into a shell. I don't condemn myself for it, but I regret it. My dad was a big advocate of my athletic career, and if I would have told him, he would've helped out financially. But I didn't tell him for like fifteen years what really happened, and to this day I've told very few people, because everybody who gets sent home has a story that they got screwed, and I never wanted to sound like that. It all left a bitter taste."

Brooks Hurst did not watch baseball for years. He couldn't even watch a movie about baseball. It all just hurt too much. His brother finally convinced him to join his fast-pitch softball team, and the old feelings—his love for the game, rather than his disgust with all the bullshit—returned.

Hurst began teaching at Crenshaw in 1969, the year after it opened, but he didn't become the baseball coach until 1975. The program was a distant second (at best) to Crenshaw's basketball team. Hurst started promoting baseball. He approached kids who looked like athletes, talked up baseball, plastered the corridors with posters advertising the upcoming tryouts. Having rediscovered his own passion, he set about finding and making ballplayers.

Most of the boys he attracted in those early years had played some baseball, or at least something like it—stickball, over-the-line, or one of the other baseball derivatives that city kids play. If a kid had never played stickball, Hurst made sure to teach it to him. He handed out broomsticks and tennis balls and told boys to get their friends together and play in the streets, believing that anyone who could learn to make contact with those tools would be able to hit a baseball. The broomsticks taught kids to whip the bat, and that's what Hurst liked, a player who used a light bat and whipped it around.

That first year, his team made the playoffs even with some players who were just about new to baseball. But after that, he started attracting kids who were already stars in their park leagues.

The word was out: Crenshaw was a baseball school. Kids started enrolling specifically to play there, to be on Brooks Hurst's team. Soon enough, you had to be pretty damn good just to earn a spot on the bench of the Crenshaw High Cougars.

*   *   *

Even at the professional level, a baseball practice can ooze along at a sleepy pace. A pitcher tosses batting practice. A batter takes his swings. The sun beats down. Players huddle in little groups in the outfield, cracking jokes, yawning, taking turns chasing after batted balls. But not at Crenshaw. Brooks Hurst knew the best way to keep the attention of young athletes was to keep them moving.

When the boys broke from their semicircle at that first practice in 1979, the old tires that Hurst had collected were already rigged up and hanging from fenceposts on the third base side. When the coach was done talking, several players were sent off in that direction to "pop tires"—take rapid-fire swings against the rubber. *Pop! Pop! Pop!* First short swings. Then inside-out swings to simulate a stroke that would send the ball to the opposite field—right field for right-handers, left for left-handers. Then full swings, but with the bat stopped on contact with the tire to emphasize proper positioning of hands, hips, and head as the bat reaches the hitting zone. Sometimes Hurst stood with a whistle, blowing it in six staccato bursts as a player moved the bat through six stages of the swing.

Elsewhere, at separate stations, some players stretched and lifted light weights. Others played "pepper," two kinds: short pepper and long pepper. Still others played long-toss, to build arm strength, or participated in "backhand drills"—perfecting the art of reaching across the body with the glove, planting on the back foot, and establishing the balance to make a strong, accurate throw. Several drills took place without balls or bats: they were just for footwork.

Hurst had picked up a few of these drills from his own playing career. Others he adapted from the little martial arts training he did have, from a fellow named Jimmy Wing Wu in Hollywood. (Hurst had no black belt, but he didn't dissuade anyone from thinking he did.)

A few of the drills Hurst had dreamed up himself. Baseball, he believed, was a game of hand-eye coordination, balance, footwork, and strength. "The first thing I wanted to do was educate their hands," he explains. "That's what the tires were for. Other drills were to educate their lower bodies and their feet. I wanted them down low, in position to do things properly."

Hurst coached the team by himself, without an assistant. He could never find anyone to fall in line with him, to "lay off their own style." After a while, the boys just moved from station to station; they knew what he wanted, and on a good day they just followed right along.

Elsewhere in black America, basketball was ascendant. It was faster. The equipment was cheaper: All you needed was a ball and a pair of sneakers. In 1979, no one had yet heard of Michael Jordan, but players like Julius Erving and Magic Johnson were becoming the icons in the black community that black baseball players had once been. A generation after Jackie Robinson, it was hard to get black athletes interested in baseball, and you could almost never get the best ones to play.

Phil Pote, a scout for the Seattle Mariners who for years worked in South Central L.A., would walk through gyms and see ten great athletes. He'd think to himself: *One of these kids could be the next Willie Mays.* Then he'd have a second thought: *We'll never find out, because the kid has never even owned a baseball glove.*

But Crenshaw High was an exception. Brooks Hurst's artistry was expressed on a canvas of marvelous athletes—Division I–quality basketball players; football stars if they had wanted to be; big, strapping kids who were the best Crenshaw had to offer. Chris Brown and Cordie Dillard had reported for baseball practice in 1979 just days after helping Crenshaw win a California state basketball championship.

"But baseball," says Dillard, "that was the game. The other stuff, we just played at."

Derwin McNealy says: "We were ballplayers, which to us meant *baseball players.*"

Baseball had long been the American game, for better and worse, the sport that seemed to speak to the soul of America, that emanated from that soul. It was the thinking man's game, so laden with strategy it was compared to chess—and also the simple man's game: See ball, hit ball. It was the city game and the rural game. The integrationist's game and the bigot's game.

Baseball was not America, exactly, but the border between them was porous. Each seemed to signify the other.

When the sport cruelly denied admittance to blacks, even as it was obvious that the greatest of the Negro League players were the equals, if not the betters, of those playing in the big leagues, baseball embodied the shame of the nation's treatment of its black citizens. And when the color line finally was broken, and Jackie Robinson emerged from the home dugout at Brooklyn's Ebbets Field and trotted out to first base on April 15, 1947, American society was changed forever.

"He brought pride and the certain knowledge that on a fair playing field, where there were rules and whites could not cheat and lie and steal, not only were they not supermen but we could beat 'em," the writer Roger Wilkins said of Robinson.

A generation later, the Boys of Crenshaw were among the last young black athletes who truly saw baseball as their own, who invested themselves in it. Rather than battling discrimination, they were fighting isolation. They lived in a small, almost entirely black world. Baseball was their bridge to the rest of America.

* * *

After Brooks Hurst took over, a trickle of pro scouts began to come calling at Crenshaw High. He set aside a little section of the bleachers for them and assigned teachers to sit close by so they would feel safe. A student manager distributed stat sheets.

His Crenshaw High ballclubs were developing a reputation for having good athletes. What Hurst also wanted the scouts to see was that his kids "played the game as it should be played." Crenshaw players hustled. They threw to the right base. They did not talk to opponents or argue with umpires. If a Crenshaw kid even looked at an ump, he found himself with his ass on the bench, sitting right next to Hurst.

Artie Harris, an L.A.-area coach and scout and a close friend of Hurst's, says: "Brooks kept them together. In talent, that 1979 team was unmatched, but they did not always play to their potential. He was very tough on them, but he would go to the ends of the earth for them."

Hurst's methods were understood by some of his players for exactly what they were. "We wanted to be ballplayers, with all that meant," George Cook says. "Some guys took that to mean you chewed tobacco. At least half the team chewed. Brooks chewed. But the main thing was, we knew we were being taught baseball the way white people thought it should be played. We not only had to be good, we had to act a certain way. Coach Hurst knew that was the only way we were gonna get people to take a serious look at us.

"But we knew what to do. Somebody's on second, no outs, you hit the ball the opposite way and moved the runner. Not too many inner-city schools played that way, but we took pride in it. When we played certain schools that were considered rich kids' schools, you could just feel it: They thought we were talented but not smart baseball players. You know, like maybe they could outsmart us and win that way. So when we played them, it had to be no doubt; we were gonna kick their butts. We had a little something special for them."

The Boys of Crenshaw even spoke the archaic lingo of baseball. Away from the ballfield, they were distinctively black kids from the inner city; on it, they could sound like characters in an old Chip Hilton novel. They knew to call a high pop-up a "can of corn." If a blooper fell in for a hit, it was a "Texas Leaguer." When a pitcher struck one of them out with a really tough pitch, a teammate was sure to say when he returned to the bench, "Hey, you've gotta tip your cap to him."

They were full of old-school references. They compared Carl Jones to the great catcher Roy Campanella, who had started his career in the Negro League before retiring from the Dodgers in 1957, before any of the Boys of Crenshaw were born. How did they know of Campanella? They just did. They were aficionados of the game, avid consumers of its history. They knew for a fact that their tough-as-nails catcher was the spitting image of the great Campanella.

The scouts, unaccustomed to finding prospects in the city, congregated in larger numbers in the San Fernando Valley, so Hurst made sure to schedule early-season games against schools in the Valley to give his players an early showcase. His hope was to lure scouts to Crenshaw for games later in spring.

It was at an Easter weekend tournament in the Valley that veteran scout George Genovese first "picked up" the 1979 Crenshaw team—meaning that he watched them for the first time and understood, immediately, that he needed to see more.

A lot of scouts look for esoteric stuff—the size of a kid's butt, what they judge to be his flexibility, the graded score of his five "tools" (running, throwing, fielding, hitting, hitting for power). But Genovese kept things simple. He wanted to know: Can a kid hit? If the answer was yes, Genovese liked him.

He was extraordinarily good at answering his own question. Genovese was the home run scout, having signed the sluggers of more than two thousand major league home runs, including Dave Kingman, Jack Clark, George Foster, Matt Williams, Gary Matthews, Garry Maddox, and Rob Deer. Some of these players were well known to other scouts, but several others were Genovese specials, discovered as he hopscotched from ballfield to ballfield in his battered, paper-strewn Cadillac—and then guarded like state secrets. "You park out of the way," he says. "You stand in the background. If you like a kid, you don't make a spectacle of yourself.

"No one heard of George Foster before I drafted him," Genovese continues, referring to the power-hitting left fielder of Cincinnati's mid-1970s Big Red Machine. "You could go through every scout's list and you would not find him. But I got on to him, and the rest is history."

Genovese played briefly in the late 1940s for the Washington Senators, then for years in the old Pacific Coast League. The legendary baseball executive Branch Rickey hired him as a minor league player-manager, then moved him to scouting and mentored him in the art of talent evaluation. Genovese kept bats and balls and a stopwatch in his car, and sometimes just stopped when he saw a pickup game in progress and organized an informal workout.

That was before cable TV and video games. Kids spent all day outside, and nearly everyone could play a little baseball. Genovese would haul the equipment out of his trunk, watch them play, and every once in a while be pleasantly surprised to find a kid who was worth a second look.

A scout can claim to be a success by signing a legitimate big-leaguer once every couple of years; Genovese once sat behind home plate at Candlestick Park in San Francisco and filled with pride as seven of his signees trotted out to start the game for the Giants. If the Baseball Hall of Fame opens up a wing for scouts, as has been proposed, George Genovese will be one of the first inductees.

He does not know how many high school teams he has watched over the years, but has no doubt about which was the best. "Collectively, the 1979 Crenshaw team was the best I ever saw," he says. "No can say for sure, but I'm going to say they were the greatest high school team ever.

Maybe not in wins and losses, but overall talent. My God, everybody all the way up and down that lineup could hit. They just piled on runs. They tore up the opposition. I saw them that first time and just stayed with them; you wanted to see how many kids you could take off that team.

"At the city high schools now, you've got a lot of Latino kids playing. Some of them are good, but they're small. But these boys had big frames. You had Strawberry, of course. And Chris Brown, who impressed me so much with the way he looked. You know who he reminded me of? A young Orlando Cepeda. He was strong like Cepeda and he could handle the bat. I could find nothing wrong with him other than a little immaturity, which if he got past that, and most kids do, I figured he would be a superstar.

"The McNealy twins were very fast, strong defensively, good line-drive hitters. Both of them were capable of making a twenty-five-man big-league roster. You had a catcher who was a very strong player. You had Cordie Dillard, who I felt was a sure thing, because he was a very good hitter. He wasn't that fast or that great an infielder, but as I say, if you can hit you can play. They'll find a position for you, even if it's DH in the American League. I had high hopes for Cordie. I had high hopes for so many of those boys."

$$* \quad * \quad *$$

Donald Jones, the older brother of the catcher Carl, should have been a member of the 1979 Crenshaw team. Should have been one of the stars. He had a knife-sharp curveball that started waist high, then dove at the batter's shoetops just as he started to swing. Plenty of good hitters missed that pitch by two feet. Donald's fastball traveled at better than 90 miles per hour, real good velocity for a high school boy still filling out.

Whenever he had to catch his brother, Carl Jones taped a big wad of foam rubber onto his left hand before putting on his mitt, for extra protection. But he still has a callus and a dark spot on the pad of his hand, a permanent mark just under the index finger, from absorbing years and years of Donald's fastballs.

The Crenshaw players, who liked nothing better than hitting, didn't even like to take batting practice when Donald was pitching. They would demur—*No, you go ahead, it's your turn; I mean it, bro', take your swings*—hoping that by the time they got in the cage, some other pitcher would be on the mound. "Ain't nobody in the whole city of L.A. who could hit that boy," says Chris Brown. "I don't care how damn good a hitter they were, they could not handle Donald Jones."

Brooks Hurst says, "Donald was awesome. He was the best pitcher we had, the best pitcher we ever had—and he was also our best short-stop."

But among the Boys of Crenshaw, Donald Jones was the first (for lack of a better word) *casualty*. The first to be derailed from his dream, the first to go down. And that was surprising, in one way, because the Jones house-hold had so much in its favor, so many of the qualities that would cause you to say, Yeah, those boys will be fine. They're a couple of the ones who will do all right.

Compared to other Crenshaw families, the Joneses were on the well-to-do end, although they hardly carried themselves that way. They re-mained sort of country folk within the city, always looking, no matter how they dressed, as if they'd be more comfortable in overalls. The boys hunted, sometimes missing school to go out into the woods when some-thing new came into season. Thedo Jones, their father, poured concrete for a big construction company and worked at two little side businesses—fixing up houses and hauling Dumpsters. He put his sons to work at an early age. On a couple of occasions, Donald and Carl showed up for Sat-urday morning practice driving big dump trucks, causing their team-mates to fall to the ground laughing.

The Jones boys usually had a little cash in their pockets. When they turned sixteen, they got cars—secondhand and dented up, but functional. Carl was particularly generous, and if you asked to borrow his car he'd usually say yes, then call after you—*Hey, you got enough money for gas?* At the Record Shop, a joint across from school where the players stopped after practice for sandwiches, Carl was always good for a couple of bucks to help a teammate who was hungry and broke.

Mr. Jones and his wife, Werllean, owned a house pretty far to the east, near Watts, which they added on to several times—it had bedrooms everywhere you looked—as well as another house a couple of doors down which they used as sort of a way station for people in need. The Jones property became a clubhouse for the Crenshaw team, and Thedo Jones a father to them all. "I don't remember any other fathers," Nelson Whiting says. "You know, actual fathers. Cordie had a father, but then he passed."

(This was not strictly true. A couple of the others did have fathers at home, but they were more like the black men in Walter Mosley's novels: too besieged to be fully present.)

Thedo tried to supplement what the boys couldn't get elsewhere. He loaded them into his pickup truck and treated them to Dodgers games. He put them on the summer baseball teams he sponsored, and on his fast-pitch softball squad, the L.A. Eagles. When he believed they might be in a listening mood, he offered his counsel. "I was kind of dedicated to all the boys," he says. "If they really needed something, I was there. I talked to them when they were having their little problems. And they would listen. They would respect me."

Chris Brown was one project. "Chris used to come around and sit on my porch," Mr. Jones says. "He had a hot temper; that was his thing. We'd talk baseball and I'd move the conversation around so that we talked about attitude—I was trying to settle the boy down, to the best of my ability."

On Easter mornings when the boys were in high school, Mr. Jones always took one of his flatbed trucks that normally hauled Dumpsters, draped it in blue and gold crepe paper, the colors of the high school, and the players climbed aboard and rode as a float in the Watts Easter Parade. There they would be, the Boys of Crenshaw, amid majorettes and drum and bugle corps, antique cars and church groups, standing and waving to the crowds lining Central Avenue.

They hooted and hollered and sang and drank soda pop. A couple of them held up hand-lettered signs that said HAPPY EASTER. And when the parade was over, Thedo Jones says, "We all came back and had a big Easter egg hunt."

Even on nonholiday weekends, the Jones house was a constant gathering spot. "They came over here and stayed till school started the next week," says Tahitha Jones Moore, younger sister of the Jones brothers. "We would be cooking pork ribs, chicken, hot links, hot dogs, a big can of pork and beans, and they would be playing catch in the backyard and talking baseball all day and all night long. Oh, baseball was the thing, baby. That's all it was around here. Baseball and more baseball. My brothers loved that game, and my father loved it more than life itself.

"I wanted to play, but my father said, 'Ain't no daughter of mine gonna play.' But I followed them so strong it was as if I *was* playing. At the end of the season we would have a big barbecue and get a cake and put all their names on it. That was a special moment, cutting that cake. They would all want to eat the piece with their name on it. I remember a lot of laughing and joking with some of them saying, You got a piece with part of my name on it! Gimme that. Don't put that on your fork! Oh my goodness did we have fun."

* * *

Just a few days into practice in 1979, before the games began, three young men climbed over the fence near the Crenshaw High gym and jumped Carl Jones. They were gang members looking for trouble, not Crenshaw students. Carl, so bighearted with friends and teammates but ferocious when he needed to be, stood his ground. He got them all. He had it handled.

The fight was over and two of them were running away, but Carl's brother Donald didn't know that. He couldn't see that his services were not needed, or didn't want to. In the years that followed, Donald's loved ones would always wish that, at that moment, he could have held back.

All Donald saw was his younger brother fighting one against three.

He ran to his car and grabbed a baseball bat from the trunk. When he got back, the one remaining assailant had been subdued by a school security officer and handcuffed. Donald ran at the handcuffed kid and cracked him over the head with the bat. Several times. It was brutal. It was unnecessary. But to Donald, it felt like justice.

A defining difference in the lives of children who grow up in privilege and those who do not, is that the privileged kids get several chances to screw up. They have good lawyers. Or the criminal justice system is just naturally more sympathetic. No one wants to see some child lose his unlimited future over one regrettable episode. A kid in the inner city, though, often gets just one chance. And Donald Jones had just blown his.

"That whole thing really hurt Donald," says Carl. "He was kicked off the team, kicked out of school. The team got really down about that because we were all like one big family, and here it was, the season wasn't even started, and we had lost a part of the family."

Chris Brown says, "As long as Donald was with us, he was good. When he got broken off from our little cocoon, he wasn't as good."

The players had seen plenty of violence and believed, more or less, in a code of the streets. Aggression had to be met with more aggression. It was unavoidable. Violence occurred, the victims were mourned, then life went on.

Donald Jones's teammates regretted his actions but they understood them. Being a peacemaker didn't seem like an option; it didn't even seem safe. Sure, the guy who got cracked over the head was already subdued, no longer any threat, but that was no reason to think he didn't deserve what Donald gave him.

Cordie Dillard had brothers. He figured that's what he would have done, what any of them would have done. If you don't stand up for your brother, who would you stand up for?

At practice the day after the Donald Jones incident, the players were in the midst of their drills, moving between Coach Hurst's stations—popping tires, playing pepper, working on fielding and balance—when all of a sudden, shots rang out.

"Get down!" someone shouted.

Several of them knew what a bullet sounded like. Like a bee buzzing by. Some of the guys who had accosted Carl were back with guns. Three or four of them. Nelson Whiting saw them as they came running from the girls' side of the gym.

Some students were playing basketball on the outside courts, and the girls' softball team was practicing on a nearby field. Everybody in the line of fire did one of two things: They ran for their lives, or dropped to the ground and prayed.

There was a lot of yelling and screaming. Then, as suddenly as they had arrived, the shooters ran off. No one had been hit.

Brooks Hurst gathered the team and hustled them into the gym, where they did some drills. About a half hour later, they were back out on the Crenshaw diamond, playing baseball.

CHAPTER THREE

Crenshaw

Anyone who has been around athletics knows of the inverse relation-ship between talent and devotion. The most physically gifted players are often the least committed. The lesser talents, those who had to fight for a place on the team and a spot in the starting lineup, are absolutely dedicated. They live and breathe the game. They stand on the driveway until dark, sharpening their eye by hitting bottle caps with a broomstick, then go inside and do one hundred push-ups. They take a break, read back through the *The Science of Hitting*, do one hundred more push-ups— and then maybe some sit-ups, too, right before bed. They break your heart with how hard they try.

The gifted boys, they break your heart in a different way. They've been damaged by all the early applause—the back-patting, the adulation, the favors in the classroom, the girls, the free chicken and sodas. It is a lot to overcome.

50

There was no mistaking what Darryl Strawberry was: a prince of the physical world, blessed by DNA.

Crenshaw High did not begin until the tenth grade. When Darryl entered, he was already six-foot-three. He was long and lean and popping with sinewy muscle, not the kind manufactured in the weight room or purchased from the supplement aisle at the vitamin store, but the real thing. He had the body of a basketball forward and the natural baseball swing—a powerful, looping uppercut—of a historic home run hitter.

Like many of his teammates, he had started out playing in the street, hitting tennis balls with a broomstick, or rocks. Before he played on organized teams, Darryl and his four siblings played together, taking on all challengers. He was good right from the start. So were the rest of his family, including the two girls; the Strawberrys didn't lose many games.

The first time Darryl went out for a real team, at age ten, with uniforms and a league and a schedule, he showed up for tryouts and started playing catch with several dozen other kids. He came with a friend who had played the previous year. A coach asked his buddy: Who's the big left-handed kid? *That's Darryl Strawberry*, came the answer.

The coach pulled Darryl aside and told him not to go through the regular tryout and draft; we'll just work it out, he told him, so that you're on our team. Even then, he was a free agent, a bonus baby. The next year, Darryl got lured to a new team by the coach who offered unlimited postgame chicken and sodas.

At fifteen years old, he had no memory of ever being anything but an exalted athlete. Playing sports wasn't hard; everything else was. He was never even conscious of learning to play a sport, struggling to perfect a skill or to keep up with better players. "I just remember always being the first one picked," Darryl says, "no matter if we were playing football, basketball, or baseball."

George Cook knew Darryl Strawberry from the third grade on up. "We played at Rancho La Cienega Park—they call it Jackie Robinson Stadium now," he says. "Even as a young kid, you can tell who has it and who doesn't, and Darryl obviously had it. He was the best outfielder. The best pitcher. He was the best at whatever anyone needed him to be, even when there were kids on the field who were a lot older. It didn't matter.

You knew he'd make it out and you'd hear about him if he didn't get murdered or something. But it went to his head. As long as I've known Darryl, he didn't want to listen to nobody. He wanted you to think that baseball needed him more than he needed baseball."

Nelson Whiting, the "scholar," was not quite as sure of Darryl's prospects. "He was kind of talented, but not polished. And he had a bad attitude. He was always arguing with coaches. I thought: This kid is not going to amount to anything. He's too messed up."

* * *

Baseball has often been said to be about fathers and sons, men across generations, uncomfortable with words, connecting through the game's quiet, timeless rhythms. "Baseball is fathers and sons playing catch, the profound archaic song of birth, growth, age and death," the poet Donald Hall wrote. "The diamond encloses what we are."

At Crenshaw, the diamond enclosed a lot of sadness and loss. It was a forum for sons to play out dramas with their fathers, bitter dramas. The fathers had passed the game down to them; in some cases, it was all they passed down. But the sons wouldn't share; they kept baseball for themselves. Baseball was what they could withhold, their singular opportunity for retribution.

Their fathers, roughly contemporaries of Jackie Robinson, faced straight-on racism in Los Angeles, and before that in some cases down South—restrictions on where they could live and work, promotions denied, the relentless accumulation of indignities and petty slights.

The sons faced a different social plague: fatherlessness. Some would say that was a legacy of racism, but such an explanation, even if offered, would not have been a comfort. For the Boys of Crenshaw, having fathers who walked out left them angry, sad, and in the most extreme case, crippled.

"When you're a kid, you want your father to be there," says George Cook. "You want him at father-and-son night, in the yard playing catch, all those things. Most of us didn't have that. I always had to call on my older brother, which left a bitterness. When I started playing baseball, and getting pretty good at it, I would tell my father, 'I don't want you to come to my games.' When I got to be a teenager and in high school, I would say straight out, 'You weren't there before, I don't really want you to come around now.' "

Darryl Strawberry, always the one for drama, for living at life's extremes, had the most charged relationship with his father of all the Crenshaw players. He fell in the middle of Henry and Ruby Strawberry's five children, between two older brothers and two younger sisters. Henry was a postal worker and a fine athlete himself, a locally famous football and softball player in sandlot leagues around L.A. Ruby was devout and strikingly pretty—some people took her to be Darryl's big sister.

When his father abruptly left home, Darryl was thirteen years old. His two brothers, Ronnie and Michael, had taken the lead in pushing Henry out the door, but Darryl says the whole ugly scene left him wounded and, for some reason, ashamed. He felt somehow responsible for it all, even though, he says, "My father drank, and he beat me when he was drunk. He beat us all." As to why his late mother denied she or the children were beaten, he says, "I can't tell you why my mom denied that. But nobody wants to admit that they're in a family where there's physical abuse."

Whatever happened inside the house, it inflicted lasting damage. Even after he was no longer living at home, Henry Strawberry attended Crenshaw games. "Michael would talk to his father when he came to watch him play," Brooks Hurst says. "But Darryl wouldn't. He would ignore him. When Darryl lost his father, he lost some part of himself. For whatever reason, it occurred at the worst possible moment in his life."

"Darryl feels everything," Hurst says. "He absorbs everything. That's how he goes through life."

Jack Novick, the junior varsity coach at Crenshaw, says: "Darryl had that smile, that beautiful smile, but there was always something sad in his eyes. You could never get to the depths of that."

When Darryl first came out for the team, as a sophomore in 1978, Hurst set about trying to remake him. Darryl was alternately sullen from the troubles at home, or too full of himself from the glory on the playground. He was a toxic mix of bluster, self-doubt, and self-pity. In any of his moods he was a handful, and uncoachable much of the time.

Hurst tried to teach him to "beat the ball to the spot" in the outfield—to run hard for balls that fell in for base hits, rather than glide to them as runners took extra bases. Darryl had that loping gait that allowed him to cover a lot of ground in a hurry without seeming to exert himself, just as he hit long home runs without having to swing from his heels. It all came so easily. Scouts loved that. But there is a fine line between athletic grace and giving half an effort—just plain dogging it.

"I had to be careful," Hurst says, "because Darryl was the kind of athlete who could look like he was not hustling even when he was. But believe me, much of the time he wasn't. I was constantly aggravated with him. I had to sit him down and talk to him a lot. I had him run laps. I would tell him: The scouts come in here with assumptions about inner-city ballplayers. You have to counteract that. Don't give them that ammunition. But finally, I just ran out of patience."

Darryl's tenth-grade season ended early when Hurst kicked him off the team. "I just said to him, 'This isn't working out. I hope you want to come back next year,' " Hurst says. "Darryl took it pretty well. He still came to games. He helped lug the equipment."

Hurst would be the last person in Darryl's life, until many years later, to try to impose discipline on him. His character and emotional frailty were either not apparent or were just ignored by the people whose business was the commodification of raw talent. For them, Darryl was a blinding, once-in-a-lifetime find, and they felt lucky just to be in his presence.

"I saw him for the first time at a high school game out in some cow patch," says Richie Bry, who would become his first agent. (I interviewed Bry not long before his death in December 2001.) "There were like twenty people standing around, and nine of them were scouts. I had my son with me, who was a student at USC. He takes a look around and says, 'What are we doing here?' And I said, 'Just wait and watch, and keep your eye on the big kid in right field. You'll remember this day the rest of your life.' "

* * *

Darryl Strawberry was hardly the only Crenshaw boy with an ego about his ballplaying. Cordie Dillard, the big-hitting second baseman, was about as cocky as they come. He took particular pride in his ability to hit curveballs. When a pitcher threw him one, he would shout—as the pitch was coming to the plate—*Curve!*, then swing and smack a line drive somewhere. Nobody had ever seen anything like that before.

His talents were not easily assessed. Cordie wasn't all that big, strong, or fast. He could just play. He had superior hand-eye coordination overlaid with the kind of supreme arrogance that serves an athlete well; the more Cordie Dillard told himself he was better and smarter than all the rest, the more true it became.

He was also a lot slicker than most of his teammates, even a bit of a con. Cordie knew how to please adults and how to make them think he was doing what they wanted, even when he wasn't. He had it all handled—the clothes, the girls, the car, the coach. Years later, Darryl Strawberry would say of his old teammate: "Cordie was Mr. Cool. He was like, Look at me, baby, it's about me. I'm *Cordie Dillard*."

Some of the other Crenshaw players would complain to Brooks Hurst that Cordie was his pet, and Hurst, who could be every bit the wiseass that his players were, wouldn't deny it. "You think I like Cordie better than you?" he'd banter. "Well, you know what? I do. Cordie listens to me, and you give me a whole lot of shit, so why shouldn't I like him better?"

Cordie tried to instruct his teammates on the fine art of coach-pleasing, which he first learned playing point guard for Crenshaw's basketball team. That team's strength was a couple of dominant big men, so Cordie was told to dribble the ball up court, throw it inside, and get out of the way. Which he dutifully did.

It was all so easy: just follow directions. The team won a state championship, and Cordie earned a ring and lavish praise for being the clever little orchestrator of it all. But this life skill of Cordie's, submitting to authority without surrendering his own swagger, did not come so easily to his teammates. They resented it as a charade at the same time they wished they could pull it off.

"Cordie seemed older than everybody," Marvin McWhorter says. "He was smooth. He was a good talker. He was like Mr. Popular. He would get on some guys in a joking way, and if you were a weak individual, he could get to you. Some people didn't care for him. He managed two worlds, the social and the athletic. He was Brooks's favorite and the favorite of the ladies."

George Cook adds: "Cordie was considered in high school a very attractive man. He didn't have any problems getting women, and he let you know that. He had this whole atmosphere about him. His brother had a lowrider which must have cost $3,000 or $4,000, which was a lot at the time. It was one of those cars like you'd ride on Hollywood Boulevard, a show car with the hydraulic lifts and the nice paint job with lacquer and the rims and all that, and sometimes Cordie would ride up to school in it and all the girls would be like, ooh, aah, Cordie, can we get a ride in that? I don't want to say Cordie was spoiled, although he was—I'll just say he had it a little easier than some of us."

Some of Cordie's sense of self, his confidence on and off the field, did in fact derive from an air of superiority. The whole Dillard clan had been plumbers back in Miscobie, Oklahoma, and had migrated en masse—his mother and father, some aunts and uncles—to start up quite a successful little plumbing concern in L.A. Poor folks needed toilets unclogged and busted pipes repaired, just like rich folks. The Dillards had several trucks, producing a good, steady income. Cordie understood that the family business afforded him a comfortable life—not, of course, that he ever planned to go into that line of work. But Cordie was never one to have to say that he "stayed" at a certain address.

"We always lived in a house, never that apartment life," he says. "I had my mother and my father at home, until he passed. And I went to one elementary school, one junior high, and one high school, whereas, you know, certain kids went to like three or four elementary schools and a couple of junior highs. I wasn't trying to get out of where I was—I had stability.

"The majority of time, if somebody was going to spend the night, it was at my house. Some people might say, 'I don't want nobody coming over my house. I don't want nobody to know where I live.' But I didn't have that problem. I was always, 'You can come over. Come on, I got my own bedroom.' "

*   *   *

Instead of taking public transportation home from Crenshaw, most of the players—after stopping at the Record Shop for their sandwiches or another nearby joint for tacos—walked out into the city together. They swapped stories, shared dreams, playfully punched each other, even wrestled on the sidewalks, until the last one peeled off and headed for home. If it took an extra hour, they didn't care.

"We just wanted to be together," Nelson Whiting says. "Once we got to high school, we even had to all go to the same park and be on the same summer team. We couldn't do nothing without each other. We were like brothers, the whole team."

And they *were* like brothers, of a certain kind: highly competitive ones, prone to bickering and even backbiting. They were as competitive as they were close. The team's titans, the boys who vied for top-dog status, were clearly Cordie Dillard, Darryl Strawberry, and Chris Brown. But every Crenshaw player thought highly of his own prowess. This was, after all, a team so good that its second-stringers would end up with pro contracts. To a player, each Crenshaw boy considered the most important competition to be the one they waged among themselves. Who could hit for the highest average? Belt the most home runs? Be the most impressive to scouts?

In batting practice, Chris Brown was usually the first to start the barrage of home run balls and the contest that went along with it. If he caught one really good, he could send it over the twenty-foot-high left-field fence, across Eighth Avenue, and into the yard of the old man who would come out and gesticulate and curse at each sighting of a ball rolling up onto his property. That was the goal: to make the old man fuss. That got the biggest laughs and the heartiest high-fives.

After Chris put one in the old man's yard, he would hand over the orange Tennessee Thumper aluminum bat, which nearly the whole team used, and flash a self-satisfied, can-you-top-this smile to the next hitter in line. And that player would take dead aim at the old man's yard, and usually hit it.

In center field, the goal was to reach the roof of the Whitney Young Continuing Education Building, just beyond the outfield fence. But that was an even more prodigious blast, a 420-foot bomb at least, and only a few of the Crenshaw boys—Chris Brown; Darryl Strawberry; Reggie Dymally, fortified by his nightly push-ups; occasionally, big Marvin McWhorter—had the manly strength to hit the ball quite that far.

In right field, the wind blew straight in most afternoons. Only one player could clear that fence with any regularity: Darryl Strawberry. The others comforted themselves in the knowledge that Darryl, batting left-handed, had a big advantage because he could pull the ball in that direction. Even so, it was more than a little eye-opening when Darryl, in a game, flew one over the fence, over the street, over two front yards, and onto the grass of the third house up the block. "An unbelievable shot," Brooks Hurst says. "Just completely unbelievable that a high school kid could hit it that far."

But as far as his teammates were concerned, this feat did not give Strawberry top billing. Nothing would have. He was just Darryl to the rest of them. If he looked like a future superstar, well, that's what they figured they all were. If Darryl got four hits, then Chris, the twins, Carl Jones, all of them wanted four hits. If he hit a home run, they all wanted home runs.

"Whatever anybody did," Cordie says, "we would say to ourselves, 'I can top that.' And we usually could. It wasn't just woofin', because everybody on that team who woofed could back it up."

All of this raging self-confidence made Brooks Hurst's job immensely difficult. To be coached, a player must have some degree of humility. He must acknowledge weaknesses and areas in need of improvement. Several of the Crenshaw players were not yet at that point.

"The guys we had were so good, and they all had egos," George Cook says. "Coach Hurst had a hard time managing the egos. The only ones he could really reach were Cordie and some of the younger guys like me and Marvin and Reggie [Dymally]. Darryl Strawberry didn't listen to him. Darryl McNealy, I would be surprised if he listened to one thing Coach said all year. Chris, he listened when he felt like it, which wasn't too often."

It can be tiresome to hear black athletes on TV going on about *respect*—earning it from other teams, from a coach, from the media. All kinds of behavior, from basketball star Lattrell Sprewell choking his coach on down, is explained by some version of: I was just doing what I had to do. As a man. But it is also true that sports is the one realm in which black men have been conditioned to understand that if they aggressively demand respect, they may actually get it. In sports—as opposed to on the job, in the maelstrom of workaday L.A., or New York, Chicago, or Philly—there is at least the prospect that talent might prevail.

For most of the Crenshaw players, baseball was where they first sought to establish manhood. It was where they had control, a sense that they operated from a position of strength. So even as little boys, they dug in. They defied. It was like practice for handling themselves in the harsh world of their parents. Sometimes it served them, but usually it didn't.

Chris Brown was ten years old when he tried out for a park-league team called the Cubs, whose players were up to three years older. He came home crying when the coach told him he was too young. "So my older brother beat me up and told me to go back out there and make the coach give me a chance," he says.

He did, and he made the team—and later that season, the league all-star team.

Chris was neither sullen like Darryl Strawberry nor smooth like Cordie Dillard. He was smart, stubborn, and mouthy—his own worst enemy. He wanted desperately to be a ballplayer, but on his terms only. And just like Darryl Strawberry, he clashed with Brooks Hurst the first time he tried out for Crenshaw's varsity, and could not keep his place on the team.

Chris was a senior on the 1979 team, a year ahead of Darryl, so he first came out for the Crenshaw varsity in 1977, as a sophomore. He arrived at practice that season a couple of days late, after completing the basketball season. "The twins were already out there, and so were Carl and Donald and some of the others," he says. "Cordie came the same day as me because he was playing basketball, but Coach had already seen Cordie play before. With me, he's like telling me right off the bat, you ain't good enough for the varsity. And him being a white guy and me being a black guy, maybe that had something to do with it. I'm like, who is this white guy telling me that? I've been playing with all of them since I could stand on my own two feet, and I felt like I was better than all of them. Even the seniors."

Chris made it through the early weeks of practice, but began the season's first game on the bench. "We were playing Manual Arts, and I'm sitting there and a girl I like is sitting in the stands behind us. And we're kicking their ass; it's like 10–0 in the fifth inning, and he finally puts me in. At Crenshaw, when you're playing third base, the sun starts setting in your eyes. Soon as I'm in the game, a guy hits a high chopper and it gets in the sun. I can't see it till the last second, and it tips off my glove. And he [Hurst] goes ballistic.

"And I'm like, Not with me you don't. And I just cursed him out and walked off the field. I mean I called him everything. I walked in the locker room, and here he comes walking behind me, and we almost get into it. Willie West and Joe Weakley [the basketball coaches] settled it down, and I eventually went back out there. In order for me to come back, I had to apologize and run like five miles. I figured, okay, I want to play baseball, so this is what I have to do.

"But a few days later we got into it about something else and I just quit. I decided, I ain't gonna play for this man anymore. I went down and played JV. I said, 'First you are telling me that I'm not good enough to play, and then I make one mistake and you are gonna chew me out in front of everybody.' I felt like, I can take anything as a man. But don't embarrass or disrespect me."

*   *   *

Brooks Hurst had complicated, not easily categorized racial views. He cared deeply about his players and students. He spent time over the summer in their neighborhoods, keeping in touch, watching their park-league games, hunting for new talent. He bought a batting cage for the school with his own money, then poured more money and his own time into repairing it after the nets were repeatedly vandalized. He was no rube, but even he could be taken: One time, he bailed a kid out of jail and kept his watch as collateral, only to find out the watch had been stolen from another teacher.

Hurst and the big-league scout Phil Pote considered themselves crusaders for the cause of baseball in the inner city, sometimes referring to the dwindling number of blacks still involved in the game as "our people."

But as much as he tried to understand the world of his students, what Hurst saw all around him—gangs and drugs, broken families, the absence of decent values—filled him with disgust. He was much too close to the ground to adopt the stereotypical liberal position that discrimination and "social inequities" were at the root of all problems in the black community. Much of what he saw he could not justify or rationalize, and in that way he was right in step with the socially conservative, churchgoing black crowd, the Sid Thompsons, Lorraine Bradleys, and all the others who had to deal with the situation at hand and did not have the luxury of dreaming of how they might make the world into a better place.

When a district policy resulted in the transfer of several of Crenshaw's veteran black teachers, replacing them with young white teachers, Hurst disdained the newcomers as naive do-gooders. "They had beautiful intentions," he says. "They just couldn't control a classroom."

Hurst didn't accept excuses. He didn't coddle. Give a kid a crutch, he liked to say, and he'll learn to limp. If someone suggested that what a certain student really needed was a good whupping at home, Brooks Hurst wasn't one to disagree. He held the two most gifted players on his team, Chris Brown and Darryl Strawberry, to the same standards as the lesser players, a rarity at any level of sports, even high school.

Anyone who skipped practice or cut classes didn't play. If they pushed Hurst too far, they were gone. He didn't give up on kids, but on the other hand, the talent ran so deep that everyone was in a sense expendable. George Cook recalls, "Sometimes one of the guys would fall out with Brooks and say they quit, and he'd say, 'OK, you quit. Goodbye. Have a nice life,' or whatever. But they came back after a couple of days, 'cause they knew baseball was their bread and butter."

When Crenshaw made the city playoffs in 1977, Hurst asked Chris Brown to join the varsity for the postseason. It was a peace offer, an olive branch, but mainly a way to get a good player on the roster. Hurst was in the character-building business, but only to a point; like most coaches, he was competitive enough to want to win ball games. Chris Brown could help him do that, but out of pique, he refused the offer to come up to the big club at the end of his sophomore season. "Chris was making his little statement," Hurst says, still sounding annoyed.

Chris Brown played for Hurst the following two seasons on the varsity, but even during the glory-filled 1979 season, coach and player never did get it right. Brown was a prodigy whose skills in the Punt, Pass & Kick competition had already taken him to San Francisco, Dallas, Atlanta, and Washington, D.C. (Some of the other Crenshaw boys had barely been out of L.A.) He didn't readily accept Hurst's instruction; in fact, the very idea that there needed to *be* a coach was an affront, a challenge to his status and manhood.

When Chris was pouting or not listening, he stood around with his baseball glove on his head. That was his sign that he was a little out of sorts. And that glove was on his head, it seemed, several times a week.

"We were always on Cordie, telling him he kisses the coach's ass," Chris says. "I was sort of at the other end of the spectrum. A knucklehead. But I still say he did not have to be on us like he was. We had all had good coaches at the playgrounds and knew what to do in baseball situations. If he just threw the ball out there we would have known what to do."

Hurst worked around Brown by keeping up a dialogue with his mother, phoning her nearly every day. "I used to call it 'the daily Chris Brown report.' I would just let her know how he was doing. Sometimes I would tell her not to give him any allowance on some weeks. For disrespect. To be perfectly honest, Chris was a jerk with me. We had a lot of problems."

His immense talent made it hard to convince him of the need to improve. Late to report to the baseball team in the spring of 1979 because of basketball, and without even one day of practice, he swatted the first pitch he saw in a preseason game for a 375-foot home run. It was almost just like his teammates said of him, that Chris could get out of bed and hit a home run. "He just walked up there and smacked it," George Cook says. "I guess he took batting practice before the game, but I couldn't even say he did, for sure. You looked at Chris and you just said: Wow, that's a baseball player."

One day in the middle of the season, George Genovese pulled his big Cadillac up to the field at Crenshaw. Hurst's team had started the season stomping teams by scores of 10–1, 13–0, 12–0. They were men among boys. Genovese had nearly every Crenshaw player on his draft list, but Chris Brown was at the top. The scout scanned the field, where the team was taking infield practice, then looked over at the bench and saw the star third baseman sitting by himself in street clothes rather than his blue-and-gold Crenshaw uniform.

He approached Hurst. "Why isn't Brown playing?" he asked.

"He's been a little frisky lately," Hurst replied. "I thought he needed a day to get himself together."

*   *   *

Every successful team has someone who is its emotional center of gravity, its rock. It is rarely the most talented player, or even the most vocal, and it may not even be someone who has such a firm grip on his own life away from the playing field. But on the field he is the leader, in total control. At Crenshaw, everyone agreed that player was Carl Jones.

"Carl was so hard core, man, he was like baseball as you imagine it seventy-five years ago," Nelson Whiting says. "He chewed that Red Man long cut. . . ."

"He chewed it like he was eating it," Reggie Dymally says. "I would say, 'Carl, can you get that shit out of your teeth, please?' "

"Of all the players I have ever played the game of baseball with," Darryl Strawberry says, "Carl Jones was the one who got me most excited about playing. He had more energy than anybody. He was always filthy dirty. He was just *into it* in a way that got everybody going."

At just under six feet tall and 180 pounds, Carl was built like, well, a catcher. He was a solid block of baseball, an exquisite marriage of form and function. When a runner attempted to steal second base, he had the upper body and arm strength to make the throw without coming out of his crouch—he fired it right from his knees. The ball arrived at second base like a BB, usually six inches to a foot above the bag.

"Guys would slide into the tag, they'd be like, Where the hell did that come from?" Nelson Whiting says. "They weren't used to the ball being there waiting for them."

Not just physically, but by disposition, Carl was a catcher. He thought of himself as the guy who takes out the trash and cleans up the messes. A practitioner of dirty jobs. That, to him, was what a catcher did. "You have to accept it or find another position," he says, "and on our team, all the other positions were taken."

On ground balls to the infield, Carl did what catchers are taught to do but rarely are dedicated enough to accomplish with real resolve—that is, sprint up the first-base line with the runner to back up first base in case of an errant throw. That's not easy to do in full catcher's gear, in the heat of a day. But Carl ripped his mask off and chugged up the line, every time.

"Carl was the type of person that did not let you quit," George Cook says. "You need to have talent on a team but you also need someone with balls. When things got rough, Carl was the one to get in your face and tell you, 'We ain't quittin', we ain't losing this game.' And, excuse my language, but he was the one to clear away all the excuses everybody might have and say, 'Fuck that, you know, fuck it all, let's just go kick some butt.'

"He kind of reminded me of Thurman Munson. He could talk to the pitchers real reasonably, but if he had to, he would get right in their face, point-blank, and tell them they were wimping out. If you needed a hit, he got you a hit. If you needed a double, he hit you a double. Carl was not that gifted athletically. He took a backseat to some of the higher-profile players. But we knew what he was about."

The second-tier players were not as focused on destiny, on what was preordained for them on the basis of their natural talent. It was not a matter of having faith or not; they simply understood, even as teenagers, that they were not God's gift to baseball and therefore had better work toward what they wanted. Having to strive and constantly assess where they fit in, or if they even fit in at all, did not permit them the luxury of self-absorption. By necessity, they had to see the bigger picture. So the lesser lights among the Boys of Crenshaw—those who were not Darryl Strawberry, Chris Brown, or Cordie Dillard—tended to be better ob-servers, and more astute judges of character.

Fernando Becker was sort of the accidental shortstop. He carried forward no reputation from the playgrounds. He was given a tiny red, white, and blue glove by his grandfather when he was ten years old, and he didn't give it up for a better mitt until it was time to try out at Crenshaw. If Donald Jones hadn't been kicked out of school after the baseball bat incident, and if a couple of other promising infielders hadn't flamed out along the way, Fernando may not have played much. He was so quiet as to be nearly invisible to some of his teammates; not all of them even knew that he was different in one way, the lone Hispanic on the team, with parents who had emigrated from Panama. Most of them assumed he was just another black guy like they were.

"I don't think a lot of the other guys were expecting me to be a start-ing player," he says. "I got my shot and I tried my best to take advantage of it. But I still kept to the background. I didn't try to have a lot to say," which was a lesson he learned early in his athletic career.

Before he got to Crenshaw, he was kicked out of a summer-league game after he argued with an umpire and threw his helmet. He had been trying to stretch a double into a triple, and thought he got in safely under the tag. His mother showed up a little later, saw him crying in the bleach-ers, and asked what was wrong. "Leave me alone," he said, loudly. She slapped him right across the face, right there in full view.

That was the last time Fernando argued with an umpire. Or a coach. And it was definitely the last time he sassed his mother in public.

To Fernando and several of the others, the ego-driven competition among the team's superstars was a source of ongoing fascination and sometimes amusement. And the ranking of those stars by scouts, and by the growing horde of media descending on the team, did not match the reality they knew.

Chris Brown, not Darryl Strawberry, was the best player among them, Fernando believes. Chris could hit for average and for power. He had hands like butter. He was, in Fernando's estimation, "a freak of nature."

The next best was the twin at first base, Darryl McNealy, who could "scoop it at first base" and do everything Darryl Strawberry could do but hit home runs. The third best was Reggie Dymally, who had "arms like Popeye from being a workout fanatic."

"Darryl Strawberry was special, don't get me wrong, but I would put him fourth behind those guys," says Fernando. "To tell you the truth, Darryl was a bigger figure to *Sports Illustrated*"—*SI* published a feature on the young star when he was still at Crenshaw—"than he was to us. He did have a knack for drama—he would hit game-winning grand slams, that kind of thing—but he was a creation of the press as far as we were concerned."

Other Crenshaw players ranked their teammates, with some minor variations, in much the same way: Chris Brown at the top, and Darryl Strawberry a little down the list. They also took careful note of the cascade of praise and hero worship that washed over their more celebrated teammates, and they understood its eroding effect. In Darryl Strawberry, particularly, traits like responsibility, humility, and accountability never took root amid the rapture.

"All those scouts, all those white guys would come around to see Darryl and it was like, 'Mr. Strawberry, hello Mr. Strawberry, may I have a word with you,' " says Reggie Dymally. "And I thought, they have no idea. You had these people treating Darryl as if he were a god. I looked at them as leeches. What if he breaks his neck the next day? They would all be gone. But Darryl never thought in that direction. Brooks handled it very well. He didn't kiss his butt, but he was about the only one who didn't.

"Chris Brown definitely had more raw talent than Darryl. Chris, by birth, could just do anything in any sport. But Darryl had the potential to

66

be a celebrity star because of his name, his height, and the way he carried himself. The name was big. I honestly believe that if Chris had the last name of *Strawberry*, he'd have been the one whose butt everybody was kissing, not that Chris didn't get plenty of that same treatment, too. But with Darryl, it was crazy; it was all out of proportion."

Even in high school, an entourage formed around Darryl—flatterers and flunkies he either pulled close to him or couldn't repel. "He had that thing about him that people wanted to be around him," Fernando Becker says. "He started having his own crew with him, guys who weren't on the team with us. Maybe he saw himself on that level. But there were times we started to not want to hang with him, because we wanted real friends. We didn't want to be part of nobody's crew."

The self-regard of the team's other two stars also wore on their team-mates at times. "Chris was loud and conceited," Nelson Whiting says. "You couldn't tell him nothing. It was his way or he would cop an atti-tude, like a little baby. He would say anything to anybody. Sometimes he would be joking—or he would just say something to get you upset. He didn't care."

Cordie Dillard, says Marvin McWhorter, could also be thoughtlessly stinging. "He was bossy. He was a spoiled brat a lot of the time. There were times I know that Chris and Cordie couldn't stand each other. It was like one of those old Westerns where the guy rides in and says, 'I don't know if this town is big enough for the two of us.' We laughed about it. It was funny."

*   *   *

As one might expect of a group of high school boys, the Crenshaw play-ers did not always use what might be called sound judgment. They had escapades. One night several of them piled into the "undercover car," a battered station wagon which belonged to the Joneses, and which may or may not have been registered, and headed for a football game at Palisades High School. Darryl McNealy drove, with Nelson Whiting next to him in the passenger seat, the Jones boys and the other twin in the row behind, and Darryl Strawberry stretched out in the way-back, in the cargo space.

When they pulled up to the game, before everyone was even out of the car, Darryl Strawberry got into a hassle with a kid in the parking lot which became a fistfight in a flash. By the time everyone turned around to see what was happening, "he was socking somebody in the face," Nelson Whiting says. "He busted him up pretty good. We had never seen this other kid before. We were like, What the hell is going on here? But we knew we had to get out of there because we were a bunch of black dudes on the wrong side of town."

Those who had made it out of the car quickly scurried back in. The old car started back up—praise the Lord!—they wheeled out of the parking lot, took a wrong turn, and promptly got lost, somehow ending up on the leafy, mansion-lined streets of exclusive Bel Air. They took a moment to catch their breath. Gave thanks for getting the hell out of there. Then turned their attention, finally, to the back of the car. *Darryl, what the fuck was that? What'd you hit that boy for?* As with so much else, Darryl had no real answer. *You don't know why you hit him? You thought he said something? What'd he say? You don't know what he said?*

They gave up on trying to get an explanation from Darryl, looked out the windows at the mansions, tried to figure out how to get turned back east and toward somewhere they recognized. Maybe they'd seen these streets on TV, but they definitely had never been on them. Someone thought to look at the gas gauge. It was on red.

You think they got gas stations in places like this?

Nelson finally navigated them out. He had been over in that direction before, to a music store, although not exactly on these Bel Air streets. "That's the way it went," he says. "Somebody was always doing something and we had to bail them out—not literally, but pull them away and get away from the scene. That was kind of my role. When I was out with the guys, I was sort of there but not there, more of an observer type who stands back and takes it all in. I was the one who laughed at everyone's jokes—and who had the cool head if we were in a jam."

Nelson was also one of the few who had his eye on something other than sports. He was not as invested in the myth of his own athletic prowess, or of sports in general. Nelson's other life, an entirely separate life, was music. He started playing the piano early in grammar school, then picked up the guitar. By junior high school, Nelson was something of a music prodigy. "I could read music before I got there, but it really got ingrained at that school. We had a very good music program. We went to some competitions—in junior high, we were competing against college-level bands."

Nelson got interested in the drums after pounding out rhythms on some moving boxes left outside after one of his family's several relocations. A drummer happened to live nearby and encouraged him. His mother soon bought him a small drum set, and Nelson joined a band that had paying gigs. "It was a combo band, a little soft jazz, some James Brown stuff. I was in the union. We went to Tahoe and did a couple shows up there and I was getting $250 a set for eleven songs, and we'd do three sets a night. That was pretty damn good money. My mom didn't get to my games because they were during the day—she might have seen me play in one Little League game—but she'd come to some of the shows. Once she was crying 'cause she was just so proud of me. I wasn't really thinking seriously about baseball all through high school and I probably didn't concentrate on it like some of the guys, although I did take it serious.

"All my dreams were in the direction of music. I didn't know if I would be performing, or have my own little music studio, or go into teaching, but it'd definitely be music."

Tellingly, Nelson was shocked to learn that the 1979 Crenshaw team was considered special, even historic—the most talented assemblage of high school talent ever. "You've got to be kidding me," he says.

He thought they were just playing baseball, that he was on a pretty good team with a couple of star players.

* * *

"I watched Julia Child," Reggie Dymally says. He was the other one who had a burning passion apart from athletics. His teammates learned how to turn the double play on *This Week in Baseball*, Reggie tuned in to his local PBS affiliate and found out what the heck foie gras was, how long to cook the choucroute, and how to dress the baby spring greens with a good vinaigrette.

He watched *The Galloping Gourmet*. Watched every cooking show he could find. He cooked for his mother, his sister, for whatever guests came into the house. "I loved cooking before I loved baseball. I didn't share that with anybody. I wasn't ashamed of it; I just don't think anyone would have been very interested."

Reggie Dymally's background was a little different than the others. His mother was from Baltimore, but on his father's side, the Dymallys had come to L.A. from the Caribbean nation of Trinidad and Tobago. His uncle Mervyn Dymally served as California's first black lieutenant governor. Reggie may have been the only Crenshaw player with a parent who went beyond high school.

"On my birth certificate, it says that my father was a draftsman, so I know he went to school. He was an educated man. On my father's side, they are all very well educated. They were attorneys and so forth."

But Reggie wasn't raised in Baldwin Hills or anyplace fancy like that. He was as poor, or poorer, than most of his teammates. When his parents split, his father remarried and began a new family, leaving his mother to raise and support the family on her own. But Reggie seemed to have come by some of the Dymally legacy: a lively curiosity, and an estimable work ethic.

"I was never pushed into sports," he says. "I didn't have brothers or uncles or cousins who played or took me to ballparks, but I was always playing, just for fun. But I didn't play organized sports. I wanted to, but I just couldn't afford it. It always cost something for an entry fee, a glove, spikes, whatever, and I didn't want to put that burden on my mother."

He played on his first baseball team at thirteen years old, very late to start. But when he finally did take it up, he did so with a steely resolve and confidence. "When I got out on the field at Crenshaw, I was in awe at first—I was in awe of the other guys. They had been playing for five, six, seven, eight years, and they were stars before they even got to Crenshaw.

They had a ton of talent, but I noticed that they didn't all put the energy into it they could have.

"Luckily, I did have some talent, and I was focused. I would work out before school, on weekends, swing a heavy bat two hundred times for strength, then swing at bottle caps with a broomstick for hand-eye coordination—or I'd throw a ball against the wall for an hour to build up my arm, which was a weak point for me. My thing is, when I do something, I have to do it all the way. Once I decided to play, there was no way I was going to sit on the bench. That wasn't even a question."

Reggie was introspective and diffident, rarely the one to cut up or make a joke. He tried to laugh at teammates' jokes, but he was one of those people whose face does not easily form into a smile, even when he might want it to. "I was the quiet one," he says. "That's what people have told me. You noticed me, but you didn't. I spoke with my bat."

Reggie was a favorite of Brooks Hurst's, for obvious reasons. He listened. He worked. He caused not one ounce of trouble. He was held in high regard by his teammates as well, who appreciated that unlike Cordie Dillard, he stayed in the coach's good graces without lording it over them or making it seem like some kind of scam.

"Reggie was a little bit of an outsider, but you'll find that he was highly respected," Hurst says. "Physically, he was like a young Steve Garvey. The other kids respected his power at the plate, and they respected the way that he carried himself."

Marvin McWhorter, always the connoisseur of hitting, says, "Reggie was a very intelligent guy. And when he got to high school, he was already like a man. He had a full beard, and he was buffed. He was one of those diehards in the weight room. We called him baby Jim Rice. He couldn't hit a curveball, but throw him a fastball and he'd just tear you up."

* * *

"When W.E.B. Du Bois was the editor of *The Crisis* magazine, he published portraits of black college graduates, lawyers and doctors on its cover and in its pages," Henry Louis Gates wrote in a 1992 essay. "Being an athlete or an entertainer was fine and good, for Du Bois, but these were not serious occupations. Law and medicine, education and scholarship—these were the pinnacles of achievement, these were the province of the Talented Tenth."

Du Bois published his famous Talented Tenth essay in 1903, segregated times, when most black communities were composed of the whole social strata, with professionals, shopkeepers, and schoolteachers living in close proximity to domestics, factory workers, and grade-school-educated laborers. It was Du Bois's hope that the "exceptional men"—"the best of this Race"—would, by example, uplift the masses.

In Gates's essay, titled "Two Nations . . . Both Black," he lamented that the spirit of Du Bois had been lost and that black America had gone down two divergent paths: One set of black folks had aspirations that matched those in mainstream America, and was willing to work to achieve them, while the other was so dispirited that it disdained future-oriented pursuits like education.

"As crazy as this sounds," Gates wrote, "recent surveys of young black kids reveal a distressing pattern. Far too many say that succeeding is 'white,' education is 'white,' aspiring and dreaming are 'white,' believing you can make it is 'white.' "

By the time the Boys of Crenshaw were growing up in Los Angeles, those whom Du Bois would have considered the black community's elite, its exceptionals, had long since separated themselves from the poorer element. As Lorraine Bradley and Sid Thompson pointed out, the Talented Tenth (and then some) had virtually *run* up to Baldwin Hills, and to other newly integrated neighborhoods even farther from the inner city. Without close-at-hand models to demonstrate what schooling might do for a person, even some of the most able students among the Boys of Crenshaw had the whole Du Bois thing turned upside down: To them, it was *education* that didn't seem like a serious pursuit.

"They pushed, at the time, other stuff to black kids rather than education," Reggie Dymally says. "It was all about, how am I gonna make some money? And who did you know who was making money because they were educated? I had my uncle, but most people didn't know anybody. Maybe they had heard about them, but they were no longer in the community."

Dymally was in a college prep course at Crenshaw. So, in fact, was most of the team. But being in college prep didn't actually mean you were going to college; it just meant you weren't in metal shop or automotive repair.

Dymally, George Cook, Fernando Becker, and Nelson Whiting pulled good grades. Chris Brown was bright but indifferent. "He had plenty of intelligence, but no interest in academics," says James Derrick, who was his English teacher.

The Jones boys, except during baseball season, were sporadic in their class attendance. "They were always in a hurry to go someplace," George Cook says. "Where? I have no idea. But they were too busy for class. It was strange."

On game days, the Joneses, the twins, Darryl Strawberry, and some of the others pampered themselves like pro athletes, taking lengthy, post-lunch naps in the school nurse's office after first claiming some trumped-up ailment. Sometimes Brooks Hurst would burst in, shake a half-dozen or so of them awake, and tell them to get their asses back to class. But if Hurst didn't happen to catch them in there, they snoozed right up until it was time to suit up and take batting practice.

"It was ridiculous," Nelson Whiting says. "Some of them, they'd get to the point where they'd be just about kicked off the team for grades. Then Brooks would talk to their teachers and he'd have to drag them into classes until they got it together. I would say to them, 'It ain't that hard.' And it really wasn't. I was encouraged to go to class. Mainly, I couldn't go home and show my mom bad grades, anything less than a B. That wasn't gonna happen. But showing up was like 80 percent of it. That's all you had to do. But they'd be in the halls all the time; I'd be sitting in class and see them out there peeking in at me."

Hurst says that he checked in with teachers about grades but never asked for one to be changed. Derrick, a longtime Crenshaw teacher, said that he sometimes considered what an athlete needed to remain eligible before submitting his grade to the central office. "Let's put it this way, they usually got the grade they earned, ultimately, but I have given breaks on midterm grades so a kid could keep playing. If that's the only thing keeping a kid in school, do you take that into consideration? I have, and I know I'm not the only teacher who has."

Cordie Dillard, another bright but unengaged student, said that he came to expect breaks because he was viewed primarily as an athlete. "And that came from the black community, too," he says. "The black community was into: If you can't make it in education, and he's this great ballplayer, why would you stand in his way? That's what the mind-set was, back then and now. We don't want him on the streets. If you give him an F, and he can't play ball, what do you think he's going to do? We're not telling you to give him an A, but let's make it so that he has an opportunity to do something with his life."

CHAPTER FOUR

No Way We Lose

The Crenshaw High Cougars spent the spring of 1979 burying opponent after opponent under an onslaught of long balls. After they clobbered University High, 16–2, the *Los Angeles Times* noted that the score was "only" 7–2 before the Cougars put together a nine-run inning that featured two home runs and five different players who had two hits apiece. "Not only that," the *Times* continued, "but after a 15–5 mugging of Hamilton, Crenshaw has now scored 31 runs in its last two games."

After another rout, a newspaper account said that Crenshaw "did what they do best: Hit . . . and hit . . . and hit." With reporters starting to follow his team, Hurst did his best to quip like a big-leaguer. Did his team's hitting surprise him? a reporter asked. "No," he answered. "I'd hate to pitch against them, although I have to in batting practice."

When Carl Jones, Darryl McNealy, and Darryl Strawberry all homered in the same inning to power a victory over Palisades, countering two home runs by the opposing catcher (future Oakland Raiders quarterback Jay Schroeder), Hurst told the newspaper, "The only problem is the neighborhood keeps all the balls."

A week later, Crenshaw again bashed three home runs in a single inning, including colossal blasts to dead center field by Darryl Strawberry and Marvin McWhorter. (This at least occurred at an away game, so some other school was out the baseballs.)

Crenshaw would lose only a handful of regular season games, in each case when Hurst had benched one of his stars for disciplinary reasons. With each game, the throng of scouts in the bleachers and standing beyond the foul lines grew thicker. Some games, there were twenty-five or more watching, about one for every big-league team, more scouts than fans. It could be intimidating, especially for the younger players. Marvin McWhorter would always tell his friend George Cook: "They're coming to see Darryl and them, but if we do something good, they're gonna see us, too."

Marvin McWhorter and George Cook, juniors in 1979, were part of the team's quiet core, best friends linked by a deep baseball devotion. Marvin would drag George as often as he could to the batting cages, hounding him mercilessly on the occasions when he tried to beg off. To George, it seemed like his friend would blurt to him about five times a day, "You've got to work on your hitting, man"—to which George, the little infielder, would sometimes reply, "Why don't you work on your running, Mac?"

Only George could tease Marvin about anything having to do with baseball. The big guy didn't like having his ability questioned. He could be fun-loving, just not about baseball. George was a bit more light-hearted, but both of them were burning to play and eager to use baseball to jump into a new life.

Marvin played behind Darryl McNealy at first base, sometimes starting as the designated hitter. George backed up Cordie Dillard at second base, often playing the late innings because he was better defensively.

Turning double plays, George could hold his ground and jump over a sliding runner, come across the bag and fire a sidearm bullet to first base, or step back and throw from behind the bag. "He was so smooth," Brooks Hurst says. "Just an absolute beauty around the bag. Every way there was to turn a double play, he could do it."

George would sometimes make suggestions to Hurst during games—tell him to move an outfielder in a bit, or position the shortstop a little more to the third-base hole. Hurst didn't treat him like he had been treated when he dared to express a baseball opinion, but he was old school enough to make clear that George wasn't helping him coach. "I would just look at him," Hurst says. "But I would appreciate it. He was a kid who could see some things I didn't always notice."

The two juniors waited their turns as best they could. Any athlete with pride wants to play, believes that he belongs on the field. But this season was, in a sense, an exception to all of that. "I tried to understand my time would come," George says. "I mean, that team was oozing with talent. The way these guys could hit, they were pros. They were pros in high school. When we got to Dodger Stadium later on, that's right where they belonged."

Marvin marked every baseball milestone as if he were punching his ticket at each station on the way up. When he started playing baseball on the city streets as a little kid—manhole cover as home plate, the light pole first base, etc.—he secretly celebrated the occasional broken window he caused, taking it as a sign of his budding power. When he first started playing in the park, for teams that didn't really compile statistics, he kept track of his hits, RBIs, and home runs on scraps of paper he filed in a dresser drawer. When his uncle took him to an adjacent neighborhood to play "over-the-line" (pickup baseball with fewer players and parts of the field closed off), he remembered the names of the couple of real good older players he met. Years later, when Ozzie Smith and Eddie Murray reached the big leagues, Marvin knew that they were the ones he had played with that day.

At Crenshaw, prospective players first had to qualify for Brooks Hurst's baseball class, an alternative to gym class. Hurst would watch kids throw, look at them swing, make sure they'd had a bat in their hands before, then put them through a little workout. The Chris Browns and

Darryl Strawberrys wouldn't fret for a moment over a little audition like this, but Marvin—always the striver, never the natural—had a little case of nerves, then a pang of elation after Hurst gave him a nod of approval.

He registered for the class in the fall of his sophomore year, knowing that not everyone got to stay in. Hurst walked past a couple of kids working out and said, simply, "You're not a ballplayer." Others just walked off after looking at the level of competition.

Marvin took his swings, played catch, then was asked to run over to the bleachers and fill out a little card that said what teams he had played on, what positions he played, where he hoped to play, a kind of baseball résumé. He put down third base, but when he went back out on the field it seemed like there were fifteen guys standing over there, including Chris Brown. So he trotted over to first, where there was hardly anyone. Marvin didn't know the mechanics or the footwork; he was just about tripping over himself.

"You've never played first before, have you?" Brooks Hurst said after watching him for a few minutes. Marvin admitted that he hadn't. That's all right, Hurst said, adding that it was a "smart move" for him to have crossed the diamond. You can stay in the class, he said, but "go get yourself a first baseman's mitt."

After Hurst walked away, "I was just standing there," Marvin says, "feeling about ten feet tall."

The association with Crenshaw got Marvin into faster summer-league competition—yet another ticket punched—and into games against slightly older players like Chili Davis and better-known peers like Eric Davis, another future big-leaguer, who played for Crenshaw's rival Fremont High.

Anyone known in local L.A. baseball played at Connie Mack Stadium in Compton; the good players were sprinkled on all the teams, but most of the Crenshaw kids played for the Compton Moose, coached by a man named Earl Brown. In the summer, Hurst basically turned his kids over to Brown. Getting on that team, says Marvin, "was like a feather in my cap. Scouts came to the games, and like in high school, you knew they probably didn't come to see you specifically, but you had the chance to be seen. The scouts would tell you things, try to give you little tips about how to improve. When you got in that kind of setting, you knew it—there was no doubt—that a pro career was possible if you were just able to perform."

The former Major League shortstop Rafael Ramirez, who grew up poor in the Dominican Republic, was once asked why he swung at just about every pitch he saw, even if it was over his head or a foot outside. "You can't get off that island with a walk," he explained. Marvin took a similar approach: "I didn't want to walk. I wanted to swing as hard as possible and use the heaviest available bat. I thought that would make you hit the ball farther."

George, too, played at Connie Mack Stadium. He had fallen hard for the game, maybe not as hard as Marvin—but who had?—and was eager to get noticed, to land on someone's draft list. Few of the Crenshaw boys had more of an economic incentive. George's parents had migrated from Arkansas to Los Angeles when they were in their early twenties, and he had five brothers and five sisters. His father worked at an aircraft manufacturing plant, moving up over time to supervisor status. "But when my dad left, we went on welfare," he says. "That kind of humbles you a bit. You pinch the pennies."

In the classroom, George was enrolled in an accelerated program, a sort of school within a school. Some classes met in offices rather than classrooms, with the students and teacher sitting on couches and talking as if they were in a college seminar. "It was cool; the teachers were like professors," he recalls. He had enough credits that he could have graduated after eleventh grade, but pointed himself in one direction only: toward baseball.

*　　*　　*

Inner-city high schools didn't contend for the baseball championship of the Los Angeles Unified School District, let alone win them. The schools in the San Fernando Valley—with their manicured fields, year-round programs, crushed brick infields, parent booster clubs, and private baseball tutors—won all the titles and put forward most of the serious contenders.

Unlike basketball, which required only a ball, an asphalt court, and a hoop, baseball had somehow become a money game, damn near a country club sport like swimming, tennis, or lacrosse. Before 1979, the last non-Valley team to win was Venice High in 1972. (And after 1979, Valley teams would win every championship right up through 2003.)

But the Boys of Crenshaw were the exception. They played with an angry desperation. They played baseball just like basketball was played in the inner city—or like baseball was *still* played, but elsewhere, in Puerto Rico, Venezuela, or the Dominican Republic, by boys with dime-store gloves and taped-up baseballs and a relationship to their sport that was equal parts joy and hunger.

The 1979 Crenshaw High team wanted to play baseball, and they were also determined to *use* it. When Marvin McWhorter's father called after him to get on the landscaping truck, and Marvin walked right out the door with his glove and his spikes, that's what he was saying: He was going to make something of baseball, propel himself out of inner-city L.A. and into a world where a man didn't need to work three jobs to make ends meet.

Brooks Hurst was thrilled that his team entered the postseason with realistic hopes for a title, but was still vexed, as any coach would be, by the various flaws and idiosyncrasies among his players that he had not yet conquered. Marvin and George, Reggie Dymally, some of the others, were no problem. But several of the stars, the big talent/big ego boys, had not been tamed.

Chris Brown, deep into his senior year, was still full of mouth. Darryl Strawberry didn't always beat the ball to the spot. Donald Jones, of course, was long gone, and his brother Carl—oh, how Brooks loved Carl; how any coach would have loved Carl—was still allergic to class.

Darryl McNealy, at first base, was another headache. He had a habit that threatened to drive Hurst insane. "When we took infield practice, Darryl, as the first baseman, was the cutoff man on the throw in from the outfield," Hurst explains. "Well, he'd get the relay throw and spin and throw it to Carl Jones, our catcher, as hard as he could—even if he was ten or fifteen feet away from him. And I'd say, 'Darryl, you can't do that!' And he'd give me this stupid look, like 'Yup, Coach, okay,' or he'd just laugh and do the same fucking thing again.

"Now keep in mind this kid could throw the ball 85 to 90 miles per hour. He was one of our pitchers. He could throw it as hard as Darryl Strawberry. One day I took him aside and talked to him calmly. I figured maybe that would work. I said, 'Darryl, you know you really have to stop doing that. You have to understand that you could kill somebody.' "

* * *

Darryl and Derwin McNealy were, like George and Marvin, a singular unit—but even more so, by virtue of being identical twins. "They were like one person," George Cook says. "They had each other's back."

When they were in tenth grade, Brooks Hurst tried to elevate Darryl to the varsity from the JV, but he refused. The hang-up was that Hurst had not extended an invitation to the other twin. The twins' mother told the coach: If they can't both go up, then neither are going. They were a package deal.

Whatever the twins did, they did together. "We didn't really need no coaches or parents or older brothers or playmates," Derwin says. "We just had ourselves and we went to war against each other. Every free moment, we were competing in some form of competition.

"We played strikeout against the wall at the elementary school probably one hundred straight days sometimes. We had a rubber ball and that square on the wall. A base hit was if you hit the ball past the pitcher. Past a certain line it was a double. Off the fence it was a triple, and over it, a home run. That's what we did. I tried to kill him, and he tried to kill me back."

Sports kept the boys occupied, then it became a cause and a hoped-for salvation. "Even as itty-bitty little boys, they were always playing," their mother, Dorothy McNealy, says. "They played in the rain, in the dark, they didn't care. And always somewhere in there it was going to be a money thing. Everybody was always talking about how good they was. That was their dream, to become pros and buy themselves a nice house. We had a house ourselves. We tried to expose them to the best, but there was only so much we could do."

The twins pulled the usual twin pranks. They switched classrooms in elementary school. They had different recess times, and somehow would work it out so they each ended up with two recesses. They took tests for each other. A great many notes came home about their clowning. Later on, they would pull the classic twin trick of taking out each other's girlfriends.

Darryl was born one minute ahead of Derwin, and through high school he was the dominant twin. "At that time, he was the more active, the more outgoing person," their mother says.

As athletes, the twins were not as big or as strong as Darryl Strawberry or Chris Brown, but they were highly gifted, and never in doubt about their abilities. "The closer we got to Dodger Stadium, the bigger the crowds got, the more scouts we had following us," Darryl says. "I would watch the scouts make their notes during the game. It didn't make me nervous at all; it made me play better."

The twins were not as suave as Crenshaw's second baseman, Cordie Dillard, the self-professed original varsity player. But they were just as confident in their abilities. They had that big-league arrogance, the good kind that serves an athlete well, and therefore were big-league material: The twins were good, and they knew it; nothing was going to stop their march to Major League Baseball.

Their teammates couldn't always tell the McNealys apart physically, but they could by personality. Derwin was compliant. Darryl was loud, wild, rude. He could be a bully.

"Darryl was unbelievably good at first base," Nelson Whiting says. "Coach Hurst would hit the ball as hard as he could at Darryl, and he would make the play every time. You couldn't get it past him, even with a fungo bat. But he did a lot of dissing."

One day Hurst got fed up with his mouth and demanded that Darryl McNealy hand over his jersey. Nelson watched in disbelief. "I was like, 'Wow, he ripped the jersey right off that twin.'"

But Nelson, the other twin, and several other players went to Hurst and said they needed Darryl McNealy, and a day or so later—after Darryl had to apologize in front of the whole squad—he was back on the team.

Marvin McWhorter says: "Derwin did some dumb stuff, just like we all did. But he was just a kid. He was okay. But Darryl, he had a little mean streak in him. He could cause some problems, either because he was being ornery or just not paying attention."

*   *   *

Crenshaw opened the 1979 playoffs in typically robust fashion, winning its first game, 12–1, and its second, 11–3. Before the third-round game— the one they had to win to reach the finals at Dodger Stadium—Brooks Hurst, as usual, stood next to catcher Carl Jones at home plate and put his team through infield and outfield practice. The game was at Cal State Northridge, which had a ballpark bigger than they normally played at, so Hurst gave extra attention to having his outfielders retrieve balls in the gaps, then work them back in toward the infield.

"We had what we called a trail," he explains. "If the ball was all the way against the fence, we had a relay man, a player backing up the relay man, and then Darryl McNealy, the first baseman, as the cutoff man. Counting the catcher, we had four guys right in a line.

"So that's what we were doing, and I hit the ball against the fence, and Darryl Strawberry runs it down, throws it to the relay man, who throws it toward the plate. I was evaluating the situation, making sure the trail was like I wanted it, and Darryl [McNealy] cuts the ball off and wings it from point-blank. Just like I had told him a million times not to do.

"You know how Ted Williams used to say he could see the seams of the baseball before he hit it? Well, I saw the seams, and then it hit me right in the fucking jaw. I do a back flip. I'm laying there. I'm spitting up blood. I throw up. My jaw is broken in two places. Carl is leaning over me; he had no chance to grab it and save me."

Darryl McNealy had done exactly what Hurst pleaded with him so many times not to do: wheel and throw the ball home, at full speed, from nearly point-blank distance. To disastrous effect.

"Darryl [McNealy] runs in, and the poor kid is frantic," Hurst says. "He's crying. He thinks he killed me or, if he didn't, he thinks I'm gonna get up and kill him. I said don't worry about it. We've got a game to play."

The other players witnessed this, in something like a state of shock, from their positions on the field. Here they were, about to play the biggest game of their lives—one more win and they go to Dodger Stadium—and their coach looks like he might be dead.

"It was horrible," George Cook says. "Everybody looked at him and said, 'Wait a minute, he's a big part of this team and he's laying there bleeding and in pain.' Even the ones who battled with Brooks, they knew in their hearts all of what he did—the time he put in, the exposure he got us, all the money he spent. What happened, to tell you the truth, took a little air out of the season."

Phil Pote, the scout and Hurst's good friend, rushed out with an ice bag. Hurst got up, his whole face and head shooting with pain, and staggered to the bench. He refused to go to the hospital until later that evening—when his jaw would be diagnosed as broken, and wired shut.

When the game started, Hurst took his accustomed spot in the third-base coaching box, gave a little clap, and, through the pain, managed to mutter a word or two of encouragement for the team's leadoff hitter—Darryl McNealy.

The pitcher's first offering was a fat one, right down the middle of the plate. Darryl—not usually a power guy—took a mighty swat and connected.

The ball lifted off his bat on a line, kept rising, and cleared the right-field fence.

Nothing, it seemed, could keep Crenshaw from hitting—not even the alarming sight of their coach lying in a puddle of blood. They overpowered Monroe High, 10–7. Next stop: Dodger Stadium.

*   *   *

The prickly Brooks Hurst was not one to attract a lot of merriment or ceremony around himself or his players. When the team started off fast and began to generate a buzz of excitement at Crenshaw, the school's cheerleading squad tried to board the bus for an away game—to hop on the bandwagon, as it were—but Hurst saw them coming and told the driver to hit the gas and not look back.

He had enough distractions; he didn't need girls on the bus. He didn't even like the cheerleaders setting up behind his bench at home games, where they cheered at the wrong times and pierced his zone of baseball quietude.

Earlier in the season, without Hurst's knowledge, a school administrator arranged for a former major-leaguer, a supposedly reformed drunk, to talk to the boys on the field one day before practice. And even that went disastrously wrong when the ex-player's remarks veered alarmingly off course. By the time Hurst arrived, he was telling the boys about all the success he had experienced playing hung over, and of his various assignations on the road, including one with a woman in St. Louis "who could fuck all night."

Every other word out of the guy's mouth was *pussy*. Every third or fourth word was *nigger*. Frequently, these two words occurred in the same sentence, since the one coherent theme of his disjointed remarks was that a black man in the big leagues could have as much sex as he wanted.

The players listened silently, stifling laughs, then made fun of him when he left. Marvin McWhorter came up to Hurst and asked, "Why did he come talk to us?" The coach said he was sorry, adding, "I didn't invite him."

What Hurst said on that very first day of practice still held: *No one else gets inside the gates. Just us, and baseball.* It was a lot safer that way.

It was not surprising, then, that the Boys of Crenshaw got a fairly modest send-off—a hundred or so students and a few relatives, but no cheerleaders or band—as they boarded the bus on June 6, 1979, for the short ride to Dodger Stadium. The players, though, were pretty revved up all on their own. Several wore cowboy hats and boots, purchased specially for the occasion.

"We figured we were playing the role, we were gonna wear the role," Chris Brown says. "We were the gunslingers ridin' in to whup some ass."

The cocky ones—Chris, Cordie, Darryl Strawberry, the twins—opened the bus windows and shouted out to the L.A. streets: *Crenshaw! City champs! Y'all come to Dodger Stadium and watch us kick some ass!*

"We were city kids, so of course we were loud," Fernando Becker says. "But some of us were a little quieter. Even the guys doing all the yelling, they had some quiet moments where I'm sure they had their own little thoughts."

Fernando was one of several Crenshaw players who had family members coming that night to see him play for the very first time. His maternal grandfather, Walter Bethune, was the one who had bought him the red, white, and blue glove, and gotten him started in baseball. He was a diehard Dodgers fan. And here his grandson was playing in Dodger Stadium. The whole Becker and Bethune clan was convinced that could only mean one thing: Fernando himself was ticketed for the Major Leagues. This was the audition, the moment of liftoff.

"I had my chest out," Fernando says. "I felt proud. But I'll admit I was real nervous. I couldn't focus at all during the school day. I was thinking, this is the biggest game of my life and I want to do good."

Reggie Dymally walked through the tunnel from the visitors' clubhouse, where Crenshaw had dressed, scanned the verdant outfield and the crowd and the big bank of stadium lights, the whole big-league feel, and thought to himself, "I could get used to this. It wouldn't be hard at all."

The opponent was Granada Hills, city champions in three of the previous four seasons. "The playoffs were a Valley domination year after year, so I didn't know that much about Crenshaw or any of the city teams," Darryl Stroh, the Granada Hills coach, says. "I made some calls and came up with a scouting report that said, basically, that Crenshaw was scary, that they really mashed the ball."

Stroh got this piece of unhelpful advice from a coaching friend whose team Crenshaw had eviscerated early in the playoffs: Pitch it and duck and hope for the best. Maybe you'll get lucky and they'll have a bad night.

Granada Hills, like most of the Valley teams, played with a crisp elegance. Lots of bunting. Good defense. Few mistakes. They played like boys who had grown up with a great deal of adult instruction.

"We had a lot of great players over the years, a lot of great teams, but this one, quite honestly, wasn't that good," Stroh says. "I didn't expect to be in the title game. We played the game well, but we had very average athletes, with the one obvious exception."

The exception was the good-looking blond kid at third base, John Elway.

The Crenshaw players, of course, could not know that Elway was to become one of the great quarterbacks in NFL history, an icon of American sports, any more than they knew what lay ahead for Darryl Strawberry, or for themselves. Most of them had heard that Granada Hills had some big deal football player on its team, but that wasn't the kind of thing that scared them.

In the three previous games of the playoffs, Darryl Strawberry had hit three triples in addition to a home run, and was the winning pitcher in two of the games. Chris Brown had two home runs, two doubles, and six RBIs. Cordie Dillard had also knocked in six runs, and stole three bases.

George Genovese, the scout, had seen both teams numerous times. "As far as I was concerned," he says, "Granada Hills had no chance."

In fact, Crenshaw's semifinal opponent, Monroe High, was considered a stronger challenge. A few local baseball aficionados were already slapping Hurst on the back, telling him that Granada Hills was going to be a cakewalk.

*   *   *

Granada Hills jumped off to a 2–0 lead, but Crenshaw stormed back with three runs in the top of the third inning, still had runners on base, and seemed poised to do what it had done all season long—obliterate and dishearten an opponent with one huge inning. Stroh was about ready, as his coaching friend suggested, to duck and hope for the best.

He had a relief pitcher loosening up in the bullpen, a dependable enough kid but, in all likelihood, raw meat for the Crenshaw sluggers. And at third base he had Elway, who had not pitched in six weeks.

The last time Elway had been on the mound, he looked like one of those frightening, discombobulated cases who one day loses all sense of the mechanics of throwing. In that outing he had bounced balls in front of the plate, sailed them over hitters' heads, issued several walks, and hit two batters before his coach came out and rescued him. It was an ugly scene, something that Stroh never wanted to see repeated.

"When I took him out of that game, I told him, 'You're not going to pitch anymore.' John was so heavily involved in football, getting ready to go off to Stanford to play, that we weren't really working with him. It wasn't really fair to ask him to pitch."

Against Crenshaw, Stroh headed for the mound intending to call in the kid from the bullpen. Halfway out, he changed his mind. He thought to himself, "This is a tough spot. I'm going with the toughest guy I have."

Elway somehow knew what his coach was thinking. Over at third base, he turned his back and stared out toward left field. Stroh had to call over there to get his attention.

Elway took his eight warm-up pitches, then struck out Carl Jones to end the third inning. Two innings later, with the score still 3–2, Elway surrendered a leadoff single and then a walk. Darryl Strawberry came to the plate with two runners on, no outs, and a chance to create the kind of mayhem Crenshaw had failed at two innings back. The previous at bat, Darryl had hit a ball to the warning track. He was looking forward to another chance to drive one out of Dodger Stadium, especially with a couple of men on base.

The Crenshaw boys had a superstition about the fifth inning—it was their lucky inning, their comeback frame if they needed one. And here it was. They were edgy on the bench, but in a good way. Anticipating something good.

Darryl's stance looked much as it would in the Major Leagues. Knees slightly bent, hands held chest high, weight forward—then, as the pitcher began his delivery, a slight rocking back to shift his weight to the back foot. It was a posture of coiled power—the relaxed body, then the unleashing of a formidable kinetic force. He was about as scary a hitter as any skinny seventeen-year-old could be.

As Elway's first pitch came to the plate, Darryl—rather than preparing to swing—edged his top hand up on the bat and squared toward the pitcher. Inexplicably, Brooks Hurst had asked his slugging outfielder to bunt.

In the on-deck circle, Chris Brown looked on in disbelief. "He hadn't done nothing all year but let us loose like wild horses. And now he is making this man bunt? The Valley kids bunted; we did not bunt."

Hurst's jaw was still wired shut, and he had lost ten pounds. "He wasn't thinking straight from what happened to his jaw," Brown says. "That's all the explanation there can be."

Strawberry got the bunt down—too hard, and straight at Elway, who threw to third base for a force-out. Next, Darryl McNealy was thrown out trying to steal third base for the second out. Then, Elway struck out Chris Brown for the third out.

That was the end of the lucky fifth inning. A bizarre bunt. A promising rally squelched. No runs scored.

Even worse, the disappointment of the top of the fifth was followed by disaster in the bottom half. Fernando Becker, who had been so nervous all day—and whose error in the first inning had let in a run—made yet another error, letting a potential double play ball roll under his glove.

The Granada Hills batters then began a tactic of fake bunts, squaring around to distract the pitcher—a Little League maneuver that should not have worked—but Darryl Strawberry walked several batters and had to be sent to the outfield. Then Derwin McNealy, and a third pitcher, Lee Mays, unraveled and issued yet more walks.

By the end of the inning, Granada Hills had scored six more runs on three measly hits—and a lot of bad pitching and shoddy fielding. From then on, Crenshaw's big bats were silenced, its gunslingers put down. In the middle of the lineup, Strawberry, Brown, and Carl Jones went hitless in a combined ten at-bats.

"John just shut them down," Stroh says. "Strawberry and Brown hit a couple of monster foul balls. The whole team must have hit a half-dozen balls to the warning track, but they couldn't do any damage."

As Stroh had hoped, his star had summoned internal resources. What he lacked in craft he made up for in heart. Elway was a warrior, and on this day, the Boys of Crenshaw were not his equal.

It is sometimes unwise to make too much of one game—especially in baseball, where even great teams don't win all the time. But this contest could be taken as a reflection of the lives the Crenshaw players had lived to that point, and perhaps a vision of what was to come.

Their opponent John Elway, a golden boy from suburbia, had been equal to the moment, worthy of Dodger Stadium. The Boys of Crenshaw, for all their bravado, were not as ready as they believed. They unraveled. The team that scout George Genovese considered, from top to bottom, the most talented assemblage of high school talent ever, could not win the L.A. city championship.

Some of them may have been just plain scared. But others were too focused on what was to come next. Too eager to impress scouts. Too hungry for personal stardom.

"The egos took over," George Cook says. "We got caught up in being 'I'm Chris Brown. I'm Darryl Strawberry. And I'm gonna jack it out of Dodger Stadium.' All those warning track shots, they would have been jacks at most of the parks we played during the regular season. At Dodger Stadium, they were big outs."

"The game itself felt like a dream," Marvin McWhorter says. "It went by real slow. It didn't seem real. And then it was over. That part felt sudden. It was like, damn, that's it? We're done?

"Darryl [Strawberry] never took losing too well. He ran out to center field and cried like a damn baby. The coach had to talk to him. Then Joe Weakley, as assistant basketball coach, had to go talk to him. The whole rest of the team was ready to go, and he had to be coaxed onto the bus."

Chris Brown was out there for a while with Darryl. "I ran to near the visitor's bullpen when they were giving out the trophies," he says. "I didn't want to even see the second-place trophy. That's how mad I was. It might have been bad sportsmanship, but I was hurt. I didn't like the way it ended. To get that far, to play the way we did—to have Brooks make Darryl bunt—I didn't like any of it.

"Our athletic ability should have taken over. I'm not gonna lie, we did have some dummies on that team. But even the dummies knew how to play baseball. All we had to do is go out there and do what we knew how to do. We had an entourage with us. Everybody I knew was there—my girlfriend, my friends from school, even my dad. I just wanted to hide. I wished I could have just disappeared."

The bus ride back was nearly silent. Nelson Whiting was among those who thought about Donald Jones, how Crenshaw would have been city champs for sure if Donald hadn't cracked that kid over the head with the bat. No way Donald would have gotten flustered by all those kids faking like they were going to bunt. He wouldn't have walked them all. And for good measure, he was just mean enough to have plunked one of the would-be bunters with a good hard fastball, and that would have been the end of that.

But Donald Jones was sitting with the rest of the Joneses that night in the Dodger Stadium seats. There wasn't a damn thing he could do to help.

Fernando Becker, the accidental shortstop, thought about his errors, especially the double play ball that dribbled under his glove. Later that night, he would turn on the TV and see his error on the evening news, then switch channels and see it *again*.

Immediately after the game, Brooks Hurst wondered if he had been at fault. Had he prepared the boys for baseball but not for Dodger Stadium? The Granada Hills kids had been to the big game before and played like it. Their band was there. Their cheerleaders. It seemed like their whole town was in the stands. But somehow, they managed to keep their concentration and poise.

As for the bunt, he almost immediately kicked himself. He knew it was a mistake. He had overcoached, maybe gone overboard with trying to prove what "good" baseball his kids played. Who was he trying to impress?

And he had sent a team out to the field that was nervous right from the first pitch and never relaxed. Hurst took responsibility for that, too. His boys were starry-eyed, overexcited—and then when things went poorly, they too quickly deflated.

When the bus pulled up to Crenshaw, Brooks Hurst turned the lights on in the gym and the players followed him in. One by one, they handed over their dirty uniforms, which he stuffed in a big duffel bag.

Hurst had no consoling words. He was better at running drills than offering comfort. And he was every bit as disappointed and angry as his players; he knew that his team was far more talented than Granada Hills, but had let the city championship slip away.

"Good season," he said quietly to each of his players as they put their uniforms in the duffel bag.

No large welcoming party greeted the team. Only a handful of parents, and Hurst's good friend, the big-league scout Phil Pote, who a week earlier had rushed forward with the ice pack for his jaw. Pote approached Hurst as he was lugging the duffel bag to his car.

"You did what you could," he said simply.

Most of the boys took rides home. A few walked, meandering through the city one last time before they had to scatter, each of them, and find their own way.

CHAPTER FIVE

Chasing Darryl

Look at any picture of Darryl Strawberry. It's remarkable how often it looks as if in the next instant he might cry. He is perpetually on the verge: of tears, laughter, a life-wrecking lapse, a game-breaking home run.

Even his batting stance was built for drama. The menacing waggle of the bat as the pitcher began his windup, the exaggerated lifting of the right leg, the explosive firing of his hips as his bat whipped through the hitting zone. There are less complicated ways to hit—fewer moving parts, a more compact swing—but Darryl always resisted them.

His approach produced towering home runs, bushelfuls of strikeouts, prolonged droughts, and sizzling streaks. When his big frame and big swing were in rhythm, the great Darryl Strawberry was fearsome. "There was a certain way Darryl looked when he was really locked in," says Hubie Brooks, a former Major League teammate. "It was like his whole body was alive. When he was like that, you just knew all hell was going to break loose."

To the other Boys of Crenshaw, Darryl was a puzzle, a frustration, a point of pride, and a source of sadness. Yeah, they knew Darryl Strawberry back in the day. Played high school ball with him. Loved him to death, and envied the hell out of him.

Who among them would not have wanted a taste of what he had? The instant celebrity, the money, the fast train to the big leagues and New York. Who wouldn't have traded some sanity, good health, even a few years of life expectancy for a shot at that grandeur? And who couldn't have played it out better and saved his own ass before his whole damn world caved in?

Whatever it was—the talent, the name, that regal stature—put Darryl way out in front. He was a beacon, but a strange one, nothing you could navigate by. All the others were chasing baseball, running hard, trying to get to where he already was. And Darryl was running, too, but into some shadow world.

One afternoon late in his senior season, a big white Lincoln pulled up beside the ballfield, and a man in an expensive-looking suit got out and approached him as he was shagging fly balls. Darryl talked to him; he was no good then, or ever, at telling anyone to go away. Brooks Hurst came sprinting out to right field.

"Who the hell are you?" Hurst shouted. "Get off my field and don't ever come back!" The man took Hurst aside, told him he wanted to be Strawberry's agent. "Would you be interested in going to Palm Springs this weekend?" he asked the high school gym teacher. "I could put you up."

The suggestion of a bribe only set Hurst off some more. "Do I come into your office, you asshole, and just sit down at your desk? Get the fuck out of here before I kick your ass."

The agent got in his car and drove off, but plenty of others, hustlers of all stripes, continued to come around to try to attach themselves to the budding star—college recruiters; more would-be agents; long-lost kin of the Strawberry clan; street preachers seeking a piece of Darryl's wallet and soul; young women in leather miniskirts and low-cut blouses. They came to the baseball field, the school, his house. They accosted him on the street—Darryl would be taking those big, loping strides, and all of a sudden he'd feel someone beside him going at a half trot, trying to keep up.

It was a circus, and Darryl was the last person who could control it. Who was the ringmaster? There wasn't any damn ringmaster. The whole thing just swirled, and right at the center of it was this big, beautiful, scared, broken kid.

In the decades that followed, other young phenoms—basketball players mainly, like the sensation LeBron James—would cocoon themselves within an inner circle of family and close friends and vow to extend trust to only to a handful of people. An uncle or older brother would step forward, or a summer-league coach. You had to talk to that person if you wanted to get to the kid, and if you broke that rule, you had no chance.

This system broke down as often as it worked because, at least half the time, one of the trusted people inside the cocoon, usually the gatekeeper, was himself a pimp. He was selling the kid off to an agent, a sneaker company, or some rogue university, and pocketing the money. But at least the phenom, aware of the sad stories that had preceded him, and knowing he was a temptation that some adults would not be able to resist, had started out with some kind of plan. He had given himself a fighting chance, even if it didn't work out in the end.

But Darryl was an innocent. He had no instinct for self-preservation, no sense of himself as a commodity. At the Record Shop one day after practice, a stranger walked in while some of the Crenshaw players were having a snack and asked Darryl if he would step aside and talk to him. They walked over to a quiet corner, talked briefly, then the man scribbled something on a piece of paper.

When Darryl returned, someone asked who the man was. Darryl said he didn't know. What had he written down on the paper?

"My phone number," Darryl answered.

Darryl neither liked all this attention nor actively disliked it. He was just helpless against it, like so much else in his life. The praise, the back-slapping, the overheated hype—he could keep none of it at a distance. It all penetrated him on a deep level, congealed, and filled up some big empty space inside him.

The press buildup as he was about to leave Crenshaw, and therefore the excitement and anticipation around him, just kept growing. Darryl was anointed the next Ted Williams. The black Ted Williams. The second coming of an American icon. Never mind that Williams was the greatest, or after Babe Ruth, the second-greatest hitter in baseball history. Or that he possessed the inner fiber to fly fighter jets in World War II and Korea, qualities not unrelated to his accomplishments in the batter's box.

When *Sports Illustrated* published a feature on Strawberry late in his senior season, the caption under his picture said, "Darryl, 18, is likened to Ted Williams."

Likened to him, yes. But wrongly. There could hardly have been two more different personality types.

Physically, Darryl certainly did bring to mind the former Boston Red Sox great. He was tall, slim, and left-handed just like the Splendid Splinter, as Ted Williams was called.

Baseball people have never liked to think of their game as one of brute strength, and for a long time, weight lifting was discouraged as an activity that could make a player "muscle-bound." (Sluggers getting strikingly bigger by pumping iron, or in some cases by injecting steroids, is a fairly recent phenomenon.) Darryl, like Ted Williams, generated his home run power with leverage, timing, and just enough muscle. For the baseball aesthete, he pushed all the right buttons.

"He's got a Williams-type physical makeup—tall, rangy, good leverage," the scout Phil Pote told *Sports Illustrated*. "He's got bat quickness, he can drive the ball. The ball just jumps off his bat." Another seasoned scout, Hugh Alexander, gushed that Strawberry was "the best prospect I've seen in 30 years."

Even Brooks Hurst, normally so careful not to feed his players' egos, and especially not Darryl's, got carried away and added to all the Ted Williams talk. Most of his Crenshaw players would have heard of Ted Williams (and big Marvin McWhorter, of course, had just about memorized his book on hitting), but the name was not initially familiar to Darryl.

"Do you know who Ted Williams is?" Hurst asked him one day.

Darryl hesitated. He didn't want to guess wrong but he didn't know the answer. "Well," Hurst said, "there's a little generation gap here. But you're going to be a black Ted Williams, because you hit just like Ted."

Darryl confessed to a writer that he had been kicked off the baseball team in tenth grade and relegated to lugging equipment bags. He deserved it, he explained, because he'd been acting like a child—but he had learned his lesson. "I changed myself over the summer, matured myself as a ballplayer, and came back," he said. "I did it myself. I said, 'The Lord gave you all this talent. Why mess yourself up?'

"I dream of being in the major leagues at the age of 20," Darryl continued. "I dream about making it to the World Series at the age of 20 if I go to a good ballclub. And I dream of coming out the No. 1 draft choice in the nation."

A couple of weeks before the Major League draft, Darryl got a call at home. It was Richie Bry, the agent who had first seen him play in the "cow patch," and who had told his son to keep his eye on the big kid in right field. Would Darryl want to go to a Dodgers game with him, then out to dinner with two of Bry's other clients—the baseball star Lou Brock and the football star Kellen Winslow? Of course he would.

Bry showed up at his door with a suitcoat and a silk tie for Darryl to wear. They sat in box seats, then Bry took Darryl into the Cardinals clubhouse after the game. After that, the agent, the two pro athletes, and Darryl and his mother all went out to a fancy restaurant and ate big steaks. Darryl didn't say much through dinner; he just sat and took it all in with a big grin on his face.

This was a taste of the big time, what it was going to feel like from here on out. A fine meal. All the attention focused on him. A certain amount of fawning. And Darryl didn't have to do anything but sit back and drink it all in.

"Mr. Bry," he said toward the end of the evening, "I just had the best night I've ever had in my life."

The next day he signed on with Bry as a client. Among the many decisions Darryl would make over the course of his baseball career, this was not among the worst. Bry was in it for his cut, just like all agents. But he was also fatherly and kind, a good man who in the coming years would genuinely try to do his best for Darryl. But winning him for the price of a steak dinner was about right. Darryl was never a hard sell.

* * *

Darryl wanted to be the first pick in the nation, and he achieved it. The New York Mets, then a lowly, bad-box-office franchise, chose him with the first pick in the June 1980 amateur draft. (Darryl was a junior on the 1979 team.) The team paid him a $200,000 bonus to forgo a college scholarship, then flew him to New York and proudly showed him off at a news conference and luncheon at Toots Shor's—an event that began with the playing of the Beatles song "Strawberry Fields Forever."

Even in his jacket and tie, and with his mother affixed to his side, he moved with a lovely athletic grace. From across the restaurant, Frank Cashen, the Mets general manager, took a quiet moment to himself and admired his new hire. Cashen had spent a lifetime around baseball but had only seen a handful of players who projected what Darryl did. The word that came to his mind was *majestic*. Darryl was majestic. He was that rare athlete who didn't even need to suit up or take the field to draw all eyes to him—all he had to do was exist in a physical space.

A few days after his Manhattan introduction, Darryl reported to the Mets rookie league team in Kingsport, Tennessee, where he began his quick ascent through the minor leagues. He got a taste of small-town celebrity—strawberry sundae promotions, strawberry shortcake give-aways, all manner of Darryl Strawberry buzz at every stop in the Appalachian League.

In Paintsville, Kentucky, any fan bringing at least one strawberry to the game got free admission. The local team presented a pint of strawberries to Darryl, sold only strawberry soda at the concession stands, and even arranged for a helicopter to hover over the ballpark before the first pitch and drop strawberries onto the field. It was all silly and funny and, for a kid just a couple of weeks removed from his cramped stucco house in inner-city L.A., altogether exhilarating.

In the minor leagues, Darryl got his first taste, as well, of the franchise player's life of entitlement. He had some money in his pocket. He was recognized and feted everywhere he went. But like a lot of eighteen-year-olds on their own for the first time, he had no idea how to comport himself and virtually no life skills—and because of his star status, he had no incentive to learn them.

It is perhaps a cliché to say that ballplayers never have to grow up, that they rarely face adult consequences. But it's true. And the bigger the star, the truer it is.

Brooks Hurst had held Darryl accountable at Crenshaw. He sat him down for a whole season, then for individual games over his final two years at Crenshaw. But after Darryl left high school and began drawing a paycheck to play ball, he was held to a lower standard. He was coddled. His missteps were excused, and the messes he left behind were quickly and expertly covered up.

Right from the start, Darryl had a particular problem interacting with women, a condition that would become chronic. On at least two occasions in the minors, female employees at hotels lodged complaints against him. The incidents were quietly handled and kept out of the news.

"The Mets would call me in," Bry said when I asked him about these incidents. "The team would talk to the maid and the hotel management. One way or the other, it would get taken care of. It would get quashed. It was never anything brutal. It was obscene language, or tiny rough stuff."

Bry says that at least once, at a hotel in St. Petersburg, Florida, police were called. He says that he gave no money to the female complainants, but thinks Cashen, the Mets general manager, might have. Says Cashen: "I don't remember much about the specifics anymore. So much water has gone under the bridge. I can't remember what we did to make them go away. But I don't think it was a financial thing. . . . I don't remember any money changing hands. If his agent paid money, I wouldn't know about it."

Darryl never missed a game as a result of these incidents. No one sought to determine what caused them; no one suggested he seek counseling. Once the incidents were "taken care of," they were forgotten.

In the estimation of his teachers at Crenshaw and of others who knew him, Darryl was of average intelligence, plenty smart enough to achieve on the ballfield. What he lacked were emotional resources, and the realm he had just entered, big-time sports, was only going to make that worse.

Pro sports takes psychologically sound people and, by giving them an abundance of free time, temptation, and money—and combining that with the intense pressure to perform, and the possibility of flagrant public failure—pushes them to their absolute limits. What it does to already-broken people is break them up some more.

On the field, a player must produce. He is held accountable. Off it, he is indulged. The disconnect is confusing, sometimes disabling.

In the winter after his first minor league season, Darryl attended a basketball game at Crenshaw with Chris Brown. They were pro athletes gracing their alma mater, returning to look in on the basketball team they had led to championships. Everyone wanted to talk to them, to get an autograph or just to get up close. In these settings, Darryl was sometimes nice—and sometimes a jerk. It depended on his mood. It depended on if he had been drinking.

During the game, Chris Brown says, a girl they had known at Crenshaw said something that annoyed Darryl. "So he says to her, 'What did you say, bitch?' " Brown recalls. "Then he draws his hand back and slaps her, right there in the gym with the game going on. He slapped her hard. I said to myself, This man left here crazy, and he came back a little crazier."

As a ballplayer, Darryl's work ethic was still sloppy, as it had always been, going all the way back to Little League, when one coach used to come into his house and pour water on his face to wake him up and get him moving. In the minor leagues, he was sometimes late—and in Kingsport that first year, he even missed a game.

A lesser player might have been handed his release and sent home, but that was never going to happen to Darryl. Because of his status as the nation's number one draft choice, and all the hype orchestrated around him, his failure, or even a less-than-rapid rise to the big leagues, would have equated to the failure of the Mets' brain trust.

In his first two minor league seasons, Darryl was no immediate star, but his struggles were not unexpected. Many of the pitchers he was facing had entered pro ball after four years of college and were substantially older. They fooled him with breaking balls and aimed hard fastballs inside, right under his hands, where he could not extend his long arms and generate power.

Off the field, Darryl was lonely. He called his mother every day, collect. For a while, he was in the habit of staying in bed all day until it was time to go to the ballpark. Finally, a teammate told him that he had to get up and get moving, go to a movie or to the mall, anything to get his blood flowing, because he couldn't expect to play well if he showed up to play all stiff and groggy.

By 1982, his last full minor league season, Darryl's immense talent had overcome all else, as talent nearly always does in sports, at least in the short term. He hit thirty-four home runs for the Mets affiliate in Jackson, Mississippi, and stole forty-five bases, exactly that rare combination of power and speed that got everyone so wound up.

The Ted Williams comparisons persisted.

"Ted Williams is an awful large order," George Bamberger, then the Mets manager, said. "But if someone asked me, 'Who coming up will be another Ted Williams?' well, I'd have to say Darryl Strawberry. I've compared ballplayers to other ballplayers but never to Ted Williams. Fifteen years from now this kid will turn out to be one of the greatest ever to play the game."

The plan was for Darryl to apprentice one more year in the minor leagues, but the 1983 Mets got off to a terrible start and the plan changed. Darryl played just one month for the Mets' Triple A team in Tidewater, Virginia, then was summoned to New York on May 6, 1983, less than two months after his twenty-first birthday. He was ready physically, but emotionally he was still immature and raw.

Frank Cashen regretted having to call him up ahead of schedule, but baseball's a business and he knew Darryl would put fans in the seats. "We were so bad," says Jay Horwitz, the Mets' publicity director. "We were dying for publicity, and we had the black Ted Williams down in the minor leagues."

* * *

As easy as it was for Darryl Strawberry to reach the big leagues, it was going to be that difficult for most of the other Boys of Crenshaw. The mathematics alone were bracing. That June, about fifteen hundred young men were drafted into pro baseball. About one in ten would make it all the way up to the majors, and even some of those would manage only to hang on for a "cup of coffee"—a couple of games, a week, a month at the outside. No one plans on having such a tragically short Major League career, but it happens.

Derwin McNealy, the rail-thin whippet of a center fielder, the quieter and more compliant of the twins, was drafted out of Crenshaw in the twenty-first round by the most storied franchise in all of professional sports, the New York Yankees. Derwin remembers the call coming into his house; his mother handing him the phone; and the man on the line asking when would be the best time to stop around with a contract for him to sign. The best time? Any time would be good. Derwin said if he wanted to come around right away, he would just sit there and wait for him.

A young man like Derwin, already drenched in baseball lore, who liked to endlessly reenact Willie Mays's famous catch in the 1954 World Series, quickly projects himself forward onto the lush green outfield of Yankee Stadium, amid the monuments and greats and ghosts of Yankees past. He dreams about speeding through the minor leagues and reaching New York in time to play alongside Reggie Jackson, Thurman Munson, and the other Yankee stars of the day. He sees himself on television on October evenings, with everyone from the neighborhood hunched forward in their living rooms, marveling at how good he looks in his Yankee pinstripes.

He does not dwell on the possible length of his journey, or the odds of ever reaching his hoped-for destination. If someone told him the odds, it wouldn't matter; he would know he could beat them.

Right up through Crenshaw, Derwin McNealy had never seen another center fielder who could run down a fly ball like he could. He hadn't seen one other player who could take a lead off first base like he could, get a fast jump off the pitcher, and steal a base. He hadn't come up against a pitcher who could throw a fastball by him, who could prevent him from stinging a line drive into one of the outfield alleys and turning it into a double or a triple. If there was one logical reason he couldn't become a member of the New York Yankees, it had not yet flashed before his eyes.

And, as always, there was the specter of Darryl Strawberry. No doubt, Darryl was good. But if he was the best player in the nation, like everyone said, then what did that make Derwin? He knew for a plain fact that he couldn't be that far behind his old Crenshaw teammate—that there couldn't be enough players between Darryl's talent level and his to keep him out of the big leagues.

Major League baseball was not a dream at this point; it was a given. The only question was how long it would take to get there. But even that didn't matter all that much—Derwin was nineteen years old; he had all the time in the world.

George Cook, the little second baseman and one of the most thoughtful of the Boys of Crenshaw, would come to think of his own yearning for baseball success as a kind of obsession—a desperate love that was not always returned. "When you get addicted to sports, that's all there is," he says. "It's like you're chasing a beautiful woman and you're gonna keep on chasing her until she downright dogs you out and says she don't want nothing to do with you. We were gonna stay with baseball until it dogged us out."

For Derwin McNealy, dogging baseball would mean spending long summers in little towns he had never heard of until he was posted to them, like Oneonta, New York, which he had just learned to properly pronounce when he was sent off to Dunedin, Florida. Some other towns along the way he had certainly seen before on maps—Syracuse, Birmingham, Nashville—and knew them to be distinctly not major league. Darryl Strawberry made these kinds of stops, too, but his trajectory, straight up, was never in doubt.

Derwin McNealy's acceleration would depend, primarily, on baseball's famously unforgiving numbers: batting average, home runs, runs batted in, stolen bases. (There had never been a doubt he could field his position.)

But that wasn't all there was to it. Derwin's progress, nearly everyone's journey toward the big leagues, would partly depend on being liked, fitting in, seeming to belong.

The Boys of Crenshaw had played on all-black, or nearly all-black teams all the way through high school. But after Crenshaw they discovered that the culture of baseball, unlike the culture of the NBA or NFL, was still distinctly white. They couldn't be fueled any more by playing in opposition to white players, by beating the rich boys from the Valley at their own game, because now they were all on the same team, playing the same game.

Baseball rosters have long tended to be top-heavy with minorities. In every season since Jackie Robinson broke the color line in 1947, black players have appeared in the league leader categories in far greater percentages than their overall representation on rosters. Four of the five career home run leaders—Hank Aaron, Willie Mays, Barry Bonds, and Frank Robinson—are black. In the National League, which integrated at a faster pace than the American League, thirty-two of the fifty-five Most Valuable Player awards since 1947 have gone to black or Latino players.

When I covered Major League Baseball in the late 1980s, I knew people in management who still believed that a team too thick with minority players was unlikely to win championships. The intangibles that were so highly valued in journeymen players—being "heads up" on the field, a "team guy," causing no trouble while waiting for a turn to play— were qualities ascribed more frequently to white players.

White managers and team executives came overwhelmingly from the ranks of nonstars. They were the pluggers, the role players who sat eagerly on the bench and prided themselves on contributing when called upon, the ones who imagined that they embodied all the intangibles. In looking for players to promote up to the next level, they tended to look for those in their own image.

Derwin was not an emerging star. He fell within that great mass of prospects on minor league rosters—good but not great players who are right on the cusp but need just one break. But he was probably going to have to be a little better than an equivalent white player to make it all the way up.

Buck Showalter, the former Yankees manager, played with Derwin McNealy in the minor leagues and later managed him. He says that Derwin was "an impressive tools guy," by which he means he had physical talent. "He was a good guy, likeable, upbeat. He was the kind of kid you root for, and you wait on for a long time. There was a lot of talent there."

Derwin McNealy in the 1980s dressed like a lot of young men out of inner-city L.A. He favored silk shirts and fairly tight pants. One season after he had reached Triple A ball, one step from the Major Leagues— and a level where players try to carry themselves like major-leaguers—he bought a sport jacket at a men's shop on the road. It was nothing too conservative, an off-white linen jacket of the kind with sleeves you can roll if you like. He wore it that evening as he waited at the hotel for the bus to the ballpark. A coach took notice. After the game, he told Derwin, "You looked good in the lobby."

Derwin wasn't offended. It made him feel good, like he had done the right thing. That season he bought two more sport jackets, including a blue blazer with three gold buttons that would have been perfectly acceptable at Princeton.

The markers of success, and of status, were not always what Derwin had anticipated. The Nashville Sounds traveled in a bus with six beds in the back for sleeping, and two of them were reserved just for the pitcher who had worked that day and the one scheduled to start the next game. The other four beds usually went to whoever could scramble to them first.

But Derwin was a respected man. He played every day. He wore himself down patrolling center field and stealing forty or fifty bases a season. One season he made $50,000, real good money for the minor leagues. When he wanted one of the beds, he got one.

Derwin liked the baseball life—he enjoyed playing a ball game every night, then bringing home a six-pack and ordering a pizza; he genuinely liked most of his teammates; he didn't bristle under coaching. He didn't even mind the nomadic part as long as it seemed he was headed somewhere.

He cherished his friendships with some of the can't-miss players who were his teammates in the minor leagues, and gave them his sincere best wishes when they went up: Fred McGriff, Cecil Fielder, Willie Mays Aikens. He even crossed paths once with John Elway, who gave pro baseball a brief try between college football seasons.

Derwin wasn't able to talk to Elway for long, because his old high school opponent was already a well-known football star, and therefore had a clot of reporters around him. But Derwin struck up a conversation and managed to tell Elway that he thought Granada Hills had been "solid, but not talented," and that Elway's team was lucky to have won that game. If we could have played ten games, Derwin said, Crenshaw would have won eight of them.

Elway didn't disagree. But he did have something he wanted to ask Derwin: Why did your coach make Darryl Strawberry bunt?

Derwin had some memorable minor league games, including one five-for-five night that ended with a game-winning double off the great relief pitcher Goose Gossage, who was then just a big kid learning to control his powerful fastball.

In 1986, six years after he left high school, Derwin McNealy went to spring training for the first time with the big club—the real New York Yankees, not one of their minor league affiliates. He wore number 73, a non–roster player's number, marking him as a long shot to go north for the regular season. At that point, he was with the Yankees by choice. He had just spent a couple of years playing in the Toronto Blue Jays' system, then was lured back as a minor league free agent by the $50,000 salary—and the chance to fulfill a dream.

Derwin had started out as a Yankee. In his heart, he wanted to go to the big leagues as a Yankee. Later he would think that maybe that wasn't the right decision. Did the Blue Jays have a plan for him that would have finally gotten him a true shot to play big-league ball? He would ask himself that question for years. What would have happened if he said no to the New York Yankees?

The Yankees, as usual, were loaded with talent, and two of the outfield spots were already taken by future Hall of Famers Dave Winfield and Rickey Henderson. That spring, Derwin got into six games and had seven hits in sixteen at bats, a .437 average. That became like a mantra for him: *seven-for-sixteen*. He had gone seven-for-sixteen for the New York Yankees.

A couple of his hits knocked in runs, and one came in the midst of a decisive late-inning rally. But the newspaper stories that speculated on players fighting for roster spots did not once mention Derwin. The other players talked to him, treated him pretty good, but on an organizational level he was just a number, a high number, passing through camp.

The sporting goods companies, who are in constant competition to get big-league players to use their products, apparently weren't following along quite as closely. Or perhaps they were hedging their bets. After Derwin started getting some hits, he found lots of free stuff piled in his locker—shoes, batting gloves, sweatbands, sunglasses.

He had been swinging bats given to him by Ken Griffey Sr., who took a liking to Derwin. But one afternoon, Derwin found different bats resting in a little stack against his cubicle. Derwin McNealy model bats. Straight from the Louisville Slugger representative, with his name stamped onto the barrel.

"It wasn't cursive writing, like the real ones are," Derwin says. "But it said my name on it."

*   *   *

The other McNealy twin, Darryl, who had nailed Brooks Hurst in the jaw with the errant throw, was drafted in the seventh round by the San Francisco Giants on the same day the Yankees chose his brother. The twins took their signing bonuses and bought matching Pontiac Trans Ams—black and gold, with beige interiors.

They drove them off the dealer's lot and proudly parked them right in front of their house. In that neighborhood, people certainly owned cars, but generally high-mileage rattletraps that were purchased used and driven right up until they coughed to a stop on some L.A. street and died. So when the twins pulled up in their new wheels—windows down, radios blasting, drivers grinning like fools—it was an event. Folks came outside to marvel at what pro baseball had already brought the nineteen-year-old McNealy boys.

That night, Darryl and Derwin, each of them with a date, drove their cars to a concert at the Fabulous Forum in Inglewood. The act was Tina Marie and the Thunderbirds, but it hardly mattered. The main event was the Trans Ams.

Within days, both twins would be off on their baseball journeys—Derwin way across the country, back East, to where the Yankees farm clubs played; and Darryl to a place nominally closer to home, but every bit as foreign.

The Giants dispatched him to Great Falls, Montana, to play on a rookie league team with two of his high school teammates, Chris Brown and Cordie Dillard. All three had been signed by George Genovese, the scout so captivated by Crenshaw talent. Genovese liked hitters; he scooped up three of them from Crenshaw—Brown in the second round, Dillard in the twelfth—and would have taken more of them if he could have.

It may have seemed like a good idea at the time, sending three kids from inner-city L.A. off to make their start together in Montana. Or more likely, no one gave it much thought.

When Darryl, Chris, and Cordie landed at the Great Falls airport, they were immediately hustled off to a hotel banquet room for a dinner with their new teammates, an annual event heralding the opening of the team's season. A couple of chamber of commerce types approached and shook their hands, and the boys mumbled their responses. They listened to speeches and ate dinner while trying to remember their table manners, and hoping not to look too dazed or terrified.

The next day they rented a three-bedroom apartment to share, although Cordie—being Cordie, a ladies' man, a player, even in Great Falls, Montana—he quickly got himself a girlfriend and didn't spend much time in the apartment.

They had all heard the expression "cow town" and were pretty sure that's what Great Falls was. Two or three restaurants stayed open past eight P.M. The one disco wasn't bad, but it operated weekends only. The team had one other black player and a couple of Hispanics, and those were about the only other people of color they ever encountered.

Being so far out of L.A. was exciting and boring at the same time. Even as they told themselves how good it was to be somewhere that they could just concentrate on baseball, they were much too young to embrace the quiet of Montana, and they missed the clatter and chaos of home.

None of that was an excuse, or even an explanation, for what was to transpire just a little more than a month into the season. One afternoon, Darryl was shopping in a department store in town. Someone left a wallet on a counter. He took it, and quickly exited. The wallet had credit cards in it. Darryl and Cordie charged some items on it—clothes, mostly, as well as a camera.

"It was all stupid stuff," Cordie says now. "It was of nonvalue to what we were trying to accomplish up there."

Cordie had signed for a couple of the purchases. "Darryl was kind of nervous," he says. "I was always kind of a smooth talker, so I stepped in."

During the next road trip, to Medicine Hat, Canada, Chris Brown— the third of the Crenshaw players at Great Falls—went out for a midday walk and stopped to talk to some girls. He was seated on a bus-stop bench when Darryl McNealy approached with a couple of teammates. They asked Chris if he wanted to go into a Woolworth's with them. He said good-bye to the girls and went on in.

The next thing he knew, Darryl had picked up a camera and was walking to the counter with it. "What's he doing?" Chris asked the others.

Chris knew about the credit card but thought Darryl and Cordie had stopped using it.

A teammate, a player whose father was supposedly a self-made millionaire, answered that Darryl had agreed to get a camera for him with the card—and that he had promised to pay Darryl half the purchase price in cash.

Chris, never one to mince words, blew up. "Why would you ask him to do something like that and get his ass in trouble for you?"

Chris could be a jerk and a loudmouth but he was no thief. After he had his say, he walked out and sat right back down on the bench. He didn't want to be anywhere near a phony credit card transaction.

In a few minutes, everyone but Darryl McNealy came back out of the store. "You left Darryl in there?" Chris asked. "If he can't get that camera in a few minutes, then something's wrong."

Chris hurried back into the store, hoping to pull Darryl out of there. He arrived just in time to see two police officers closing in on Darryl McNealy. Then he heard that distinctive *click-click* that any child of inner-city America would recognize—the sound of handcuffs being fastened onto his friend's skinny wrists.

*   *   *

As Chris Brown and Cordie Dillard arrived at the ballpark for pregame practice, Darryl McNealy was around the corner at police headquarters, being interrogated. He was a frightened kid in a foreign country—no family around, no lawyer in the room, not even a coach—with nothing to say for himself but that he had done a bad thing and he was sorry.

About an hour before game time, as Cordie stood out at second base taking ground balls, he heard over the public address system: *Cordie Dillard, please report to the press level.*

He walked off the field, put his mitt on the bench, and climbed the stairs to a tiny minor league press box. He was awaiting such a call, and already regretting that he had ignored something his father told him repeatedly, Don't do wrong, but if you do wrong do it by yourself. His father reasoned: If you do bad things in concert with others, and they get caught, then you will get caught, too—because they will not take the punishment themselves.

And that is exactly what happened. Under questioning, Darryl gave up Cordie, told law enforcement agents that his old high school teammate had signed for some of the purchases and kept some of the goods.

The fact that the credit card had been stolen in the U.S. and then taken into Canada and used made the whole thing a bit more serious. Waiting for Cordie when he arrived upstairs were his manager, a coach, a couple of police officers, and two men they understood to be FBI agents.

Cordie admitted what he had done. He felt sick to his stomach. He couldn't wait for the whole thing to be over so he could go somewhere and throw up.

Of the three Crenshaw kids playing for Great Falls, Cordie had been the lowest draft pick—a twelfth-rounder. (Chris was taken in the third round, Darryl McNealy in the seventh.) All three were playing well, but Cordie was the one really exceeding expectations.

George Genovese was right—Cordie sure could hit. He handled high school pitching. He was handling minor league pitching. He could have hit anywhere. He had not yet shouted *curveball!* before taking a whack at one, but he was getting pretty comfortable—he might have done that in due time.

"It was a shame what happened, because they were liking Cordie more than they were liking me," says Chris. "The twin, he had a chance to make it up to a big-league club, a legitimate chance. But Cordie, he was definite. You could see it; it was just obvious that he was better than most of the other guys."

Neither Cordie or Darryl McNealy played again in Medicine Hat, or anywhere. They were not charged criminally, but team executives in San Francisco decided that as soon as the team arrived back in Great Falls, they would be put on the first available flight and shipped home. A few days after they got back to L.A., they each received registered letters saying they had been unconditionally released. Fired.

The Boys of Crenshaw were sometimes victims of racism. They were victims of society's inequities. But that was not the case here. What they fell victim to was their own foolish behavior.

Darryl McNealy reaching for that wallet, and charging up the card along with Cordie, had the same effect as Donald Jones's impetuous decision to set upon his brother's assailant with a baseball bat. It was the end of baseball.

"We did wrong and paid for it," Darryl McNealy says. "We went all that way and got our hearts broke."

When word got back to their old high school teammates, they were incredulous. They were sad about Darryl McNealy but not entirely shocked. But Cordie, who always had everything handled—Cordie, who was so good at staying just clear of trouble—Cordie, whom they so admired and so resented for these traits—being led astray by one of the twins? And by the twin that any one of them would have known to steer clear of? It didn't make sense.

Cordie was angry at Darryl McNealy, but much more so at himself for being so foolhardy, and especially for disregarding his father's advice.

Chris Brown was angry about the whole thing, too. There had been three Boys of Crenshaw, all together, and now there was one. He found someone to take it out on.

That night in Medicine Hat, the player who had encouraged Darryl to charge the camera for him knocked on Chris Brown's door in the team hotel. It was well after midnight. He wanted Chris to protect him, not to tell team management of his involvement. Chris said: "You want me to do what? You want me to roll over on my buddy to protect your ass? You know doggone well you was in that store, and why you was in that store."

"I was so mad that I grabbed him, and I started beating on him so bad that I woke the whole floor up and some of the guys came running from their rooms and pulled me off of him. If they hadn't showed up, I might have killed him. When the team found out his part, they fined him fifty bucks. *Fifty bucks.* And Cordie and the twin done lost their whole careers."

*   *   *

The star among stars of the Boys of Crenshaw was struggling, too, but in an entirely different way.

Everyone was so exhilarated by the whole Darryl Strawberry package: Massive Darryl who could hit long home runs and steal bases. Darryl the outfield gazelle who glided after fly balls in right field, who gunned down base runners with his powerful throwing arm. They were so excited that they failed to take proper notice of a disturbing fact. Darryl himself—the accidental grand prize winner of some genetic lottery—was not so celebratory of his great gift. He treated it cheaply. It felt like a burden. He was even oddly resentful, bemoaning that he was not loved for being just plain old Darryl Strawberry.

That was his one true insight into the world of professional sports— no one loved him for just being Darryl. But it wasn't personal; pro athletes are loved for what they do.

His mother came to visit him in New York not long after he joined the Mets. On the streets of Manhattan, they passed a homeless man curled up on the sidewalk, asleep. Darryl lingered, then expressed a shocking thought. "I wish I was that bum because nobody would bother me," he told his mother. "If I didn't have all this money, I wouldn't have all these pressures, all these expectations."

New York baseball fans, and a great many fans nationwide, had fallen hard for Darryl before ever seeing him play. They fell for the name and the hype and the hope of following a historic career. That's what sports fans do. They hook onto a young player, the showier and more bally-hooed the better, and give him their devotion. So Darryl's fans tracked his progress through the minor leagues, awaited his New York debut, then celebrated when he seemed in the beginning to be everything that was promised.

Who among them would have guessed that even for a fleeting mo-ment the young Darryl would have wanted to trade places with a bum passed out on the street—or that years later, he would all but achieve that transformation?

Nearly everyone in baseball expected Darryl to fulfill his destiny, de-manded it. The particulars changed in one small way: Instead of being compared to Ted Williams, the legend more often invoked was Willie Mays.

Like Mays, and unlike the more one-dimensional Williams, Darryl could win a game with a home run, a stolen base, a running catch, or a strong throw to nail a base runner. But Darryl didn't know much more about Mays than he did Williams. "I'm not familiar with the things Willie has done," he told one reporter.

His innocence—just a wide-eyed kid from L.A. who didn't know that much about Willie Mays—made for pleasant enough newspaper copy. But looking back, his lack of zest for baseball lore could have been taken as a tip-off to his limits.

It's hard to make history, after all, if you have no knowledge of it, no reverence for what preceded you, no marker to point toward or push beyond. But none of this dampened the excitement or the expectations. A defining feature of Darryl's early career was that he caused veteran baseball men to lose their normal caution. He made them take leave of their senses.

"He can go as far in baseball as any man living," Frank Howard, his second Mets manager, said.

John Stearns, a catcher for the 1983 Mets, took one look at his new teammate and proclaimed: "If Darryl works at it, he could be the greatest player ever."

But Darryl didn't work at it. Even after he reached the big leagues, he was still trying (although not too hard) to master some of the things Brooks Hurst had tried to instill. Before a game in Philadelphia in his rookie year, Mets coach Jim Frey stood with a bat along the first-base line and hit ball after ball to Darryl in right field. Just like at Crenshaw, Darryl was being drilled on "beating the ball to the spot," cutting off hits before runners could take extra bases. He hadn't been doing this very well—he had the speed but not the will—and Mets pitchers were fed up with watching Darryl amble after balls while runners scurried from base to base.

That afternoon with Frey, Darryl fielded a couple of dozen balls and then came trotting in. "I've had enough," the rookie told his coach.

"What do you mean, you've had enough?" Frey asked.

"Had enough," Darryl repeated as he passed the coach and continued on into the clubhouse.

*   *   *

"I live in a hotel near Shea Stadium," the twenty-one-year-old Darryl Strawberry told sportswriters. "I don't stay out late or run around. I'm not into that." The following season, *Sports Illustrated* wrote that he was not "a partygoer or a carouser."

Darryl had a gift for telling older white men—coaches, writers, his agent, would-be mentors and saviors—what they wanted to hear. He could fool people, not forever but for a while.

His production as a young Met was not immediately Williams-esque: between twenty-six and twenty-nine home runs in each of his first four seasons; a batting average no higher than .277. But he did enough spectacular things, and showed such a measure of raw physical talent, that his future still seemed boundless.

In 1986, he helped lead the Mets to a World Series championship— the series in which Bill Buckner famously flubbed a routine ground ball and kicked away what looked like a clinching Red Sox victory in Game 6. Darryl was still just twenty-four years old. His lean, supple strength had matured into a man's muscle. Few in the big leagues would have wanted to tangle with him.

In addition to strength, he had developed some savvy in the batter's box. When he was slumping, he still swung at balls a foot outside and scratched for them in the dirt. But when he was hot, no pitcher wanted to face him. St. Louis Cardinals manager Whitey Herzog once walked him with the bases empty, a tactic that would be employed in later years fairly regularly against Mark McGwire and Barry Bonds but which back then was almost unprecedented.

On the field, Darryl was maturing; off it, his behavior was worrisome.

In fact, he was drowning right from the start of his big-league career, and in such plain view that even some members of the city's other baseball franchise could see it. "You would hear things; players, you know, we talk a little bit," says Willie Randolph, the Yankees' second baseman when Strawberry was a young Met. "You would see Darryl out with his entourage; even then he had a lot of people around him. It was a shame the things that happened, but it wasn't a surprise. You knew as a player that it was only a matter of time.

"As a pro athlete, you can have a good time but you cannot be having a party every single night until the sun comes up. When you see someone who is, you say to yourself, 'Uh-oh, there's trouble down the road.'"

Baseball is night work. The games end at ten or eleven o'clock, sometimes close to midnight. Few players can go right home and get to sleep, so they stay out late. They drink, and some do drugs.

Allan Lans, the Mets longtime team psychologist, talks of the machismo of pro sports. "There's a whole scene that goes with being an athletic hero in our society," he says. "The spoils of it are women, drink, and drugs. The thing they always say in baseball is 'have fun.' Gimme a break. The game isn't that fun if you struck out three times that night, or you're a pitcher and you got knocked out in the first inning. It's hard. What they do to replenish the soul is drink and do drugs."

Richie Bry, Darryl's agent, wondered if his client might have a drinking problem. Darryl would have three or four drinks before dinner, usually mixed drinks—rum and Coke, or Jack Daniel's and Coke—then maybe a couple of beers with dinner. But Bry told himself that Darryl was probably fine. He was big; he seemed to be able to handle it. But Darryl's increasing off-field troubles, combined with the ever-present pressure to achieve on the field, heightened Bry's concern.

In one way, Darryl's life looked increasingly easy. He had ascended to that class of wealthy celebrity who pays for almost nothing. It is one of life's paradoxes: To whom much is given, more is given. Restaurants and nightclubs comped him. Sporting goods companies lavished him with free apparel. Every time he went back to his locker at whatever ballpark he was playing at, somebody had loaded more free stuff into it. Very little came with a cost, or consequences. (Years later, even his expensive stays in drug rehab centers would come for free, as a benefit of the players' union contract.)

Darryl married for the first time in 1985, at twenty-two, to Lisa Andrews, a lissome, tempestuous beauty he had met the previous year at a Lakers game. The wedding itself was like a coronation, befitting Darryl's status as a young prince of professional sports.

But Lisa's family could not afford such a celebration, and the groom was not digging into his own pocket to cover the full freight. Richie Bry paid for the big rehearsal dinner at Trader Vic's, and, he figured, for about half the reception in Beverly Hills. It was the kind of thing an agent does to cement his relationship with a superstar client. An investment.

And besides, Darryl was like family. Bry's wife came to the wedding; his kids danced.

Darryl was ambivalent about the marriage right from the start. On his way to the church near Pasadena, he surprised his groomsmen by telling the limousine driver to intentionally take a wrong turn off the 210 Freeway. Some of the other passengers, including his Crenshaw teammate Chris Brown, tried to get the driver to turn in the right direction.

Darryl told his friends to shut up. To the driver, he said: Keep going. The wedding was supposed to start at eleven A.M.; the groom and his party arrived well after noon.

There are many bad marriages in baseball. Darryl had a disastrous one. Two years into it, Lisa filed assault charges against her husband for allegedly breaking her nose after a National League Championship Series game against Houston in 1986, the series that preceded the Mets–Red Sox matchup in the World Series.

Darryl had starred in those games, hitting two crucial home runs, but on-field exploits clearly did not equate with off-hours tranquility. Just the opposite, it seemed.

Darryl and Lisa fought, separated, reconciled, and fought some more for the whole of their eight-year marriage. Bry feared that Darryl was beginning to crack from the accumulated pressures of his career and his home life.

"I'm not your father, but I'm about as close as you're going to get," he said during one of several attempts to get Darryl to level with him. He asked Darryl directly if he was using drugs; Darryl denied it, as he would in several other conversations. But of course he was.

Darryl's teammates had their own suspicions, but a Major League clubhouse is like a lot of workplaces: People go their own way, live and let live, overlook nearly any behavior that does not interfere with the product. "What you have in baseball are baseball friendships," says Dave Magadan, a longtime major-leaguer and former Met teammate of Darryl's. "I've played for a lot of years, and there's guys who when I played with them, I saw them every day, and I went to lunch with them every day, and we went out after games every night. And I don't even speak to them now. That's just how it is. You move on."

Says Hubie Brooks: "Everybody says the camaraderie is the best thing about playing, but that's for 162 games. And camaraderie and closeness are different. Closeness comes under different circumstances. How close are you to your teammates really? Usually, not very."

Besides the natural inclination not to meddle in a teammate's personal life, the other reason Darryl's behavior went unchecked was because so many of his teammates were living the same fast life he was. Even by baseball's loose standards, the Mets of the mid- and late eighties were free-spirited and notoriously hard-living. And even by Mets standards, Darryl was over the top. (Their nicknames—Nails, Mex, El Cid, Straw, Doc—made them all sound like dead-end kids.)

"A lot of us drank too much," says Keith Hernandez, the former Mets first baseman. "I drank too much. You're on the road. You're with guys. They feed you in the clubhouse after the game, and then what do you do? I could close a bar at two A.M. and be in bed by two-thirty and have no trouble being ready for batting practice the next night."

Hernandez was one of the older players, and he had some tread on him, having just kicked a cocaine habit before coming to the Mets. "I found out later that many of my teammates were running around till four A.M.," he says. "I found out they were crazier than I was."

And things got even crazier after the Mets won the World Series. They became, literally, the toast of Manhattan—or of wherever town they happened to be. Drinks came free. For those who were interested, so did women and cocaine. The Mets of the Strawberry era were lavishly talented, chronic underachievers. They never returned to a World Series. "We had the best team in the division by far, and we went to the playoffs just one more time," Magadan says. "It was inexcusable."

Even Darryl, rarely introspective and almost never one to make harsh judgments—of himself or others—acknowledges the source of the problem. "We didn't win more because we partied too hard," he said to me in one of our conversations. "Whoever wants to can deny it, but that was our downfall."

Darryl was no thug—he has mainly hurt himself and his loved ones—but he could be a mean drunk. On team charters, a lot of players drank and played cards. Sometimes Darryl played; sometimes he just sat in the back and drank, often with pitcher Dwight Gooden, whose own career would be sabotaged by drugs and alcohol.

One on one, Darryl could be charming and generous. He was great with kids. After games, he sometimes signed autographs until every last person in line had left. But on team flights with a few cocktails in him, in a grouping with his teammates, many of them also liquored up, he could be vicious.

There were unwritten but clearly understood limits to what you ribbed a teammate about. His clothes, but not his wife or girlfriend. Some pratfall on the field, but not his overall performance. Darryl didn't observe those niceties.

A particular target was catcher Gary Carter, a star of the 1986 championship team who in the late eighties had a couple of woeful seasons as he struggled to reach three hundred career home runs. Darryl stayed on him about money and production—not the usual jocularity, but much closer to the bone. Darryl had yet to cash in, and the older Carter was making better money.

"I've got thirty jacks," Darryl would say, meaning thirty home runs, "and you're hitting a buck-seventy (.170)." It was not friendly ribbing but aggressive verbal abuse, the last thing a struggling teammate needed to hear.

Going all the way back to Crenshaw, and even before, Darryl had never had much of a sense of self. What was he beyond a big guy who could play some ball? He wouldn't have been able to tell you, aside from some platitudes about loving his mother.

The Strawberrys were not churchgoers, so he had no grounding in faith. (His abiding faith, like so many of the Crenshaw kids, was in the redemptive quality of sports.) They did not have a large extended family, so there was no real Strawberry family tradition to cleave to. His father had walked out. His older brother, Ronnie, was chronically in trouble with the law.

More than any of the other Boys of Crenshaw, Darryl was unmoored, a child of inner-city Los Angeles whom everyone fawned over, many admired, some envied—and no one thought to try to help. What could anyone that gloriously talented really need? What could the world offer Darryl Strawberry that pro baseball and all his fame and money wasn't already providing?

But those who really knew Darryl were never sure he even liked playing ball, at least not at the level expected of him. Lans, the team psychologist, thought Darryl "liked shooting hoops in the backyard."

Darryl would later tell me, "Baseball was fun. I loved it from the time I was a kid just starting out. But I never thought there would be pressure attached to it."

Over time, the hype around Darryl utterly defined him. He lived the life of a superstar, and took on all the most unsavory trappings and affectations, even though he only periodically performed like an actual superstar. His worst instincts were tolerated, even encouraged. He wasn't cruel by nature, but abetted by alcohol and drugs he became so at times.

A player of Darryl's magnitude attracts not only a devoted fan base but a following among other players who want to be around him for the fun, the free drinks, the women, the perceived security of being known to management as part of the inner circle. So he had a clique of teammates who laughed at his jokes, even when they weren't funny. He had teammates who agreed that he was underpaid and underappreciated.

"If you went out with Darryl, you were probably going to have a good time," Magadan says. He adds: "Some guys were afraid of Darryl. They were afraid of his stature on the team. I think some were afraid of him physically."

Darryl had, as well, a growing cluster of nonbaseball associates at his side—buddies, mainly from back home, who traveled at his expense, rode in his limos, accompanied him to clubs. One friend in particular, a childhood buddy from L.A., was suspected by teammates and some Mets officials of procuring drugs and women for him.

Darryl paid for his buddy's flights. The Mets booked his hotel rooms, and Darryl paid the bills. His only job seemed to be to go to clubs with Darryl. Mets executives didn't like the situation; it worried them. But Darryl was a man in his twenties. He was from inner-city L.A. They didn't think they could tell him who his friends should be.

*   *   *

Chris Brown took just a little longer to reach the big leagues than Darryl Strawberry. After Great Falls, he played five more minor league seasons, making nearly every stop in the Giants farm system—Clinton, Iowa; Shreveport; Fresno; Phoenix.

Chris didn't like this long climb, of course. Hadn't expected it. He had been the athletic whiz kid who was first at everything. But after this long wait was imposed on him, he turned it into a point of pride. He told himself that he had been raised right in baseball—schooled, refined, and polished until he was premium big-league material.

He finally arrived in San Francisco in September 1984, two weeks after he turned twenty-three. He had filled out to a rock-solid six-foot-two, 210 pounds. But he was still the little hardhead who at eight years old marched out to third base and claimed it as his own. He considered himself half a football player, and just assumed, and told anyone who would listen, that if he had chosen football, everyone would be watching him in the NFL. (Years later, Chris's line was that if he'd had three more inches of height on his blacksmith's frame, he would have been Charles Barkley.)

In San Francisco, he was an instant star. In 1985, his first full season, he made the all-rookie team, and the year after that, the National League All-Star team—whose starting right fielder was Darryl Strawberry.

At the end of June of that season, Chris was hitting a robust .348, the best average in the league. When his manager Roger Craig called him into his office and told him he had been selected for the All-Star game, he felt an actual physical sense of elation—a tingle down his spine, and tears in his eyes. Chris knew he was good, but there's nothing like a big honor—National League All-Star, in just the second season of a big-league career—to authenticate it.

His teammate Chili Davis, a veteran and another L.A. guy, had also been named an All-Star, and was asked by Roger Craig to help guide Chris through the experience. Chris had not been voted onto the starting team, so he had no guarantee he would get anything beyond a chance to pinch hit. A cameo.

Whatever you do, Chili Davis told him, don't swing at the first pitch when they put you in the game. *Make it last.* Chili spoke from experience: A couple of years earlier, he had been chosen an All-Star, traveled to the game, practiced the preceding day, waited eight innings for his chance, then swung at the first pitch and dribbled the ball weakly to the shortstop.

When Chris got his chance in the fifth inning, he was seized by a voice other than Chili's. "When I got up there, I said, 'Hey, I didn't get here looking at pitches.' My mind said to listen to Chili, but my heart said to get up there and hack."

The pitcher was Charlie Hough, a knuckleballer. His first pitch came fluttering in, and Chris, whose Crenshaw teammates believed he could get out of bed anytime and smoke a line drive, took a mighty swing and smacked that knuckleball against the Astrodome's center-field fence. He stood at second base with a double, beaming. He had just about jumped on top of the bag.

He looked into the dugout and there was Darryl Strawberry, up on the front step, shouting out something he couldn't hear. Chili Davis was so doubled up with laughter he hadn't even been able to get off the bench. Chris looked in and saw Chili, and he started laughing, too.

He stayed in the game, replacing starter Mike Schmidt at third base, and grounded out in his only other at bat. It hardly mattered. The night had been a triumph.

Chris had gotten married in the minor leagues to his high school sweetheart. They had a son, Chris Jr., but had split on more or less amicable terms. He was in Houston with a girlfriend, and they had plans to meet Darryl and Lisa Strawberry after the game and go together to a club—the two Boys of Crenshaw, teammates in the National League All-Star team, celebrating together.

But nothing involving Darryl Strawberry was ever that simple. Darryl and Lisa got in a spat before the limousine even pulled away from the Astrodome. Chris was afraid Darryl might hit her. He thought to himself: I've seen this too many times. I'm not even going to try to break it up.

Chris and his date got out of the limo and went to the club themselves. He didn't see Darryl the rest of that night.

*   *   *

The greatest Giant of them all, Willie Mays, normally came to spring training in Arizona for a few weeks to serve as a kind of freelance instructor. He didn't do all that much. Talked with the younger players, threw in a suggestion here and there, showed up fairly late in the day and left early. His role was mostly ceremonial, but just having Willie Mays around was enough.

In 1987, however, Giants management asked Willie to do something specific: spend time with Chris Brown. Try to figure out, basically, what the hell's wrong with him. What's he thinking? What's eating at him?

At Crenshaw, everything was easy for Chris. Baseball. Basketball. The classroom. His mother made life easy at home, waiting on him, cooking for him, pressing his baseball uniforms—in the estimation of his teammates, spoiling the hell out of him.

Swaddled in this comfort zone, Chris was gregarious, if a bit hard to take. In pro baseball, and especially after he came up to the majors, Chris was a different person. He lived inside a shell. He didn't extend trust. If he didn't like you, he just didn't talk to you.

His 1986 season, that All-Star year that had started so gloriously, turned sour and ended badly. After a doubleheader in Chicago—which had started at one P.M. and ended close to seven P.M.—Chris was handed a note to contact family back in L.A. When he called, he learned that his father, whom he had reconciled with after years of distance, had suffered a stroke and was fighting for his life.

When Chris looked again at the note, he saw that the message had been taken at ten A.M. He blew up at everyone in sight, figuring that the team had wanted him to play the doubleheader before attending to business at home.

Chris flew back to L.A. and stayed for nearly a week. When Giants officials called, he wasn't glad to hear from them. "My father's in intensive care," he said, "and you want to talk to me about baseball?"

After he came back, he injured his left shoulder. Medical tests and X-rays revealed no obvious injury. He sat out some games. He took hydrotherapy treatments. When he returned to the lineup, he couldn't hit for power. He took several more games off. The team's general manager, Al Rosen, wondered why he didn't seem to care about winning a batting championship. Chris looked at him like he was speaking Chinese. Did this man really think winning a batting championship was more important than his health?

In fact, he probably did. Al Rosen had been a legendarily tough player, and a batting championship probably *would* have been more important to him—but it wasn't to Chris Brown.

The team's suspicions, that Chris was malingering, began to make their way into the press. When he did play, some fans booed. When he made a routine play in the field, they cheered derisively. Chris, a golden boy from the moment he started playing ball, had never been the object of anything like that.

When the team fell out of the pennant race, he sat himself down for good. He did so, he believed, with the encouragement and support of the team's veteran players, although that is not how some of them would remember it.

That off-season, the source of the shoulder problem, a torn tendon, was identified and corrected in surgery by Dr. Frank Jobe, a renowned sports orthopedist. Chris felt vindicated. But it was following that off-season that Willie Mays was assigned to crack open the shell around Chris Brown.

"We were like two peas in a pod," Chris says. "Everywhere I went, Willie went. He was cool with me. He understood that I was a private person. He just said be yourself, play baseball, produce what you're supposed to produce on the field, and everything will take care of itself."

Chris wanted to believe that was true. Just stay healthy. Hit the ball. Everything would be okay then, right?

*　*　*

Chris Brown had one problem in common with Darryl Strawberry: He couldn't accept the part of baseball that was a cold-blooded business. It may have had something to do with growing up without a father at home. Both of them looked for some kind of approbation in the game apart from what they did on the field. (Darryl looked everywhere for father figures.) They wanted to be loved as well as written into the lineup and paid. When that wasn't forthcoming, it made them unreasonably angry.

But Chris had an additional issue, a problem that was in many ways the opposite of what plagued Darryl: He did not drink, smoke, or do drugs. He was a straight arrow and something of a prude. Much about the off-field baseball scene—especially in the 1980s, when a criminal trial in Pittsburgh involving several players lifted a veil on only a small slice of drug use in the game—made Chris distinctly uncomfortable.

"I saw so many crazy parties in the Major Leagues," he says. "I was at parties where this room was all cocaine, this room was all alcohol, this room was all weed, and this room was all naked women—and you could have as much sex as you wanted. I would go in there and say, 'That's not me,' and I'd leave.

"I never dated a woman who smoked. If she drank, it was just a little social drink, okay, I have no problem with that. I got criteria for a woman, I guess, that she be like my mother. She has to be churchgoing, God-fearing, don't drink or smoke, don't go around cursing."

Chris could not, as Willie Mays suggested, just be himself and play ball and let everything else fall into place. Professional baseball didn't agree with him physically, or in any other way. He kept getting hurt, sitting out, disappointing his employers.

The Giants gave up on Chris and traded him on July 4, 1987, to the last-place San Diego Padres, whose manager was Larry Bowa, a fiery, easily agitated former shortstop in his first year at the helm of a Major League team. It was, to say the least, an unfortunate fit. Playing for Bowa was like playing for a deranged man. Bowa's own book about that dismal season was titled *Bleep*, because Bowa communicated almost entirely in expletives.

Late that season, Chris hit a line drive that nearly nailed star right fielder Tony Gwynn, who was on second base. Gwynn strained a muscle taking evasive action. Bowa, who had wanted Chris to hit the ball to the right side to move Gwynn over to third base, started screaming at Chris as soon as he got back to the dugout. He blamed him for causing Gwynn's injury. They argued again in the clubhouse after the game.

"He was screaming at me, like I somehow guided the ball right at Tony, like that was even possible," Chris says. "I went right after him. I said to him, 'My father doesn't curse at me that way, so you better well not.' I told him, 'If you want to fight, I'll kick your ass. I may not ever play baseball again, but if you don't respect me now, you will respect me after that.'"

It took several players to pull Chris away and out of trouble. Several weeks later, he came down with an eye infection and was out of the lineup. Bowa told reporters that his third baseman had "slept on his eye wrong," which was duly reported in the papers. Chris figured if it had been anyone else, it wouldn't have come out that way. Later, a toothache was listed in the team's media notes as a "bruised tooth."

In 1989, the Padres traded Chris to the Detroit Tigers, who were managed by Sparky Anderson, the legendary manager of the Cincinnati Reds Big Red Machine. Chris came down with yet more injuries. He didn't play much. He and Sparky didn't get along. That same season, years of baseball pressure caught up with Sparky, and he left the team, taking time off for exhaustion, and some of that got reflected back on Chris—as if he had somehow driven Sparky over the edge. There was even a rumor, untrue, that Sparky and Chris had gotten into a fight.

By 1990, Chris Brown, twenty-eight, was out of baseball, a stunningly premature departure from a game he had played as a kid with such joyful exuberance. Four years earlier he had been an All-Star; now, not one team wanted him. Injuries undermined him, but no more so than what looked like a mystifying lack of resolve.

But that is not how Chris saw it. Shouldn't the surgery after the 1986 season, after the team didn't believe he was hurt, have settled everything? Shouldn't everyone who thought he was dogging it have come up and apologized to him, or at least gotten off his back?

Maybe if he could have made friends of the writers, no one would have written that he had "slept on his eye wrong" when he had a damn eye infection. But Chris, so comfortable with himself at Crenshaw, talking all the time, the center of every scene, had no idea how to handle himself in the big-league milieu. Specifically, he had no clue how to talk to the baseball writers and how to get his own slant on things into their stories. Some of the other players could do that; Chris never figured it out. Whatever language they all conversed in, he didn't speak it. Chris, blunt and impolitic, had long felt safer keeping his mouth shut.

He attempted a couple of comebacks, but his reputation for indolence carried more weight than the memory of his prodigious talent. "It got to the point that I was disheartened," he says. "There was a roadblock everywhere."

In 1995, a labor impasse caused Major League Baseball to recruit so-called replacement players, what the union called scabs. Chris talked to some friends still in the game, and they gave their blessings for him to try to get back in baseball by becoming a replacement player for the Cincinnati Reds. Even after five years off, he came back hitting line drives. Five games into the exhibition season, he already had two home runs.

Then he sat out with an injury, which became a source of great fun for baseball writers already grumpy about having to write about watered-down strike baseball. Now they had Chris Brown to kick around again. What a godsend!

"Quite the action-packed day for our favorite malingerer, Chris 'Downtime' Brown," the *Philadelphia Daily News* wrote. "You remember Downtime, the good-hitting third baseman who exhausted the Giants' and Padres' patience with his excuses for sitting out, like the time he slept on his eye wrong."

Chris's biography in the online Baseball Library is withering. He had the talent to be an MVP, it says, "but the enigmatic Brown showed little desire to play like one, or often to play at all. Instead, he would infuriate both managers and teammates with a careless attitude and a litany of nagging, minor injuries that were usually described as imaginary. From 1984 to 1989, Brown missed over 250 games with ailments as ludicrous as a 'bruised tooth' but was placed on the DL only once, when a Danny Cox pitch broke his jaw."

The bio goes on to say that Chris was called "the Tin Man" both by his teammates and opponents—a nickname he was unaware of.

One day, after Chris had given up all hope of getting back into professional baseball, George Genovese, the scout who had first signed him, was out driving in the L.A. area. Genovese stopped his car beside a field where a Sunday game was in progress, something between an informal league and a pickup game.

Most scouts would drive right by such a game, but he figured he would watch for an inning or two. Every once in a while, he'd even find a prospect at one of these Sunday games, or at least someone worth a second look. As Genovese walked up to the field, the muscular-looking guy at third base, crouched in his fielder's stance, attracted his attention. He looked like a ballplayer.

It was Chris Brown. The scout felt a twinge of sadness.

How long had it been since he first saw Chris as a seventeen-year-old at Crenshaw, playing for Brooks Hurst—firing perfect throws to Cordie Dillard at second base to start double plays, batting third in the lineup right in front of Darryl Strawberry? Not that many years. Chris didn't belong back here, not now. He belonged up in the big leagues.

There wasn't one thing Chris couldn't do on a baseball field. He had power, soft hands, a great arm, good speed. Genovese thought he should have had as good a career as George Brett, the great Kansas City Royals third baseman.

The scout stayed long enough to see Chris loft a home run over a short left-field fence. He walked over to the bench and tapped him on the shoulder.

"You can still hit, Chris," he said. "You could always hit."

Chris smiled. As Genovese headed for his car, he told him, "If you were ten years younger, I'd sign you again."

*   *   *

At Crenshaw High, George Cook was the clever little infielder with the sweet footwork around the second base bag, the coach on the field who whispered suggestions to Brooks Hurst—the kid stuffed into the little house with his ten siblings who dreamed of living on a ranch with horses to ride and hundreds of acres to roam. It was a baseball dream and a money dream combined, an escape dream, like the dreams of most of the Boys of Crenshaw.

Through most of high school, it wasn't clear that George would ever get big enough to be taken seriously by scouts. But he grew late, and on graduation day was just short of six feet tall, and a spindly strong 155 pounds. The Baltimore Orioles selected him in the thirteenth round of the Major League draft. In a draft that stretched for fifty rounds, that wasn't a hopeless place to be picked, but after the first couple of rounds players aren't offered a lot of money, nor do teams invest a lot of time in them. Middle- and late-round picks either quickly show promise in the minor leagues or are sent packing.

An Orioles scout came to George's house after the draft with a contract in hand and the bonus offer of $2,500 already penned in. Even in inner-city L.A. that wasn't going to buy an acre, let alone a ranch. Darryl Strawberry had just signed for $200,000. George knew he wasn't in that class, but was Darryl really eighty times better than he was? He had been playing with Darryl since he was eight years old, and he didn't think so.

That was not, of course, the way pro baseball people made their calculations. But just knowing what money was put in front of Darryl, and thinking he could improve his draft position by playing well in college, was enough to make George spurn the Orioles.

He enrolled at Los Angeles City College, figuring he'd either jump directly from there to pro ball or move on to a four-year college. The coach at LACC was Phil Pote, Brooks Hurst's old friend, who doubled as a scout for the Seattle Mariners.

Pote was blunt about his players' pro prospects. To George, he said: Field your position. Turn double plays. Hit for a high average and steal bases. Run the sixty-yard dash in under 6.6 seconds. Fail at any of those, and the scouts won't give you another look. You won't be drafted again.

George's good friend Marvin McWhorter, Big Marvin, ended up with him at LACC. He had not been drafted at all out of Crenshaw, and was crestfallen about it. Phil Pote's mission statement to Marvin: You're big. You're slow. You're strong. See those fences out there? Hit a bunch of balls over them, and they'll like you a lot.

This was like telling a fish to take in oxygen through its gills. Marvin really didn't need any prompting to swing for the fences.

In his first season at LACC, Marvin crushed the ball—hit close to .400, set a California junior college record for doubles, made all-conference, led the team in home runs. The Oakland A's chose him in the seventeenth round, after which Marvin, like George, had a decision to make: Continue in school, or go off to play minor league baseball?

Marvin's big extended family, a council of elders, gathered to advise him. Some said he should sign with the A's and go off to the minor leagues. Others said to stay in school. His mother didn't weigh in on either side, advising him to just follow his heart.

The decision he finally made was not an entirely rational one, because it flowed from that old drama between father and son. Marvin McWhorter Sr., who had played catch with him every Friday evening, but had told him so many times there was no living in baseball—that it was a waste of time and he ought to get on the landscaping truck and earn some money—suddenly had a change of heart.

"My father never came to any of my baseball games," Marvin says. "Not one time, not even when we played for the championship at Dodger Stadium. But when baseball became something with money behind it, he got interested. As soon as I got drafted, he started coming to my junior college games and bringing his friends around to them, too. It bothered me."

Marvin's father said sign. So, naturally, Marvin decided *not* to sign.

"It sounds terrible now," he says, "but I was at a point in my life where whatever he said, I wanted to do the opposite just to spite him. I was undecided what to do, so what he said made up my mind for me."

*　*　*

Marvin was playing basketball in the old neighborhood a couple of years after high school when Chris Brown came wheeling up in the car his bonus money had bought—a black Camaro Z28, fully loaded. Leather interior. Gold-spoke wheels. Marvin had an overwhelming urge to get behind the wheel.

"Can I drive it?" he asked.

"You can if you beat me playing one-on-one," Chris said.

They played to five baskets. Marvin scored the first three, then Chris started lowering his big butt, backing Marvin under the hoop, then rising up and shooting over him. Marvin was a big man, but Chris was a little taller and more explosive.

Chris beat him five baskets to four. Then he threw him the keys.

Darryl Strawberry and Chris sometimes talked about "big-footing," lording their success over others. Big-footing was bad, but sometimes could not be resisted. Especially if it was in good fun, like making Marvin think he couldn't drive the car unless he won at basketball.

Chris knew there was no way Marvin was going to beat him. And he knew that after he whupped Marvin he would of course let him take a spin.

The Boys of Crenshaw had always measured their own success in terms of how they stood against one another. How many balls they could hit over the fence and out onto Eighth Avenue. How many times they could hit it onto the old man's lawn and make him stomp out and fuss. Who could be the one to hit the roof of the Whitney Young Building, a 400-foot blast to dead center field.

Marvin hardly needed to see Chris's car to know that he was losing the big competition, the one that had engaged them from the moment they saw themselves as ballplayers. Chris, at that moment, was pointed toward the big leagues. Marvin was stalled; his copy of Ted Williams's *The Science of Hitting* was getting dog-eared, his window of opportunity to play pro ball closing fast.

Having spurned the contract offer from the Oakland A's, he transferred to Pomona College, a California baseball power about ninety minutes east of L.A., almost to the mountains. It was a mistake to go there, and Marvin knew it instantly.

The first day of fall practice, a coach—one of what seemed like about a dozen assistant coaches—walked over to Marvin as he was loosening up and told him he'd have to cut his sideburns, mustache, and Afro.

Marvin explained that he wasn't from the area, didn't know any local barbers who could cut his hair, and could it wait until the weekend when he could get back into L.A. for a trim?

Fine, the coach said, so long as Marvin understood the rules: hair nice and short, no mustaches, no beards. In their green-and-gold baseball uniforms, Pomona players were all supposed to look pretty much alike.

Marvin took a look around. There were some fifty players spread over three diamonds. He saw two other black players. How was he supposed to make himself look like the rest of the Pomona players?

While the culture of professional baseball was white—the customs and traditions, the ways of speaking and relating—the whole reality of college baseball was white through and through. There wasn't anything subtle about it. The coaches recruited almost entirely from white suburban high schools, where the baseball talent was presumed to be. Black players who were legitimate prospects were expected to go straight to the pros.

The assistant coach told Marvin that there was one other thing that he needed to understand: It didn't matter anymore that he had been a high school star, a junior college star, a draftee of the Oakland A's.

He told him: "Before, you were a big fish in a small pond. Now, you're just a little fish in the ocean."

For the first several weeks of practice, Pomona players were not allowed to take full swings. They had to swing as if playing a leisurely game of pepper. Coaches were trying to cut down on strikeouts, and this was supposed to focus hitters on making contact. In another drill, Pomona players swung wooden bats that had been cut off at the barrel, so they were like mini-bats, then let them go so they sailed toward a mesh soccer net. The idea was to have them fly as evenly as possible in flight, to facilitate a smooth swing.

Marvin had participated in all of Brooks Hurst's drills and understood the point of most of them, even when they made him impatient. But these he didn't get at all. They just seemed weird and pointless. "I was like, 'Let's go hit. Let's play.' I didn't buy in, basically."

The coaches had also, for some reason, decided to try to change big, lumbering Marvin from a first baseman into an outfielder. Under the watchful eyes of the several assistant coaches assigned to tutor the out-fielders, he ran what felt like an endless series of sixty-yard dashes.

"Are you hurt?" they would ask him.

"No," he would say. "This is how I run. I'm just *slow.*"

Marvin was told the team might redshirt him, have him sit out a year. They had a theory of "stacking," lining up talent at every position in excess of what was needed, so some players had to wait their turns.

Marvin responded that redshirting might suit their schedule, but it didn't suit his—he intended to be drafted again, and for that to happen he had to play a season of college baseball rather than pass the year ambling around on the practice field doing silly drills.

Marvin had always been an easy guy to get along with, an ideal teammate, but even that wasn't going well. Pomona was a suburban college full of suburban kids, many of them wealthy. It didn't give athletic scholarships—Marvin had been coaxed out there with the promise of campus work to pay his tuition. While his teammates were lounging about in their frat houses or drinking in local bars, Marvin raked the baseball fields and swept out racquetball courts.

"Some of the guys would say to me, 'Why don't you go out with us and drink beer?' They tried to be nice. But I couldn't do it. I just felt totally out of place."

Marvin hadn't felt racism at Crenshaw or at Los Angeles City College, where the majority of students were black or Hispanic. Pomona, though, was different. He still remembers the jokes a teammate told, the ones that everyone—except him—laughed at.

One of the jokes was: How do you kill a black guy?

Answer: Aim for the radio.

"That was when guys in the inner city were carrying those big radios around," Marvin explains. "Pretty funny, huh?"

There were jokes aimed at other ethnic groups, none of them any funnier. *Why don't Mexicans barbecue? 'Cause the beans slip through the grill.* The last straw was: *How do you stop five black guys from raping a white woman?* Punch line: *Throw them a basketball.*

After Marvin heard that one, he spoke up. " 'You know what, don't tell that joke again or you're gonna have to deal with me,' " he said. " 'In fact, don't tell any more jokes like that.' Everybody just looked at me. I think they were surprised, or scared, or whatever, but I didn't care. I'd had it."

Marvin hung in as long as he could—"I refused to quit"—and lasted through that first season at Pomona. But he didn't go back. He played a season of minor league baseball in Florida, for an independent league team not affiliated with a big-league organization. Then he returned home and enrolled at his third college in four years, Cal State L.A., but he had to work a graveyard shift at a reform school to support himself and pay the tuition. He would drive from work to a campus parking lot, sleep a couple hours in the car, go to class—then come home and study, get a few more hours sleep—and go back to work and do it all again.

He was never drafted again after he declined the offer from the Oakland A's.

He had become, at last, his father's son. A hardworking man. There was no time anymore for baseball.

* * *

The gritty catcher Carl Jones had always been a little unkempt, but mostly just in that country way of his. The wad of chewing tobacco. All that grime that collected on him from hauling Dumpsters and working the little construction jobs with his father. That was just Carl, the blue-collar catcher who was the heart and soul of the Boys of Crenshaw, the team leader who marched out to the mound and demanded of his pitchers: "Punk, throw a fastball."

Now, though, he looked dirty in a different way, like he hadn't been sleeping in a real bed or eating real meals. It was 1988, nearly a decade since high school, and Carl was hanging around the ballfield at Harbor Park—where starting in January each year, the guys who had made it into pro baseball gathered to start working out for the coming season.

They called it the Program. Darryl Strawberry and Chris Brown started it, along with Eric Davis, a close friend of Darryl Strawberry's who had starred at Crenshaw rival Fremont High, then gone on to a career with the Cincinnati Reds. Davis's teammate Barry Larkin sometimes came in from Cincinnati for a week or so to work out, and on any given day a half-dozen or so other major-leaguers were taking swings, fielding grounders, and shagging fly balls at Harbor Park.

A whole mythology had been incorporated into the Program. The big-leaguers told themselves that playing on the crude field deep in L.A.'s inner city took them back to their roots and reminded them of how blessed they were to be making millions for playing a kid's game. It showed them how high they had risen, and how hard they could fall if they did not put in their work.

Darryl, Chris, and Eric Davis were all living in big houses in the far eastern reaches of the San Fernando Valley. Their homes had more bedrooms than they could ever need, big kitchens, two-car garages, and generous yards with sliding boards and swing sets for their kids. When the grounds needed tending, a truck pulled up and a bunch of Mexican American guys jumped out with lawn mowers and pruning tools.

The young big-leaguers hadn't literally moved west, toward Beverly Hills and the beaches, but they had accomplished the equivalent: They were way out of the old neighborhood, in the foothills of the mountains, ensconced in more luxury than they could have imagined.

Coming back into Harbor Park, they believed, was a kind of pilgrimage.

Brooks Hurst had stopped around the Program a couple of times and considered the whole thing mostly nonsense, a bad baseball workout preceded by a parade of luxury automobiles. The players coasted up in their Benzes and BMWs, sound systems booming, made a show of taking off their gold jewelry and putting it in little felt pouches, stretched for a moment, then took big swings at soft batting practice pitching. They signed some autographs, exchanged handshakes and manly hugs, then climbed back in their vehicles.

By tradition, Darryl Strawberry and Chris Brown, along with Eric Davis, hit in the first group. Whichever major-leaguers were around—Barry Larkin, sometimes Royce Clayton, David Justice, Shawon Dunston—hit next. Then the minor-leaguers (usually including Derwin McNealy) and local high school players took their turns.

Carl Jones was part of a third group—former players, young kids, hangers-on—who watched the workouts and chased down balls in the outfield, often without benefit of baseball gloves.

Carl used to keep his baseball mitt as close as possible, stuffed between the waistband of his pants and his lower back. Now, he had no idea where his glove was. He may have sold it.

In his senior season at Crenshaw, Carl hit .355. When the team absolutely needed a hit, he was one of the players who could be counted on to deliver. He handled the pitchers, blocked the balls in the dirt, threw out nearly every would-be base-thief who was foolish enough to test him.

He was shocked when he went undrafted. So were his teammates. Fifty damn rounds and nobody wanted Carl Jones? How the hell could that be? It was a joke. If you wanted to win baseball games, then you wanted Carl Jones on your team. That should have been obvious. Carl wasn't the biggest or fastest guy; he was just a pure ballplayer, a winner.

After the others got into pro ball, they came back and told Carl he was better than the catchers on their teams. And they meant it. But that's how baseball is: subjective. Unlike in basketball, you don't get to go to some Nike-sponsored camp and play head-to-head against some other hotshot and establish who's best. In baseball, someone has to draft you, put you on a roster, give you at-bats and a chance to shine.

Carl didn't get that chance. And he was one of several of the Boys of Crenshaw who seemed constitutionally unable to deal with disappointment. From the moment he went undrafted, Carl began spiraling down.

In contrast to Darryl Strawberry, he did so entirely out of public view and concern. No one but his baseball-loving father, the rest of the Jones family, and a few friends had any investment in Carl Jones.

On this day, after their workout at the Program, the three big-leaguers—Darryl Strawberry, Chris Brown, and Eric Davis—were to stop back at Chris's mother's house to shower and change, then continue on to a Lakers game.

Carl jumped in the car. He was riding again with his buddies. He was happy. He figured he was going to the Lakers game, too.

But Darryl felt Carl was too disheveled to take into the glitzy atmosphere of game night at L.A.'s Fabulous Forum. He could easily have bought him some new clothes; that's what Darryl did for himself plenty of times after working out at the Program—bought new clothes if he didn't have the proper threads for where he was going next. He just stopped somewhere, pulled out a credit card, and emerged with a new outfit.

But Darryl, who was driving, stopped the car at Western and Exposition, near the Forum. He opened his wallet and pulled out a twenty-dollar bill. He reached around to the backseat where Carl was sitting. Handed him the twenty. And told him to get out.

That was not at all like Darryl, whose nature was to be generous and kind. But Darryl's own problems were taking a toll on him. Changing him. He had the money and the presence to not be out in public all unkempt like his friend Carl, but otherwise they had plenty in common at that moment.

That said, this was a particularly ugly example of bigfooting. Chris Brown, always competitive with Darryl, sometimes resentful and often at odds with him, didn't like how he had put Carl out of the car. After they left Carl behind, he confronted Darryl: *What did you do that for?*

*   *   *

The depth of Darryl Strawberry's personal problems first broke into public view on January 26, 1990, when he was arrested in Los Angeles after a horrific domestic scene—he had punched his first wife, Lisa, in the face and menaced her with a .25-caliber semiautomatic pistol. The argument that preceded it, Darryl would later acknowledge, was over his "drinking" and "fornicating." (Blood tests had just established that he was the father of a son born to a St. Louis woman.) Dr. Allan Lans, the Mets team psychologist, flew out to Los Angeles, holed up for a few days in a hotel with Darryl, then flew back east and lodged him at the Smithers Alcoholism and Treatment Center on Manhattan's Upper East Side.

This could have been a turning point for Darryl, but he approached his twenty-eight-day interlude at Smithers more as a scam than an opportunity to get well. He mainly viewed it as a convenient way to dodge prosecution for assaulting his wife, admitting only to a drinking problem. "Going to Smithers was my cover-up," he said. "I never even bothered telling them about the drugs." He also said: "The Mets had a counselor, and he figured if I got away, it would take the pressure off."

That was Darryl. A decade in professional baseball had conditioned him to believe that he could always get over, that no situation was so serious that it could not be finessed. He wasn't all that clever a liar; the people at Smithers almost certainly knew or suspected his drug use. The Mets may have, too. But when Darryl lied, he was almost always lying to people who desperately wanted to believe him, who had some economic incentive to do so.

When he would say to his baseball employers he was fine, no problem, no drugs—praise the Lord for this new sobriety—they were happy to have him back in the lineup, hitting home runs and luring fans through the turnstiles.

He left Smithers in time to play the 1990 season in New York, his last with the Mets before signing as a free agent with the Dodgers. In 1994 he failed to show for an exhibition game, disclosed that he was addicted to cocaine, and spent the next month at the Betty Ford Center in Rancho Mirage, California. After the Dodgers bought out his contract, he spent 1994 with the San Francisco Giants. He then lost that job after testing positive for cocaine in February 1995. He had played all of twenty-nine games for the Giants before being unceremoniously dumped.

That same year, Darryl pled no contest to federal charges of tax evasion for failing to report income from memorabilia and autograph shows—basically scooping up cash without telling the government, the same thing that six years earlier had landed Pete Rose in federal prison.

But Darryl drew a more sympathetic judge than Rose, and instead of the jail time prosecutors expected, he gave Darryl "six months home confinement without electronic monitoring."

Writing in *The New York Times*, columnist Dave Anderson said the judge had given Darryl the equivalent of a soft batting practice pitch. "Darryl Strawberry really got nothing except being confined to his $1.2 million home with a swimming pool among the palm trees of Rancho Mirage," he wrote. "And when his sixty-day suspension ends on

June 23, he will be eligible to join any major league team that wants a troubled, 33-year-old, left-handed swinging felon with 294 homers."

And he did, of course, play again. But Darryl's inventory of troubles over his last decade in professional baseball were staggering: knee and back surgeries; arrests for spousal abuse and for failure to pay child support; the tax conviction; serial episodes of substance abuse. It's hard to say what is the greater marvel: that he laid waste to his career or that he managed to have one at all. Only his prodigious talent kept him in the game.

"I never had a problem hitting," he told me. "I had a problem living."

New York Yankees owner George Steinbrenner first came to his rescue in 1995, after Darryl was no longer young and after he had undermined his body and career in a dozen different ways. With Steinbrenner behind him, Darryl began his Yankee habit of resurfacing at some point in the summer to make memorable late-season contributions. He even began 1996 with the St. Paul Saints of the independent Northern League, a baseball equivalent of dinner theater in Trenton.

In St. Paul, he made $2,000 a month and rode buses to away games in such towns as Duluth, Winnipeg, and Thunder Bay. But there was no reason for Darryl to feel humbled, because he inspired the same kind of awe he always had and received the same star's treatment.

The St. Paul manager, a baseball lifer named Marty Scott, watched him take batting practice his first day in town and marveled at how the ball jumped off his bat. "Amazing," he called it. Then he said it again. "Amazing."

Scott said he had seen some good hitters before, but had never witnessed such a pregame home run display. It was like Darryl was eighteen again, fresh out of Crenshaw, captivating seasoned baseball men and perking up minor league towns.

During a roadtrip to Sioux City, Iowa, a memorabilia dealer set up a stand outside the Lewis and Clark Stadium with nothing but Darryl Strawberry items for sale—Strawberry autographed jerseys, 500 Strawberry baseball cards, and a stack of Crenshaw High yearbooks.

By the end of that 1996 season, Darryl was swatting home runs in the Bronx and leading the Yankees into a World Series. At thirty-four years old, even after his stays in rehab and his brushes with the law, he still had that quality that Frank Cashen put a name to years back: He was majestic—*still* majestic. Maybe even more so than ever, because now he also seemed indestructible.

Who else but Darryl Strawberry, after all that he had done to himself, could dig in at the plate, wave the bat menacingly, and stand in against 95-mile-per-hour heat? Who else but Darryl could turn the pitch around and send it on a magnificent arc over an outfield fence?

"Some guys have a presence at the plate," Yankees right fielder Paul O'Neill said of his new teammate. "Darryl has that sitting in the dugout."

In October of 1996, Darryl Strawberry, once the most famous New York Met of them all, put the Yankees on his back and carried them into the World Series. He hit .417 in the League Championship Series against the Baltimore Orioles, including three home runs in the final two games.

The last home run was epic, pure Darryl, a space shot to right-center field that was launched as if headed for the stratosphere before falling back to Earth and into the visitor's bullpen at Baltimore's Camden Yards. Mark Kriegel, writing in the New York *Daily News* the next day, described the blast as if it were something out of *The Natural*.

"For a moment, a long moment, it seemed as if the ball would just stay up there. The guys in the bullpen started to giggle. Finally, the absurd dimensions of the trajectory became apparent: Darryl's ball was headed straight for them. . . .

"The home run was measured at 448 feet. But that seemed entirely insufficient. The distance should not have been calculated in feet, but in years. Yes, it was as if Darryl Strawberry smacked that sucker through time, a full decade in fact. It was as if Strawberry hit that ball all the way from 1986 into the present, into the bullpen at Camden Yards, where for just a few moments, it delighted grown men as if they were children."

The nation's drug czar, presidential appointee Lee Brown, had chastised Steinbrenner for giving Darryl another chance in 1996, saying it sent a "terrible message." But it seemed like everyone else in America was charmed by his resurrection. The press surrounded him after the game, everyone seeking quotes on how it felt to return to a World Series a full decade after getting there with the Mets.

140

Unlike Chris Brown, Darryl knew how to talk to the press. He could be colorful, contrite, confessional—whatever the moment demanded. What Darryl lacked in actual wisdom he could often cover up with glibness.

"Ten years, I took some rough roads," he told the writers circling his locker. "Just didn't figure any of them led back here."

Darryl was remarried, to Charisse Simon, and they had two children (and later, a third). He made it a point to assure reporters that his postgame celebration would bear no resemblance to the blowouts of the old days.

"I know people don't believe what they hear about me now, that I go back to the hotel after games and don't run around and carouse," he said. "That's okay. I only have to answer to myself, my family, and my God."

Darryl said that he had learned where not to go, what kinds of places might drive him toward his old vices. "I had to learn that I can't go to those slippery places no more. I can't go to the TGI Fridays and sit there and fool myself and sit at the bar. I can't go to Hooters and fool myself that I'm just going there to have a bite to eat, you know, and, you have the little girls running around with the shorts on and the little tight shirts. You know, come on. See, these are things that people in recovery, and especially athletes, have a problem with."

That was the other reason Darryl was so believable: When he pledged to straighten up and do better, he believed it so deeply himself.

*   *   *

The big New York stage and late-season heroics only served to highlight what could have been. Darryl Strawberry was a starter in the All-Star Game in each of his first four full seasons in the Major Leagues. Not one player in the century-long history of baseball had ever accomplished that. In his first six seasons, he hit the same number of home runs (188) as Hall of Fame slugger Reggie Jackson had—and more than Mickey Mantle or Hank Aaron.

But in his eight seasons after turning thirty, Darryl played a substantial portion of only one, when he played 101 games (of a 162-game season) for the 1998 Yankees. In six of those seasons (including two shortened by strikes) he played in fewer than fifty Major League games. After 1992, he hit just fifty-two home runs.

He would finish his career with 335 career home runs, far short of the two players he had been compared to in his youth. Ted Williams hit 521 despite missing nearly three full seasons while serving in two wars. Willie Mays, sidelined for nearly two full seasons during the Korean conflict, hit 660 career homers.

Even the best scouts sometimes get it wrong. They miss on a player; they vastly overestimate his potential. But nobody missed on Darryl Strawberry. Based on pure physical talent, it was not a stretch to believe that he could have had a career like Mays or Williams.

Frank Cashen entered his seventies as Darryl Strawberry played out his twilight. He never once believed that he had been wrong about Darryl. Cashen said he had seen some "hellishly good ballplayers" over the course of fifty years, but Darryl "had more talent than any player I had ever seen."

In what should have been the prime of Darryl's career, the ballparks were getting smaller, the pitchers more hittable, and, by many accounts, the ball livelier. Five hundred home runs punches a ticket to Cooperstown. Six hundred places a player with the greats of the greats, a pantheon reached only by Ruth, Aaron, Mays, and Bonds. How many, in the natural order of things, should Darryl have hit?

"Six hundred," says his old Mets manager, Davey Johnson. "He had the swing, the grace, the power. When he wanted to be, he was as good as it gets. But the thing is, I don't think he was hungry or mean enough to do the six-hundred-home-run deal. Darryl is no dummy. He was comfortable hitting thirty home runs a year and stealing thirty bases. He knew what it would take to do more, and he didn't want to do it. He made a calculation. To be one of the real greats, it has to be your whole world, and Darryl had other worlds going on."

All the Boys of Crenshaw had missed out on certain things in their childhoods. Darryl had seen people around him struggle, but he had never really seen anyone strive. In many cases, there wasn't that much to strive *for*, no apparent payoff at the other end.

That is part of the legacy of his youth that Darryl carried into his baseball career: Given a little success, he got comfortable very quickly.

A real superstar is mean in a particular way. He is Michael Jordan or Cal Ripken, greedy for records and history. Armored and self-contained, his inner core is a hard knot of physical talent and fierce will. Nothing penetrates that core, and anybody or anything that gets too close is out of his life.

Darryl had none of that. Not the inner core or the greed, and especially not the armor. Sometimes he was too nice. Always, he was too sensitive.

Fans, particularly those of opposing teams, sensed this. Big as Darryl was, you could get at him. Bother him. He was vulnerable, even weak. As early as 1984, Chicago Cubs fans were derisively chanting "DAR-ryl, DAR-ryl," a haunting chorus that was picked up by crowds around the league—even in his home park.

Much of what he felt so intensely, and could not repel, were the wants and needs of those around him. He could not distinguish between friends and opportunists. He was no better at protecting himself than he had been at Crenshaw, when the stranger approached him in the sandwich shop and walked out with his home phone number.

His friend Eric Davis used to tell him, "Darryl, forget trying to make everyone else happy. Do what you have to do for yourself." Darryl would agree. He would promise to take Davis's advice, but in the end he could not.

The financial devastation of Darryl's life is nearly as astonishing as the emotional devastation. And they are connected: Whatever belonged to Darryl—his career, his good name, his money—he did not adequately value. Everything that was his, he let others get at.

He made about $30 million in baseball and at the end of his playing career had virtually nothing left. Much of what he made he gave away. To his mother, his father, and four siblings. To his first wife, Lisa, whose clothing business, Strawberry Patch Kids, hemorrhaged money.

He gave to Darryl Strawberry Enterprises, another money pit, which provided salaries for his mother and siblings after Ruby Strawberry convinced him that his fame made it impossible for his brothers and sisters to get jobs.

Richie Bry tried to tell Darryl that this was ridiculous—that usually people want to associate with the kin of well-known people and were more likely to offer them jobs than disqualify them. Darryl nodded, as always. He seemed to agree. But he didn't take the advice.

The Strawberrys had been hardworking people. His mother had a good job at Pacific Bell. The family house near Crenshaw was nothing special, but it was neat and well-kept. But after Darryl hit the big time, his mother quit her job and numerous family members went on his payroll.

"They started a business with Darryl's money," says Bry, "and all it did was suck money from him."

Darryl's brother Michael was an L.A. cop. He quit that job to try to tend to his baseball star brother on the road, to keep him out of trouble. But it didn't work; all it did was put another Strawberry on Darryl's payroll.

Darryl emptied his pockets almost out of habit, like some people stop and hold the door for others to enter first. Half the time, Darryl giving away money wasn't even anything personal. It was more like a common courtesy, extended to people he barely knew.

Eric Goldschmidt, who would become Darryl's second agent, had the same kind of frustrating conversations with him that Richie Bry and Eric Davis did. "What happens with players is they become the sole wage earners of a huge family, and that family expects the player to support them in perpetuity," Goldschmidt explains. "The player has to say: Okay, I'm going to buy you and you and you a house and a car, but that's it—and you have to pay the insurance and the maintenance and the property taxes and the utilities, and don't keep on coming at me for more money. That's a hard thing to say. But if a player can't say it and mean it, it's never ending. And it was never ending for Darryl."

As often as not, Darryl did not have to be asked; he just gave. He gave away a Mercedes, a Jeep, and, after he got tired of living in it, a house. He gave to his inner circle of friends and to his outer circle. (Even Darryl's estrangement from his father did not prevent him from lavishing a car and other goods on him.)

Darryl was hardly the first or last athlete to turn his pockets inside out for those around him. But his giving was extreme. He was a big, generous sap in the Joe Louis mold, helpless against grasping hands.

"I gave from my heart," Darryl tells me. "If people took for the wrong reasons, that's on them."

Court documents show that in one month alone, April 1992, he wrote $22,000 in checks to various relatives. That same month, he paid an American Express bill of $65,616, wrote an $11,650 check to a BMW dealership and a $20,000 check to a jeweler. This was during the peak of his playing and earning power—Darryl in 1992 was in the middle of a five-year, $20 million contract with the Los Angeles Dodgers—but even so, the ballplayer and his first wife "basically blew through every penny they had," says Robert Gaston, who was Lisa Strawberry's divorce lawyer.

"Darryl picked up the tab for everyone," Gaston says. "If he wanted to go to Las Vegas, he would charter a jet and fly a bunch of people with him. He would think nothing of it."

As Darryl began to negotiate a new contract during his last year with the Mets, team executives privately urged him to get a divorce before he signed new deal, regardless of whether he was to re-sign with them. He told them that he and Lisa were working on their marriage, that it could be salvaged. In November 1990, he signed the $20 million contract with the Dodgers, by far the financial highwater mark of his career. Two months later, Darryl and Lisa separated, and in May 1992 she reactivated a dormant divorce petition.

When the divorce became final a year later, they split assets that included three houses and no fewer than eight luxury cars (the court seemed to have a hard time keeping track of them), including a whole category termed "the Jaguars." Lisa says that under terms of the divorce settlement, she received slightly more than half the value of his $20 million deal.

To back up her petition for $50,000 per month in spousal support, which was granted, Lisa filed papers with the Superior Court of California saying that she had been spending $20,000 a month for clothes; other monthly expenses included $5,000 for shoes, $1,600 for a gym membership and personal trainer, $1,500 for a maid, $400 for dry cleaning, $200 to cover care and grooming of her dog, Slice—as well as an additional $7,000 for periodic purchases of jewelry, "which I have been free to indulge myself in as desired."

Lisa Strawberry knew that many in baseball considered her a contributor to her husband's demise, if not the outright cause. "How am I the culprit?" she asks me. The court had wanted to know her standard of living. That was part of the California divorce code—that she and the couple's three children be able to maintain the standard of living to which they were accustomed. And that had been their standard of living.

Darryl, she says, insisted that she wear a new outfit to each game, with new shoes to match. "He wanted to have an arm piece. And I was that arm piece. People would say: 'Look at the way Lisa spends. She shops, she shops, she shops.' But why am I shopping? Because every game I had to have a different outfit. And I had a budget that reflected that."

Darryl's squandering of talent, career, and money were all of a piece. "It drained him financially, and it drained him emotionally," says Eric Grossman, who became Darryl's third and last agent. "There was always this pull on him to be a gravy train even when his own life was in chaos." By the time he came back to New York in 1995, "He was paying debt after debt after debt. They lived paycheck to paycheck."

In the late nineties, Darryl, his second wife, Charisse, and their three children lived in a rental house in Fort Lee, New Jersey, while he played for the Yankees. It was a modest place that shared a driveway with a next-door neighbor—hardly a deprivation, but a comedown for a lavishly paid superstar.

Two decades into one of the most celebrated baseball careers in modern times, Darryl was just trying to stay ahead of the bills. He was a working man, maybe not quite like his postal worker father or some character out of Walter Mosley, but the idea was the same. He had made millions, and those millions were gone. Entirely.

Without baseball, he couldn't pay the electric bill.

"He got hurt by family, friends, everyone," Jay Horwitz, the Mets PR man, says. "It's a shame what happened. So many people fed off Darryl. Even his mother, may she rest in peace."

So eager to please with easy money and companionship, Darryl had one area of stinginess: baseball. He was miserly about parceling out his talent. It flowed irregularly, and never in the heaping quantities it could have.

"He had thirty-nine home runs in 1986 and had no interest in hitting forty," Johnson says, speaking of the final weeks of the season, after the team had clinched a playoff spot. "He had some nagging injuries. But he could have played. It was hard for me to understand."

Darryl never hit as many as forty home runs in a season and drove in one hundred or more runs only three times. He never won a Most Valuable Player award, the game's most coveted honor; stunningly, in only two seasons did he even receive any votes for the award. Elite athletes are never satisfied; he was easily satisfied.

Some attributed this to a lack of character, but there was something more specific he lacked—courage. The courage to put himself on the line and find out if he was really as good as people believed. Or maybe that he wasn't.

Over time, Darryl's off-field behavior put all the questions and expectations to rest. Games and weeks and then whole seasons vanished. He was not going to be Ted Williams or Willie Mays. He was not going to hit five hundred career home runs or go to the Hall of Fame.

He was a soaring talent, one of the greatest physical packages ever, but he would not be a once-in-a-lifetime ballplayer. No one had to ask him for that anymore.

His old high school teammates could read right through the quotes that he fed the sportswriters, all the promises that followed each lapse about having finally found God, sobriety, and good sense.

They knew Darryl. They knew he was hanging by the thinnest of threads.

CHAPTER SIX

Leaving L.A.

Perhaps I was overly receptive to sports-as-life messages, but I never doubted my coaches when they said we were engaged in something beyond just playing ball. Hitting the cutoff man on a throw from the out-field wasn't only about preventing a runner from taking an extra base—it was a *detail*, and paying attention to detail was one of those important things in life. Running out a ground ball, even when it was clear you were going to be out, was another test of character. You owed it to yourself, owed it to your teammates, probably owed it to the Lord himself, al-though our coaches couldn't say that in public school.

Everything we were asked to do—hustle at all times; practice our foul shots; knock the hell out of anything that moved on the football field—earned us currency to spend later in life. We were learning self-discipline and self-respect. Learning to work. And putting it all in the bank as a de-posit on becoming future leaders and winners.

Only later did I come across some strong dissenting voices to all of this—suggestions in literature and popular culture that the more a young man bathes himself in sports, and particularly the more success and acclaim he achieves, the more handicapped he may become.

John Updike's Rabbit Angstrom cannot parley his small-town basketball fame into an existence that feels anything but empty. The former college track star in John Cheever's "O Youth and Beauty" makes a habit of getting drunk at parties and hurdling the furniture in suburban living rooms. The actor Dennis Quaid, playing a former football star in *Everybody's All-American* (based on a novel by Frank Deford), ends up back home with a failed sports bar, a failing marriage, and nothing to offer but old stories. "I've told those stories so many times," he says to his wife, "that I've almost forgot it was me who had those things happen to him. It seems like somebody else." Bruce Springsteen sings of a baseball pitcher who could "throw that speedball by you" but passes his time in a roadside bar, recounting his "glory days."

This is the athlete not as a winner in life, but as something different, an opposing archetype: the washed-out sports hero, boozed up and adrift, stuck with the sad realization that he reached his apex at about the age of eighteen. (Rabbit's wife would conclude that even before their marriage, which took place just after high school, he was "already drifting downhill.")

In literature and film, these characters are without exception white men. Yet the pull of sports, the all-encompassing urgency of it, is strongest in the black community. There, sports exists more in the present.

The myth is that sports somehow fills in the empty spaces. If a boy is missing a father, he finds a surrogate one in sports. If he lacks direction, discipline, or a reason to show up at school, sports gives him all that.

In the black community, sports is less about character building for the distant future and more about a path to direct, tangible reward.

The Boys of Crenshaw knew to run hard to first base because somebody might be watching who could offer a pro contract or a college scholarship. Fail to hustle, and you might never get out of South Central.

Teachers cut them breaks because everyone was so easily convinced that it was sports or the streets. As Cordie Dillard told me, the thinking was: "If you give him an F, and he can't play ball, what do you think he's going to do?"

But that left open the question: What was anyone going to do when there were no more games, at whatever moment that came to pass? If playing sports is a means, what happens when it ends?

*   *   *

When I began researching this book, all the Boys of Crenshaw had either recently turned forty or soon would. Except in the case of Darryl Strawberry, I had no idea what I would find. I knew of Chris Brown's abbreviated career and his poor reputation, but nothing of his life after baseball. As for the others, I knew which ones were drafted into pro ball and how long they played, but beyond that, little else.

I wasn't even sure if all of them were still alive, and considered it a distinct possibility some might not be. Life expectancy for black men, nationwide, is about six years shorter than for white men, and an alarming number die young. For any of those who stayed in inner-city L.A. or returned there, the chances of succumbing to either disease or violence would have been greatly increased.

At a demonstration in the spring of 2003 to protest a string of gun deaths in South Central, one person held a hand-lettered sign that said, simply, "Live a Long Time." That was a sadly meager plea, but perfectly understandable within the context of all that can befall a man on the streets of L.A.

But all the members of the 1979 Crenshaw High Cougars reached the age of forty. That alone, I suppose, could be construed as a minor victory, some small measure of success. They had stayed clear of the crossfire of the Crips and Bloods. They had not stepped into a convenience store at just the wrong time. Not put any fatally dirty needles in their arms. Kept themselves out of the kind of trouble that can get a person shot.

Several of them, though, were not easy to find. Brooks Hurst had kept in touch with some of his former players, and was able to provide phone numbers and introductions. But a few of the others seemed to have just melted away after high school. They were not hiding; they were invisible.

As a point of reference, only three of the players from that 1979 Crenshaw High team showed up on Google, the huge Internet search engine that has become a symbol of some status, or at least belonging, in American society. If you are famous, your name is all over Google. If you have been listed as a survivor in an obituary, or if someone in your family has posted on one of the many websites dedicated to genealogy, that might produce a hit. If you teach school, sell model trains, get engaged, serve on the board of your church, make the honor roll, belong to an alumni association, you're probably on Google. If you are a stay-at-home mom who likes to run, your name comes up after you cross the finish line in your local 10K. A Google hit is a digital footprint, a sign that you have been present.

A search for Darryl Strawberry or Chris Brown, not surprisingly, produces hundreds of Google hits—their baseball statistics, stories from their playing days, Darryl Strawberry memorabilia being hawked at dozens of sites. But when I ran the names of the others, only one of them showed up, and it was more of a trace than a hit: Reggie Dymally appears on a long list of new employees at the California Institute of Technology. He had been hired as a chef, a job he no longer holds.

When I managed to track Reggie down, he directed me to another website, which provided one of the more startling moments of my research. The website is for a company called Kosher Expeditions, which operates expensive tours for Orthodox Jews who want to travel to far-flung locations while still adhering to their dietary laws.

The site touts nature trips to Costa Rica and Alaska, scuba diving in the Caribbean, safaris in Zimbabwe and Botswana. A picture of Orthodox Jewish boys in black cowboy hats leads into a description of a "Ten Day Passover Dude Ranch Adventure" in Wyoming, with a seder led by an on-site rabbi. As on all the company's tours, the food at the Passover Dude Ranch is to be glatt kosher, strictest kosher, served family style in the ranch dining room.

And this was Reggie's niche: cooking for these Kosher tours.

The quiet, focused strongman of the Crenshaw outfield, the boy who sharpened his eye by hitting bottle caps with a broomstick—who watched Julia Child while the others tuned in to *This Week in Baseball*—has taken one of the more elaborate journeys of any of the Boys of Crenshaw. Ballplayer to epicure. From the fields of Crenshaw to a movable kosher feast.

* * *

There is no reason I should have been expecting Reggie to look like some kind of he-man. It's been a long time since high school. Maybe I was hoping he would, because I had heard so many stories and wanted to see this phenomenon for myself.

Reggie had been the team's workout fanatic, the young man who built himself up with morning-and-night regimens of sit-ups and push-ups. His teammates were impressed by his muscle, but even more so that he had manufactured it himself—they had never known anyone who worked so hard to attain something.

His strength was the stuff of legend. I was told in some detail about the long bus rides Reggie took to the suburban gym where he lifted weights, and how he borrowed the Nautilus membership of Darryl Strawberry's older brother, Michael, to gain entrance. Two hours one way, pump a lot of iron, then two hours back. That's how dedicated Reggie was.

Except that it didn't work that way, according to Reggie. He had some old weights around his house. He did a lot of push-ups. He got real strong. Maybe he went to that gym once; he doesn't quite remember. But the whole process was nothing as heroic or exotic as his teammates want to remember it.

The day we have agreed to get together turns out to be a glorious Southern California afternoon. Mid-seventies, light breeze, no smog. I meet Reggie at his twin sister's house, where he stays when he's not traveling. He suggests we find somewhere outside to talk, and we end up around the corner, sitting side-by-side on a set of bleachers near the Crenshaw High baseball field.

Reggie, at forty, is in fact a little soft-looking. Doughy and rounded. His eyeglasses and soft-spoken manner lend him a kind of bookish air. You can still see the strength underneath, but of all the former Crenshaw players, he is about the last one you would imagine was an elite athlete. It could be that because he was so self-made, it all fell away quickly when he turned his energies in another direction.

Reggie tells me that he still works out some, but his line of work presents particular challenges, and not just from sampling what he cooks. Being a chef tends to rearrange a person's posture. "You stand up all day long, and you always have your neck bent down and your shoulders hunched," he explains. "You're looking at a saucepan, or you have a cutting board below you, or you're putting things in or taking them out of an oven. You could be in that position for twelve hours sometimes. Everything you do, you're bending over or looking down. You can get real messed up. I've been to chiropractors, I've had acupressure."

About one hundred yards away, a game is in progress on the Crenshaw field, a couple of teams from a local summer league. We glance at it during pauses in our conversation; we hear the *clink* of aluminum bats making contact with baseballs. The Boys of Crenshaw played in the aluminum bat era, too, but these are particularly tinny clinks. Not solid contact.

The players look to be about fifteen years old. Even from a distance, you can tell they are still trying to get the hang of baseball. They move around the field mechanically, without the ease and ingrained instincts of boys who started playing around the time they entered first grade. You can almost see them trying to remember their steps. At bat, they lunge and chop at the ball.

The neighborhood beyond the outfield fences—black, inner-city L.A.—had baseball in its blood when the Boys of Crenshaw were coming up, but no more. So many of the men who brought the game up from the South are gone. Their sons, even the ones who did play baseball, have their television sets tuned now to basketball and football.

I tell Reggie that I had been at Crenshaw a few days earlier and happened upon a gym class playing softball. Some of the boys were huge—six-footers, two hundred pounds and up. And they swung so inexpertly that they couldn't hit the ball out of the infield. I wondered if a couple of them might be swinging a bat for the very first time—fifteen, sixteen years old and never played an inning of baseball.

"They don't play that much baseball around here anymore," Reggie says. He looks over toward the Crenshaw field. "Those kids playing right now, I doubt that any of them know about the team we had. They have no idea what kind of baseball was once played out there. I'm sure most of them have heard the name Darryl Strawberry—but that's more a celebrity thing than a baseball thing. They might have seen something about him on the news."

Reggie was in the graduating class of 1980, so he remained at Crenshaw after Chris Brown, Cordie Dillard, Carl Jones, and the McNealy twins departed. The baseball team in his senior year was not quite as richly talented as the historic 1979 group, but it was pretty darn good.

Reggie was named most valuable player of the Los Angeles city schools' Western League in 1980, besting, among others, Darryl Strawberry—in the same year that the Mets would make Darryl the nation's top draft choice. Darryl Strawberry might have been the mother lode of baseball potential, but at that moment, he was not a markedly better ballplayer than the future kosher chef Reggie Dymally.

Reggie had every baseball skill but one. "He didn't throw well. He had a below average arm," says Artie Harris, an L.A.-area coach and now an employee of the Dodgers. "But boy, could he hit. I saw him in a game at Ventura College, which had fences longer than any big-league park. He hit three home runs in one game. One to left field, one to center, one to right. It was an unbelievable performance. Reggie should have been a big-time major-leaguer, but scouts couldn't see beyond the arm."

Reggie's uncle, the politician, was an educated man, as was most everyone on his father's side of the family. Reggie had always known he would go to college, and by the end of eleventh grade had completed his prerequisites.

"I had to get out. Out of the so-called inner city," he says. "Baseball was the stepping-stone for me to get out."

He went from Crenshaw to the University of Hawaii, the only one among the Boys of Crenshaw to go directly to a four-year college. He got a full ride, a baseball scholarship that paid tuition, room, and board, and travel to and from the island. That felt like a fair deal. He'd play ball, give the university his skill and sweat, and in return would receive a free education.

Except that the university athletic establishment didn't see it the same way. Reggie was coming in from South Central; what the hell did he need an education for?

Of all the Crenshaw players, Reggie had always been the most politically aware, the one who took note of the cleaner baseballs in play in the Valley and the tattered textbooks at Crenshaw that seemed to be hand-me-downs from the richer schools to the west.

When he arrived at school for freshman year, he signed up for an English course, a couple of business courses, and a computer course. The last choice was a particularly bold one: In 1980, an interest in computers was still sort of unusual. When he got his printed schedule, it was all different from what he'd filled out.

"They had changed all my classes," he says. "I had a class on how to coach football. I had a class on how to coach soccer. I had a swimming class and a military science class. That was the most asinine thing of all. They taught us how to shoot a rifle. I didn't leave L.A. to learn how to shoot guns."

The Hawaii team had five black players on a roster of twenty-five. Reggie recalls the white players taking the courses they wanted. They had majors in liberal arts, business, marine science. Reggie figured he was being pointed toward phys ed—or maybe the Army, what with the rifle training.

"It was a terrible insult," he says. "I was like, no, you want me to play baseball for you, you give me something that's not baseball. People don't see that. They wonder why black athletes don't have an education, but it's not always because they don't want one. Coaches direct you into easy classes so they're sure you'll stay eligible to play—which is different from them being interested in you learning something so you can succeed in life."

He played one season at Hawaii and then transferred to Los Angeles City College, a two-year school. He played one season at L.A. City, then transferred to the University of Nebraska. Like so many of the others, he was still chasing baseball, dogging it until it slapped him in the face and rejected him.

"I had these other interests, cooking primarily," he says. "But of course I wanted to play in the big leagues. That's what we all wanted, wasn't it? You weren't going to do anything else seriously until you played that out."

At Nebraska, he made all-conference in what was then the Big Eight. The Milwaukee Brewers selected Reggie in the eighth round of the 1984 winter draft, sent him to Arizona for minor league spring training, then released him after less than a month.

He had hit well. But he had not received even a dollar of bonus money—all he got was an invitation to show up—so the organization had no real investment in him. Reggie, never one to draw much attention to himself, didn't feel that he had made much of an impression before pro baseball issued its snap judgment.

"I wasn't loud, I wasn't boisterous," he says. "Sometimes I had that look that seemed unapproachable, so coaches could easily overlook me or pass me by. Especially if people don't feel like they know you, they can give up on you quick."

Ken Medlock, a former minor leaguer and Brooks Hurst's best friend, used to pitch batting practice to the Crenshaw team. He thought Reggie was the best player Brooks had. "A manchild," he called him.

"The thing about Reggie," says Medlock, "is that he was a powerful young man physically and emotionally. He had the composure that most of the others lacked."

Not long after Reggie was cut by the Brewers, he went to a game with Medlock at Dodger Stadium. The Mets were in town; Darryl Strawberry was playing right field and batting cleanup. Reggie was well raised, well mannered. He thanked Medlock for taking him to the game. But for the next three hours, he said almost nothing. He just stared and stared. Stared the whole time toward right field.

"He had his eyes glued on Darryl," Medlock says. "I don't think he looked in any other direction. And I knew what he was thinking: *That could be me out there*. And I agreed with him. It could have been him, should have been him. But it's such a fine line. Fortunately for Reggie, he had a game plan. He had his eye on something else."

*   *   *

Reggie Dymally once cooked a private dinner hosted by Condoleezza Rice, President Bush's national security advisor, when she was the provost at Stanford University. He does not know who the guests were. When you cook for a living, you learn which clients like you to circulate, talking about the recipes, suggesting wines—and which want you to stay in the kitchen. The Condoleezza Rice dinner was one of those of the stay-in-the-kitchen jobs.

He has been in charge of preparing a Passover seder for 280 people. He has catered dozens of events, where he has been able to put his gift for observation to effective use.

"When you're cooking," he says, "it's always about more than one thing. There's a lot to keep track of, and I like that. Say I'm doing a wedding, and there's a cocktail hour with hors d'oeuvres. It has to go in a certain way. Some crowds, fine, you send out the trays and don't worry about it. But you have to go out and look at the room first. Sometimes, you identify ten people, and they're going to eat enough shrimp for fifty people.

"You get an instinct for that. You send a few shrimp trays out, wait twenty minutes, then send more out. You let those ten people fill up with some other things."

Reggie sold real estate for about eight months after the Brewers cut him loose. He tried some other things. He went to acting school. Worked in a supermarket. Did some modeling until the agency that represented him went bankrupt.

In 1987, he moved to San Francisco and enrolled in a sixteen-month program at the California Culinary Institute. After he paid the tuition, he had $200 to his name. He had been a self-schooled chef; at culinary school he learned food chemistry, the business of food, health codes, nutrition. He learned to cook dishes from Brazil, Indonesia, Thailand.

After earning his certificate, he got jobs in a couple of restaurants, a hotel kitchen, a catering firm. He liked the strategy involved in the food business, the multitasking. "If you're feeding a lot of people, you have to figure out: How much labor will it take? What are the costs? What are the best ingredients out there? How do I set up the tables? What's the traffic flow?"

Working as a professional chef even suggested to him that when he played baseball, he was in the wrong position: He should have been an infielder rather than an outfielder.

Cooking is like playing second base. There's always something to do—hold a runner on base, back up a bag, exchange a sign with the shortstop to establish who will take the throw on an attempted steal. It's like having several dishes cooking on different burners.

The outfield, Reggie now thinks, didn't hold his interest because it didn't challenge his mind. There wasn't enough going on, not enough to look at or do. He was a fierce hitter but no better than an average outfielder, and maybe that was why. "I never told anyone I was bored in the outfield," he says, "but to tell you the truth, I was."

When he got the job at the California Institute of Technology, Reggie befriended a chef in an adjacent kitchen who prepared food for students and faculty who kept kosher. The kosher kitchen was sort of closed off, but Reggie edged his way in. He asked questions, tasted the food, and after a while made some suggestions.

"Why don't you try adding this spice?" he'd say.

His friend would give it a try, and some dish that had been coming out the same for a couple of centuries would get spruced up.

Reggie left Caltech to do private catering; so did his friend. They both ended up working for Kosher Expeditions. He has been back to Hawaii. To Alaska. All over the Pacific Northwest. He has experimented with mixing the Southern soul food recipes he ate growing up with traditional kosher food—making barbecue out of kosher brisket, for example, rather than pork. Kosher soul food.

The money is good, and Reggie, personally conservative by nature, is not a spender. If he works a ten-day trip, he can earn enough to keep himself going for a month or two. He does some private catering jobs on his own. He cooks for free at a local church in return for use of their catering-quality kitchen.

He has not been tempted to convert to Judaism and, in fact, has suffered what he considers some unkind remarks. "Most of the people I cook for are very nice," he says. "But there are some who are prejudiced. It's not a big deal. You hear these smart remarks, like why is this black guy cooking the food? It's the exception.

"If I don't like what I'm hearing, this is what I do: Just keep my head down, keep quiet, and cook."

Reggie has not played baseball since the Brewers sent him home from Arizona. He has not even played softball, nor has he been tempted to coach any Little League teams. He thinks he's played catch twice. Once the hardest working and most dedicated of all the Boys of Crenshaw, he has separated more completely from his athletic career than any of his old teammates. He just let baseball go, and moved on.

If he gave any thought to how it ended for him, he says, it would make him bitter. So he doesn't. "The only thing I'll say is that I was better than a lot of guys who made it all the way up and made a lot of money," he says. "I'm sure about that."

Baseball, he says, "wasn't the only thing I did. I was relieved in a way when I stopped playing. I feel more comfortable cooking than I ever did playing ball. It's something where I can control my own destiny. I can be my own critic. I can praise myself, make my own mistakes—and correct them."

He adds, "Food has no color. It's not black or white. It's not prejudiced. It's the greatest form of communication ever. Food and music. Those are the two greatest forces in the world for bringing people together."

Like most chefs, Reggie watches the cleared plates that come back to his kitchen to see what was eaten and what was left. It is an instant and honest critique. He even sometimes looks out into a dining room and watches people as they eat. He laughs. "I know it sounds really gross. But if you watch someone chew food, you can tell if they like it or not."

On the day we sat in the bleachers and talked, Reggie was a couple months away from his wedding, which he planned to cater himself. He had not been married before, and has no kids. (Something else that sets him apart from all of his former teammates.) Being raised without a father made him determined not to have children until he was part of a marriage, and at home to raise them.

His fiancée worked at UCLA in the finance department, and also volunteered teaching computers in inner-city L.A. as part of a program called Project Hope.

Reggie had left Nebraska for pro baseball short of his degree, and is back in school, too. In addition, he is putting together a cookbook specifically for inner-city residents. He has hundreds of recipes, hundreds of ideas. What he has, most of all, is a passion beneath his quiet exterior.

"You can make soul food that doesn't have to be dripping with fat—you can get all the flavor you want through herbs," he tells me. "There's cookbooks that tell you how to do that, but the problem is, they have ingredients in them that you can't always find in minority communities. Chives. Fresh marjoram. Where the hell are you gonna find those? You can grow them, but most people won't. My book will tell people how to adapt with ingredients they can get in their own supermarkets.

"You can educate people, but it has to be in very small steps. But it's worth doing. We've got all these people on these streets getting fat, getting diabetes, dying really young. It doesn't have to be that way."

As Reggie talks, it is clear to me why he was so admired at Crenshaw. He is the same quietly determined person who made himself into a late-blooming ballplayer. And he achieves without self-promotion or posturing.

Like all the Crenshaw players I talked to, Reggie wanted news from me. Most of them are not in close touch. They hear things, bits of information from someone's cousin or sister-in-law or from a friend of a friend.

Inner-city L.A. is still that way, tightly woven on one level, a word-of-mouth village even as it is pulled apart by drugs, gangs, and violence. You see someone you know, you never just hurry off. You stop and talk and share information.

If something big happens to any of the Boys of Crenshaw—marriages, breakups, fatherhood, trouble with the law—word gets around. But that's about it. Life is busy, sometimes crushing. Even some of the guys who were real tight have fallen into very occasional contact. They may, as Nelson Whiting said, love each other like brothers, but even brothers sometimes lose touch.

They all wanted to know: Who had I talked to? How were they doing? This book helped reconnect them—or at the very least, served to catch them up.

Reggie Dymally had been as out of touch as any of them. No one had known where he was, and he had very little information about the others. Reggie wanted to know: Had I found Nelson Whiting? I told him that I had. How about Fernando? Yes. Chris is down in Houston, right? He was.

"What about the twins? How are they doing?" he asks, but the tone of his voice tells me that he already, on some level, knows.

*   *   *

A few years ago, the *New Yorker* writer Malcolm Gladwell wrote a story about people who are natural "connectors." Even without serving in any official capacity, they seem to know everyone, to talk to everyone, to be the repositories of all kinds of useful community intelligence. If they can't help you directly, they know someone who can. If they don't know where a certain person is, they probably know where he was last. They are conduits, clearinghouses, switching stations.

To find the McNealy twins, or to at least gain a clue and start down a trail, I began with what seemed like an obvious source, someone who bears a resemblance to the connectors whom Gladwell wrote about.

Tahitha Jones Moore, the sister of the catcher Carl, is a big-boned, round-faced, garrulous, beaming woman. She goes by several different nicknames, one of them being "Big Trunk," which many women would surely object to, but she embraces. When you ring her at home, she picks up the phone and says, "Big Trunk in the house."

Growing up as the only girl in a house full of boys, and as the daughter of the baseball-obsessed Thedo, she doted on the Boys of Crenshaw. They were her extended family, every one of them an honorary big brother. She went to every game, every team cookout in her parents' backyard. When her brothers' teammates were around, she invited her friends over and all the girls flitted about and put together heaping trays of food and tried to get the older boys to take notice of them.

After that heartbreaking loss at Dodger Stadium, Tahitha took it just as hard as any of the players. She cried in the car ride home. Cried that night right up until she drifted off to sleep.

Tahitha has her own children now. Her two boys are baseball players and all-around athletes at Crenshaw High. She goes to school with them nearly every day, then plants herself in a corridor to help keep watch over student life at Crenshaw.

"You keepin' up with your schoolwork, honey?" she asks a passing student.

"How is that prom dress comin'?" she asks another. "Is your mama helping you sew it or are you doin' it all yourself?"

To one of her sons' baseball teammates: "Hey, baby, you gonna hit me a home run this afternoon? I just know you are. You're due, baby, you been in a little slump lately."

The students call her by a different nickname. In football, her older boy came to be known as "Black"—so she is called Mama Black.

It is not all good tidings and quips with Mama Black. Crenshaw High was never any paradise, but in certain ways it has become more grim. It's not just kids being raised by single moms anymore. Now, as many as half the students do not live with a mother *or* a father—they are in the care of aunts, grandmothers, older siblings, or the foster care system. Some are just on their own. It is a place of lost children.

The old ideal of Crenshaw High becoming a model school, integrated by race and class, is something out of the distant past. No one even talks any more about how the kids from Baldwin Hills and View Park don't come down the hill to go to Crenshaw.

You get a certain feeling when you walk into a school. If there is litter on the floors, students living in the corridors, and clocks that don't tell the right time, you know immediately that you've stepped into a defeated, hopeless place. Crenshaw felt just the opposite on the days I visited, despite all the challenges faced by its students. It was clean, orderly, and surprisingly cheerful.

But it takes many people willing to step into surrogate parent roles—teachers and administrators, as well as volunteers like Tahitha—to keep present-day Crenshaw High from going over into despair and chaos. "They know that I'm their friend when they need a friend," Tahitha tells me. "And they know I am their worst enemy if I see something goin' on that should not be goin' on. When they see me, they know they better get in class. If they are doin' something they should not be, they know they better stop. Believe me, they do not want to tangle with me."

Tahitha is a social being, the type to be out in front of her house a lot, mixing with neighbors. One day when I stopped around to visit with her, she was still steaming over a recent incident. A man she knew casually had coasted up in his car in front of her house on Ninety-third Street, gotten out, and struck up a conversation.

"You still married to Ernest?" he wanted to know.

Ernest is her high school sweetheart, the father of her four children.

"Yeah, we sure are," she answered. "Ernest ain't goin' anywhere, and neither am I."

"But Ernest wouldn't mind if you took a ride with me, right?"

Tahitha told him that was not the question—the question was, did *she* want to take a ride, and she most definitely did not. The man had a handful of rock in his hand, crack cocaine. She smacked his hand from underneath, sending the rocks flying onto the sidewalk.

"I was insulted. I was insulted by the whole thing," she recounts. "He was so mad at me, he looked like he wanted to hit me. But there would be some trouble then, and I'm sure he knew it. I'm not a small or a weak woman, and there's always baseball bats nearby. Had he hit me, I would have gotten my hands on one and used it on him."

As she is telling me this, a little boy is bounding around her living room. He bumps up against my knee. It is her godson, Marvin. Little Marvin, she calls him. "His mom is out there on crack, so I keep him with me most of the time," Tahitha says. "I love him like he's my own. He's three, so we're just starting him on baseball right now."

The Joneses are their own little social service agency. Faith-based. When they see someone in need, they try to give them baseball.

*   *   *

As I figured she would, Tahitha does have some information on the Mc-Nealy boys, a sighting from about a year back. She tells me that the last place anyone had seen them in L.A. was just a couple of doors down, at the house on Ninety-third Street that her bighearted parents, Thedo and Werllean, had turned into a refuge for whoever needed shelter and a clean bed.

Tahitha takes me outside and points to what had been the twins' room. "You see that window right up there? They were staying right in there."

Along with her family, Tahitha had been helping to look after the McNealy twins. But one morning, the Joneses found a ladder up against that window and discovered that the twins had fled—just ran off somewhere.

Some people were up and about pretty late that previous night. And others were up early in the morning. They put their heads together and came up with an estimate: It was decided that the twins must have come down that ladder somewhere between three and four A.M.

The twins owed money around town, including several hundred dollars to Tahitha's mother, and apparently had grown concerned that someone, although certainly not Werllean Jones, was coming to collect a debt.

I had already heard some stories about the McNealys. After baseball ended for them, they were just sort of around, usually without jobs or a permanent place to live.

"I don't know where they are," Cordie Dillard tells me. "But I guarantee you, wherever you find one, you'll find the other."

Nelson Whiting says that for years the twins worked only when Thedo Jones put them in some kind of construction jobs. They were all close, the McNealys and Joneses—Darryl and Derwin were almost like two more sons in the Jones household. But Nelson remembers telling the twins they had to do something for themselves, that Mr. Jones's sons were his sons, and that when there was only a little work to be had, he was going to make sure his boys got it first.

"When they didn't have any more baseball to play," Nelson says, "it's like they got stuck. They didn't have the first idea of what to do with themselves."

Thedo Jones says, "The twins, they had a little problem, and they just started fadin' away with it. They had been over near Inglewood, but I brought them over here so they could be a little closer to me. I had one of my softball teams at the time. They got those teams now where they have two girls on it, and they don't pitch it as hard. So I got them involved on that just so they could get out of the house and do something."

I asked him if he had thought playing softball could help turn them around. "I would try anything," Mr. Jones said, his voice cracking a bit as he answered. "I had been trying to help them for a long time."

As we stand out on the sidewalk, looking up at the twins' last-known address, Tahitha throws one of her big arms around me and sort of chuckles. "You gonna go lookin' for them twins?" she says. "I'll tell you what, brother, you bring them back here to me and I will give you half the money they owe us. Um-huh, we'll split it right down the middle."

She laughs again, then turns serious. "No, really, if you do find them, you tell them twins to come on home. We are forgiving people, and they should already know that. We're always gonna be here for them. You make sure to tell them that, okay?"

Cordie Dillard has something more direct that he wants me to pass on. He knows of someone named Charlie, a creditor of the twins. He says the twins owed Charlie $500.

"But Charlie got shot and he's dead," Cordie says. "So tell the twins that wherever the hell they are, they can come on back."

The ladder stayed up against the window for a couple of weeks. It became a conversation piece. Someone would look up and say: That's where those twins came down.

And the other person, invariably, would say something like: Where do you think those twins ran off to?

* * *

I found a Derwin McNealy on Google, but I was pretty sure it was not the one I was looking for. The name was on a student web page, which seemed to have been assigned as a project in a computer science class at an institution I had never heard of—LeMoyne-Owen College in Memphis.

The online picture of this Derwin McNealy showed him wearing a baseball cap and what appeared to be a baseball jersey. The brief text included an entry titled "Three Things That I Want in Life," and then the answer, "Family, money, and a nice car!"

I knew that my Derwin McNealy, who had bought that black-and-gold Trans Am with his baseball signing bonus, liked nice cars. But nothing else I knew about him led me to believe he would be enrolled in college. (Although if he wanted to stay out of sight after climbing down that ladder, LeMoyne-Owen certainly seemed like it could be a good place to hide.)

I looked again at the picture—the man had a lean, angular look, just like the pictures I had seen of the fleet, line-drive-hitting center fielder of the Boys of Crenshaw. When I was able to reach the Derwin McNealy at LeMoyne-Owen, I got confirmation of what I was hoping.

"The person you're looking for is my father," he tells me over the phone.

He says his father and mother had been married back when Derwin was playing in the minors, but had split up several years ago. Derwin Jr. was raised in Atlanta. He is a college baseball player, a pretty good one, with hopes of playing pro ball.

Several months earlier, he had visited with his father. They worked out together, played catch—then Derwin threw him some batting practice and passed along hitting advice. Told him to keep his hands back, and his front shoulder in.

Derwin Jr. is a fast runner like his father, and no home run hitter. Just make contact, his father advised him. Sting those line drives and put your speed to use.

"He got real close to making it all the way up," Derwin Jr. tells me. "He played a long time in the minors, so he has that knowledge."

His father has moved around some, so Derwin Jr. holds on to his baseball keepsakes. "I have all his stuff in a shoe box—pictures and old programs and stuff," he says. "I have his whole baseball life story in there. He lets me keep it."

Derwin Jr. tells me that his father is living in Las Vegas with his twin brother Darryl. It is just as Cordie Dillard promised: Where I found one, I would find the other.

I can't call them because they do not have a telephone. But Derwin Jr. puts me in touch with an aunt in Las Vegas. She goes to see the twins on my behalf, tells them what I am up to, and passes word back that they would be happy for me to pay a visit.

*   *   *

Darryl and Derwin McNealy live in the interior of a sprawling garden apartment complex on the outskirts of Las Vegas, about two miles from the Strip. The two-story buildings are connected by a maze of sidewalks. Between the walkways, stubborn patches of grass struggle to survive in the desert heat.

The whole place seems to circle on itself. I walk from building to building, past people drinking beer out of cans—past children zigzagging on bicycles, and others splashing in plastic wading pools—trying to find my way, and trying to understand why Building L seems to be nowhere near Building M. No one can offer directions; people seem to know only how to get between their own front door and where they park their cars.

When I finally get to the twins' ground-floor unit, a little later than I had promised, they both are at the door to greet me. I get the feeling that they have been waiting—waiting, in some sense, since I first made contact through their aunt a couple of weeks back.

"It made us feel so good when we heard about you wanting to come here," Derwin says. "It made us feel blessed that somebody wanted to write something about our team. I said to Darryl: Whoever this guy is, he knows something about Crenshaw."

The twins are still lean and athletic-looking, and still nearly identical in appearance. I quickly figure out how to tell them apart: Derwin's hair is processed and sort of longish, so that it falls down the nape of his neck in a sort of 1970s Billy Dee Williams look. Darryl's hair is a little shorter, and he is also slightly stockier.

The apartment is clean and furnished. It consists of a living room big enough for a television, a couch, and one chair. Beyond that is a small dining area and a galley kitchen. Down a short corridor are the two bedrooms and one bathroom.

It turns out that the twins are living with their parents. Napoleon and Dorothy McNealy occupy one of the bedrooms; Darryl and Derwin, at forty-two years old, share the other. "Just like always," their mother says. "If one goes one place, the other likes to go."

We are seated at the small dining room table. Dorothy McNealy has pig's feet cooking in boiling water on the stovetop, and the pungent aroma permeates the apartment.

Darryl goes into his bedroom and returns with a book—the 1979 Crenshaw High yearbook—opened to the team picture. The twins, with great animation, begin to point out their former teammates, each of them with an index finger on the team picture.

"That's Darryl [Strawberry]," Derwin says. "Look how skinny that boy looks."

I ask why Darryl Strawberry is not in uniform. "He was suspended for that game," Derwin says. "On the day of the team picture. That was Darryl, man, always in some kind of trouble."

Derwin puts his finger back on the page. "That one's Chris. And there's Cordie. Fernando. Carl. And that's Coach Hurst, of course."

Darryl McNealy points out Nelson Whiting, the little left fielder. Nelson had lived a couple blocks away from them in L.A. Nelson and the twins were pretty different—Nelson was the musician, and a serious student—but they all hung out together.

Nelson didn't have any brothers. The twins cracked him up. In his own way, he looked after them, tried to keep them in class and out of trouble.

"Nelson, has anybody told you about Nelson?" Darryl says. "He was our best clutch hitter as far I was concerned. You needed a hit, Nelson got you a hit. He used that orange bat. The Tennessee Thumper, it was called."

Derwin jumps in. He remembers the Tennessee Thumper. "Yeah, that was a *hit* bat. That had nothin' but hits in it. We all started swinging that."

They ask me if I have heard about the fifth inning, the famous Crenshaw fifth inning. The rally inning. "Somebody must have told you about that, right?" Derwin says. "We might be losing 3–1, 5–1, it didn't matter. We would come storming back."

The twins are enjoying themselves. They are reliving some sweet, sweet times, better times than now. They talk some more about Nelson. They haven't seen him in years, but still feel close to him. They miss him.

Am I going to see Nelson? they want to know. I tell them yes—I'm headed his way soon.

For some reason, it is important to them that I tell Nelson what a great player they considered him. What an underrated player. He wasn't one of the guys who got all the publicity, the write-ups in the community paper that covered the Crenshaw games and even sometimes in the *Los Angeles Times*. He didn't get that credit like the twins did, or Chris Brown, or Darryl Strawberry. But he was, Derwin says, "one of the best clutch hitters in baseball." Always in the middle of those fifth-inning rallies.

As we talk, I notice something. Darryl in high school had been the spokesman for both of them, the assertive twin. Darryl led; Derwin followed. That's what everyone said. But right now, Derwin is doing most of the talking.

Later, their parents tell me that a reversal of roles has indeed taken place.

Derwin—who played eight years of minor league baseball, who made some money, who saw dozens of different cities and got to within one level of the big leagues—is the leader now. And Darryl, who got himself caught up in the credit card mess while playing for Great Falls, who didn't last even one season, who came back to L.A.—separated, for the first time, from baseball and his twin brother—now quietly follows.

"It changed their personalities. It changed the way they were with each other, to tell you the truth," Dorothy McNealy says. "I would say to Darryl, why don't you go to where your brother is playing and spend some time with him and watch his games. But he wouldn't do it.

"He was in too much pain to do that, is what I believe. He would never sit down and tell me he was in pain about it, but I knew he was. A mother can tell."

Napoleon McNealy says, "Them being such an integral part of each other, you know, being twins, for one to get called down from the minors and the other to continue on, that was hard. It made Darryl sad. Because we're his parents, we could watch his expression, and we could see how hurt he was. And we felt bad for him, too. Darryl was the more outgoing, more active, more talkative person. Then he just started staying in the house a lot."

I asked if they thought Darryl had felt ashamed to lose baseball so abruptly, to be so quickly separated from what he assumed would be his life's work. "I don't know, maybe a little, but I would say more saddened and disappointed," his father says. "It stopped him in such early, early years of his career. They both had high hopes for themselves. Being born and raised up in poverty, it's hard to grasp how excited they were. They got thrown into that arena of millionaires, and they thought that's what was going to happen for them."

Dorothy McNealy interjects. "It wasn't just family or the twins who thought that," she says. "I believe everybody had those high hopes. When they got drafted out of Crenshaw, everybody was saying the sky is the limit for both of them. And we believed that, we really did."

The twins and their parents are all but marooned in Las Vegas. Stranded in the desert. Dorothy McNealy's mother lived in Vegas and fell ill. Then her father got sick. Dorothy commuted from Los Angeles to help, but after that got too hard, she took an apartment.

Napoleon joined her, then the twins followed. Not one of them has a job. They have no telephone.

"It's okay here, but it's not an area we would choose to stay in," Dorothy says. "We're all sort of starting over."

They all talk of going back to Los Angeles and starting some kind of a business. Dorothy could do hair. Open a shop like the ones she had, selling clothes and jewelry on the side. She'd call it D's and Things again. Some people would remember that name.

Napoleon calls himself an entrepreneur. He'd like to get back into something, too, maybe a little janitorial service that the twins could help out in—but it couldn't be in Las Vegas.

"This is just a temporary place," Napoleon says. "We have always had like a four- or five-bedroom. When we go back I'm gonna look into buying a place. We still like California. There's a lot of opportunities out there."

Los Angeles, in their abiding faith, remains the land of opportunity. But it is a long way from being in Las Vegas with no telephone to owning a business in Los Angeles.

Somehow, they believe that just getting back west and reconnecting to their L.A. dream is going to bridge that gap. The dream is stronger than things like bank balances and income and credit ratings.

The McNealys always had something they were reaching for in California, something off in the distance. Plans and dreams, not all of them foolish or unattainable.

Dorothy moved her boys out of Richmond, California, all the way down the coast to L.A., specifically because they were ballplayers and needed to be in a place where ballplayers got noticed. They were eight years old. Some people would have called that foolish as hell, but it worked out.

The twins played at Crenshaw with dozens of scouts watching. They got noticed, got drafted, got paid to play baseball. All those hours of playing strikeout against the wall, of imitating the famous Willie Mays catch, and they ended up drawing a check for playing their kids' game. But it didn't end how they all thought it would, which is why they are all having to start over again. They are slower-moving now. The new dream will be a struggle to achieve.

Dorothy and Napoleon have diabetes-related health problems, and draw government disability checks. Darryl had some kind of benign cyst removed from his brain several years back. His mother says it had something to do with getting hit in the head with a pitch. Darryl says that had nothing to do with it.

Darryl draws a government check, too, for a disability related to the brain surgery. So that's three checks in the house. The McNealys subsist by pooling that money. It leaves them enough money to live, but too little to relocate.

Dorothy McNealy says Las Vegas was exciting at first. The bright lights, the promise of casino winnings, the "twenty-four-hour life," as she calls it, captivated her for about a month. She played the slots. Now, she's cut back to once-a-week bingo.

Napoleon, he never did much gambling at all. But the twins still like it, not the gambling so much, but the change of scenery.

The apartment complex is wedged between two highways lined with unalluring strip malls. They have a cable hookup, and three or four TVs. The twins will put a game on each TV, Dorothy McNealy says, and walk around from room to room, following each one. But that can get old.

So when the twins have a little money in their pockets, they go down to the Strip, put some change in the machines, have a drink, look at the ladies, then get on the bus and come back home.

There's a ballfield at the edge of the apartment complex. Many days, they walk down there and watch the games. Their mother thinks they should find a team of young boys to coach.

Her boys have been playing since they were "itty-bitty little boys," Dorothy McNealy says, using a favorite phrase of hers. All those years of baseball. Derwin has passed some of it on to Derwin Jr., but he only gets to see his son now and then.

She tells her sons: Go down to the park. Give some of that baseball knowledge away.

At their Las Vegas apartment complex, they use the pay telephone across the sweltering courtyard, the one installed against a brick wall of one of the buildings. It's close enough, but not convenient. And just not quite right.

None of the McNealys like standing in line, waiting to use a pay phone. They don't see themselves in that particular line of people, but then again, probably nobody else does, either. It's a sure bet that every single person waiting for the pay phone would rather have something that rings in his apartment.

Napoleon considers getting a phone in the apartment. But then he thinks: We're leaving. We're going back out to L.A., so what would be the point?

*   *   *

One night, I take Darryl, Derwin, and Derwin's girlfriend out to dinner at a Tony Roma's, a chain rib restaurant just up the highway from the apartment complex. They have not been there before, and seem thrilled just to be anywhere—in the same way they were so happy to see me at the door.

Thinking about Crenshaw, remembering it, talking about it, puts them in high spirits. Certain other things they have blotted out, forgotten, or just don't care to talk about.

Darryl remembers Brooks Hurst's jaw being broken before the semifinal playoff game, the one that preceded the championship game at Dodger Stadium—but he doesn't remember it as some others do, that he was an unbridled kid who had been repeatedly told to be careful about those throws into the plate, especially when he was positioned just about point-blank distance from the plate.

"I felt so bad about it," he says. "I liked Coach Hurst. But it was just a big accident; I don't remember them ever saying I shouldn't throw it like that."

The credit card incident in Great Falls is also not a subject that he wants to dwell on in any detail. It was a couple of young kids in a strange town who made a terrible mistake. Darryl doesn't have much more to say about it, and, really, what more is there to say? It was a prosaic way to blow a couple of baseball careers, something he and Cordie Dillard would take back if they could—would rewind the tape and splice in a different scene.

"It was dumb," Darryl says. "Just dumb. The man left his wallet out and I took it. I've felt real down about it every single day of my life since it happened."

Derwin tells me several times that he feels "blessed" about his baseball career—blessed to have known players like Ken Griffey Sr. and Dave Winfield; blessed to have lasted for eight years; blessed to have lived the baseball life; blessed to have earned the respect of his teammates; blessed to have had Eric Goldschmidt, the agent for Chris Brown and Darryl Strawberry, agree to represent him.

That was a milestone of sorts. Goldschmidt usually took on only hot young prospects, so Derwin felt good about becoming his client, hopeful that maybe having a big-time agent would finally get him his chance.

I was "this close," he says, holding his index finger and thumb a fraction of an inch apart. "This close."

But then he signed back with the Yankees—he wanted to go up to the big leagues as a Yankee—and maybe that was his own wrong turn. It wasn't anything like what happened to Darryl McNealy in Great Falls. Not a blunder. But it was a mistake, possibly a career-killer. The Yankees had too much talent; he couldn't rise above it.

The post-baseball years for Darryl and Derwin cannot easily be accounted for, because they have little to show for them. Darryl wants to talk mostly about softball. That's comfortable, talking about softball.

He played for one of Mr. Jones's fast-pitch teams, the Eagles, a very good team that traveled to tournaments. Derwin didn't start playing softball till later on, after his eight years of minor league ball. So he never got as good at it, Darryl says, because it's a whole different deal trying to hit a softball.

"That's right," Derwin says. "I could never hit that softball like Darryl could. Darryl got real good at it."

We talk a long time about softball. Then I bring the conversation back to what the heck they've been doing for the last decade or so.

Both of them worked some construction. Darryl poured concrete for high-rises in downtown L.A., and so did Derwin after he was finished with baseball. The work was sporadic and they rarely kept those jobs more than a couple of months at a time.

I ask them about owing money around L.A., and the story I heard about them sneaking down the ladder in the middle of the night. Blank stares. They don't know anything about it. Can't remember ever sneaking down any ladder or owing money.

"We never had no troubles like that with anybody," Derwin assures me.

Derwin's girlfriend has mostly just been listening quietly to their old stories. Her name is Stephanie. She has three children, ages fifteen, eleven, and seven. She is pregnant with Derwin's child.

As we walk back out to the parking lot after dinner, Derwin takes me aside. He says that Stephanie needs prenatal vitamins, which they can't afford. He apologetically asks if I could help out, and I give him $50.

"We're all trying to get ourselves back together," he says.

It is the first time he has acknowledged that all is not right in the world of the twins. He wants to go to Memphis to see Derwin Jr. play, but he hasn't been able to manage that. He wants to figure a way to help his parents. All those years he was playing, whenever he came back to L.A., they were always there to take care of him.

Now his parents could use his help. And Derwin has this child coming, with a woman already struggling to care for the three she already has.

"We're fightin' it," he says. "You know what I mean? If we could just get set up back in L.A., I think we could get back on our feet."

*   *   *

Nelson Whiting, like the twins, lives in Nevada—but nearly four hundred miles north of Las Vegas, in a town called Fallon that is set down on a stark, desolate landscape. Just as I pull into town, I find myself in the kind of driving sandstorm that I did not know existed outside of places like Iraq; at three P.M. the wind picks up, it turns dark as night, and every inch of my rental car becomes coated in a thin layer of grit.

There is no water that I can discern in Fallon—Lake Tahoe is about eighty miles to the west—but there is a Navy base, a facility that trains pilots and offers endless acres that can be repeatedly practice-bombed with few people caring or even noticing.

Nelson Whiting works at this base. He is a Navy man—at sea, a firefighter trained to put out blazes aboard aircraft carriers; on land, a police officer charged with protecting the perimeter of a military base and making sure no one inside of it misbehaves.

In Fallon, he has faced down many a hotshot pilot—young men, usually younger than him, well-educated, well-trained, and, to their minds, above his station in life, who on their off hours like to drink and raise hell. Fallon is home to the Naval Fighters Weapons School, more commonly known as the Top Gun school. By necessity, these men are full of themselves, roaring with arrogance.

The pilots don't know that Nelson played for the Crenshaw High Cougars with the great Darryl Strawberry, that he was the clutch-hitting left fielder for the greatest assemblage of talent in the whole history of high school baseball. If he told them they probably wouldn't believe him—and even if they did, they still wouldn't give a damn.

When he encounters one of them—driving drunk; beating on a wife or girlfriend; smashing spent beer bottles in public spaces—Nelson approaches with all due deference. He tells them that in the military there is rank, but there is also such a thing as the law, and they are currently on the wrong side of it.

If that doesn't work, and frequently it does not, he will borrow from the L.A. streets and say something like, Let me tell you something. There ain't but one place you can go with this. You know I'm saying? You can listen to me and we'll get along, or you can go in the other direction, in which case I'll have to handcuff your sorry ass and turn you over to your command.

Depending on his mood, he might add, in more military-sounding jargon: You can make the choice, sir, and I'll respond accordingly.

Among the base's nonpilots, he deals with some very young men, some of them fresh off their high school football and wrestling teams— eighteen-year-olds, hormones still raging. Nelson outranks them, but they don't tend to listen too well, either.

Nelson is not a big or imposing man, but he keeps himself fit. He plays basketball twice a week, Tuesdays and Thursdays at seven A.M. He plays on a base softball team that has reached the all-Navy championships. And he religiously lifts weights, not to build bulk, but so he can take a man down if the need arises.

As we talk, Nelson and I are sitting at a restaurant in town, a decent Mexican joint that he had been wanting to try. The waitress comes to take our drink orders. The bar across the room looks pretty fully stocked— three long tiers of bottles.

"I'm gonna have a shot of Hennessey," Nelson says.

Hennessey is a cognac—not a black drink per se, but one that is popular in African-American communities. (The liquor trade publications report that the sale of "brown" alcoholic beverages, otherwise on the decline, are being kept afloat by sales of cognac to "urban" consumers.)

"What's Hennessey?" the waitress asks.

He tells her. She checks. They have none. Nelson just chuckles.

"I guess I'm pretty far from home," he says to me. "If it wasn't for the Navy, there wouldn't be one black person here. To tell you the truth, there wouldn't be anything here at all—you wouldn't even have that Wal-Mart."

Nelson loved baseball. He played on some semipro teams after high school, and went over to Harbor Park a couple of Januarys and shagged fly balls at the Program, taking his turns at bat after Darryl Strawberry and the boys were done with their hitting.

It was a point of pride for Nelson that unlike so many others out at Harbor Park, he never asked Darryl or any of the pros for money. Not to tide him over for a week, not for some business scheme, not for lunch.

Not that he couldn't have used some money at times, or that he wouldn't have been given some. After his workouts at the Program, Darryl Strawberry would give away so much money that he always had a little crowd around him, like he was some American tourist in a third-world capital.

Nelson was there for the exercise and the friendship. "Darryl and I were teammates," he says. "If I start begging him for money, that takes away from what we had."

Nelson never had any illusions about making it in pro ball. He wasn't good enough. His life was going to be music. He had those gigs in high school, good ones that paid him union scale. When he was in tenth grade, some records he made with his combo were playing on the radio.

He could play the drums, piano, clarinet, saxophone. He was like a celebrity. He had girls calling his house, begging to come over just to hear him play. He had every reason to believe he would have a career as a performer, a producer, a music industry executive—maybe all three.

He certainly didn't imagine himself in the military, out in this barren landscape—not one radio station worth listening to; the piercing sound of F-16 and F-18 Harrier jump jets overhead; and on the ground, the low hum of disorder from too much boredom and beer.

But he has made his peace with this, going wherever the Navy sends him. He has more than made his peace; he is *thankful*. Los Angeles, he believes, swallows people up. Good people. Promising people. Given the chance, he thinks it might have swallowed him up.

"Let me tell you a story about L.A.," he says.

Nelson has already told me about his father, who sold TVs on the street corner that were not actually TVs but boxes filled with rocks—the father who finally had to flee from angry customers all the way down to Texas, where he died. He has told me about his mother, who raised three children by herself—two girls, and Nelson, the baby—and took in foster children to help make ends meet.

This story is about his big sister, Crystal, the oldest one. "She was a cheerleader at Manual Arts," he begins. "She won the most-spirited award. She was always winning some kind of award. And she was smart,

I mean real smart. Straight A's every report card. She was attending Chico State. She was gonna be a lawyer.

"But she got in with the wrong crowd. One summer she came back, and she was working at the Hamburger Hamlet in the Wilshire District. And she got into something, some kind of drug—PCP, I don't know what—something that made her crazy. And I come home one day, and all the plants in the house are cut up. My mom had a lot of plants, and they were like shredded.

"My mom comes home and sees this, and her and my sister get into it. My mom was real strict. And I was glad she was. My sister ran outside of the house, and I started chasing her. I chased her all the way to Exposition Park, which was like three blocks from where we stayed, near USC. And then I let her go. I figured I'm not gonna run all the way around L.A. after her. I figured, I'll go back and talk to my mom and let her know she just kept on running, and she'll come back when she comes back.

"But she didn't come back. We didn't see her after that for two years, when she came back pregnant. That first child of hers is disabled. She's never walked a day in her life. And then my sister had another baby, and that child is healthy. But my sister got AIDS, and she passed on in 1997, on her second daughter's sixteenth birthday."

Nelson tells me this almost matter-of-factly—as a way of explaining how he can be so content in Fallon, Nevada.

*   *   *

The strict definition of poverty, by federal government standards, is based on income: Are you above the line or below? Nelson, and almost the whole Crenshaw team, was well below it. And that had implications way beyond the quality of their housing or the reliability of the family car.

Poverty for them was limiting. Most of them did not take family vacations. They didn't go to the beaches, which were about five miles west. They didn't go east into the San Fernando Valley to ride horses. They lived in one of the richest, most cosmopolitan cities in the world, but experienced only a tiny sliver of it. They almost never mixed with anyone much different from themselves. In a multicultural mecca, they lived a monocultural existence.

And because they had no practice at embracing the new or different, their instinct was to spurn it—and along with it, opportunity.

Nelson was a gifted visual artist as well as a talented musician. Some of his murals still grace the walls at Crenshaw High. Late in his senior year, he was offered a full scholarship to Otis Art Institute and Parsons School of Design in downtown L.A.

"My art teacher liked me a lot," Nelson says. "She really went out of her way to get that for me."

He enrolled at Parsons but stayed only a couple of weeks. The whole scene was utterly different from anything he had ever experienced. "There were too many gay people there. I didn't know how to adjust," he says. "That sounds like a very stupid thing to say now, but I was young. It seemed like most of the guys were gay. It made me really uncomfortable."

Nelson started taking courses at a music institute in West Hollywood. On Fridays, he jammed with artists he would have paid to see, like B.B. King, George Benson, the Average White Band. (And some he wouldn't have, like Twisted Sister.)

But for whatever reason, paying gigs were not as easy to come by as they had been while he was still in high school. He thought he would be making money and building toward his dream of owning a recording studio; instead, he was subsisting by working as a clerk for the Equal Opportunity Employment Commission, then later as a security guard for Bonwit Teller.

"I got off to this kind of slow start," he says. "I would go one place and do something, get involved, and change my mind and do something else. I was just kind of stumbling around."

He thinks now that having a father would have made all the difference. A father, he imagines, "is the person who lays out a plan for you—or checks your plan to see that it makes sense, that it's thought out."

Nelson didn't have a plan. All he had was a hope to make it in music, and a sort of onrushing fear of the things that might happen to him if he didn't get out of town.

While he was still in high school, he had gotten beaten up pretty good by gang members who tried to steal his friend's jacket. ("It wasn't even leather; it was *pleather.*") He missed a week of school with facial bruises and a jaw too swollen to eat. He still had those memories of the bullets whizzing over the practice field at Crenshaw on the day after the Jones boys mixed it up with the gang members. He had seen his sister fall to drugs. And his aunt got caught up in them, too.

Increasingly, L.A. just scared the hell out of him.

While Nelson was bouncing between jobs he didn't like and the rare paying music gig, a friend of his got shot and seriously wounded in a robbery. He had just been out on a date with his girlfriend.

"After that," he says, "I was like, you know what, I gotta get out of here. I didn't feel like I was gonna get a break. I felt like there was a better chance of me getting killed than catching some kind of break."

Someone, Nelson's still not sure who, made an appointment for him with an Army recruiter while he was in his knocking-around phase in L.A. The recruiter called with a time, and Nelson showed up and immediately signed on.

He was an Army supply clerk, which he found boring. He left after a couple of years, hung around L.A. for four months, then enlisted in the Navy. He has served, so far, for eighteen years. On board the aircraft carrier *Dwight D. Eisenhower,* he sailed throughout the Mediterranean—to France, Italy, and Spain—as well as to South America, the Cayman Islands, and the Virgin Islands.

His job on ship is damage control—containing fires, floods, any machinery malfunction that could threaten the vessel. The *Eisenhower* carries about a hundred aircraft and more than five thousand sailors. It is longer than the Empire State Building is high. Voids below decks contain torpedoes and missiles, so a lot can go wrong.

Nelson was the last line of defense against chaos, fire, and death, and he loved the work—loved the constant onboard training against any possible eventuality, and didn't even mind the all-night watch duty.

"Keep that ship on top of the water," he says. "That was our role."

He is divorced, with a nine-year-old son, Nelson Jr., back in Los Angeles. The marriage survived his tours of duty on aircraft carriers, although barely, but broke up after they all moved to Fallon.

At home, he is a man of routine and relentless self-discipline. Having escaped the the anarchy of the L.A. streets, he has thrown a security blanket of order and predictability around himself.

Nelson starts every weekend with a ritual Saturday-morning washing of his car and pickup truck. That was the case even when his family was in Fallon; the vehicles had to be clean before any family outings could commence. He inspects his vehicles often for what he calls "dings"—nicks, little dents, scratches, or smudges on the paint.

The car-washing precipitated a memorable marital spat. About the same time in the morning that Nelson liked to wash his cars, several women at his apartment complex were usually outside, exercising together. A couple of them were eye-catching, particularly in their leopard-print leotards. "They were friendly, we used to speak," he says. "I didn't think anything of it."

His then-wife saw him chatting with them one day. She got angry, and they had a big argument. "She went on and on about it in the way that a woman will do when she's upset, yelling and screaming and all of that. I told her my focus was on washing the cars, but she couldn't accept that."

Nelson makes about $51,000 a year, and pays rent of just $685 on his three-bedroom apartment. He pared down his phone bill by cutting off long-distance service and using a phone card. Every month, he puts away $2,000 in savings.

There are slot machines everywhere in Fallon, as well as a casino. Nelson has not put so much as a quarter in one. A friend who works at a nearby Amazon.com warehouse has tried to induce him into the casino—the friend won $2,000 recently—but there is no chance Nelson will accept.

He is obsessive about protecting his nest egg, looking to the future—making sure, actually, that he has a future. After he read that divorced people who live alone have a shorter life expectancy, he changed his diet and stepped up his regimen. "I had a thing for junk food and fast food," he says. He packs his own lunch now, a sandwich and raw vegetables—allowing himself, each day, a bonus of two chocolate chip cookies.

Nelson gets up each work morning at three A.M. without the benefit of an alarm clock. He has long gotten what he calls "broken sleep"—he's wakeful, always thinking of something he has to do, some task or detail, so even on the rare occasions when he has set an alarm he's up waiting for it to ring.

At 3:40 A.M. he leaves for the base, where he is the equivalent of a shift commander at a precinct house. When he arrives at four A.M., he first checks to see what weapons and ammunition have been signed out and are still in the possession of officers making the rounds, and what weapons remain in the locked weapons closet. If everything checks out, he passes out guns to his officers and sends them out.

The job got a lot tougher after September 11, 2001. The Fallon Naval Air Station sprawls over 240,000 acres, and has five entrances. Reservists were called to active duty to help guard against any encroachment onto the base, so Nelson now supervises twenty people on a typical shift. Immediately after the terrorist attacks, he went weeks without a day off, and he's still working more hours than before.

He deals with all the base security, with plenty of "domestics"—the spousal spats that are the bane of any law enforcement officer, and which can be particularly nasty on a military installation—and he does his best to finesse the "khakis," the base's higher-ranking officers.

Several months before I visited him, Nelson had a little run-in with his superior officer and had been written up for what was perceived as an incident of brutality. He was working at night when he got a noise complaint about a party on a balcony at one of the barracks. He drove over and found a half-dozen Marines "drinking and smoking cigarettes and having a good time."

He told them, It's after ten P.M. Take it inside or go across the street to the park, but by the rules of the base you can't be out on the balcony making noise.

"We had this one Marine who just kept spitting over the railing, and there were some people right down below. They were just quietly enjoying themselves and they were like—hey, don't do that? I said to him, 'Stop that. As a matter of fact, just stop spitting altogether.' But this dude is just smoking his cigarette, being all bad, treating me like a rent-a-cop. I'm used to that.

"So I said to him, 'Gimme that.' And I took his drink and I poured it out. And then I cuffed him and put him on his knees, and he still kept spitting, so I put his face down. And I didn't mean to put his face in his own spit, but it might have come off that way. And then it came up that it was police brutality. I got like a minor warning. But I told my superior, you're home in bed, man, and we're running around after these idiots.

"And I want to come home safely. And I want my people to come home safely. I'm not gonna let nobody out here take my weapon. I'm not gonna change nothing. If the same thing happens, I'll do the same thing. They drink and act crazy and they're rednecks to begin with—and I gotta take care of their feelings? Uh-uh, not me."

*   *   *

Nelson has one small area of his life that resembles what he once imagined for himself. It is upstairs in his split-level apartment, a spare bedroom converted into his music room. He has his synthesizer up there, along with a drum set. A big leather couch is soon to be moved up from the living room so friends who visit will have a place to sit and listen to him play.

Instead of sleeping, he composes music, plays it on his synthesizer, taps quietly on his drums. If he doesn't have to work the next day, and sometimes even if he does, he's up most of the night. "Sometimes I'll just be doing my music until I fall asleep," he says. "It's never like work to me. It's like walking or breathing. It's just natural."

This part of the world where Nelson lives is a pretty spooky place, what with the bombing range, and the lunar landscape; rates for childhood leukemia and other cancers are nearly off the charts from all the things that have been bombed or dumped into the ground. The bombing range is so ideal that the military is thinking of moving the disputed practice bombing operation at Vieques, Puerto Rico, to Fallon.

Nelson is not too interested in going out in his current environs and exploring. He's not that social to begin with, and is definitely not interested in mixing with this group of locals. He believes he has been run off the road a couple of times just for being black.

Except for working and exercising, he spends nearly every moment bunkered in his music room. He is no less hungry for music now than when he was fourteen and playing and traveling with Phase, the little combo band that got the gigs in Reno.

"The Navy, right now, is taking me away from what I feel I should be doing," he says. "What you see right here"—the music room—"this is my calling. But I've been in the Navy this long, I might as well stick it out—get my twenty years in and get all those benefits. I'll be forty-four or forty-five, but it's never too late to get back with the music."

Even now, Nelson is more connected to the music industry than you might imagine a full-time Navy man stationed in Nowhere, Nevada, could be. The onetime musical prodigy still composes music—background tracks, mainly, for rappers—and sells his work to producers in Los Angeles and San Diego.

When I was visiting with him, the Houston rappers Lil' Flip had a song getting radio play (titled "The Way We Ball") with Nelson's beat in the background. That was a good break for him. He was able to raise his price some, and had just sold his most recent composition for $1,200.

"That was big," he says. "Twelve hundred dollars, that's not too bad considering I'm sitting out here and the whole music world is somewhere else."

Lil' Flip's lyrics on the "The Way We Ball" reflect an updated version of the ticket out: rap, not baseball.

> *I'm thinkin—Jaguars and a Bentley Rolls*
> *I'm thinkin'—bein' rich before I'm 24.*

Nelson doesn't take it too seriously. "It's sort of like a bunch of nonsense" is how he puts it. At home or in his car, he listens to jazz, R&B, occasionally some classical. The only time he listens to rap is when he's in a club and can't avoid it. Rap "doesn't carry, musically," he says. But the only money to be made is by marrying his musicality to commercially viable rappers.

It takes a pretty formidable and determined talent to be sitting where Nelson is and selling music that gets radio play. Up in the music room, he plays one of his latest thumping, bass-heavy compositions for me, one he hopes to sell to some hip-hop producer.

"What they sing is usually pretty dirty," he explains. "So the way it works is, I lay down the music—and they curse over it."

* * *

"Boy, come over here and give me some sugar," Nelson's grandmother would say when he was little, which was his prompt to come over and plant a big kiss on her cheek.

He was raised in a world of women—his mother, grandmother, aunts, two big sisters. The whole family was close and affectionate. His mother doted on him and pushed him to achieve. His grandmother taught him how to meditate. Everywhere he turned, women were hovering, hugging him, telling him to keep his grades up and his manners minded.

"Our whole family was just a hugging and kissing, talking-all-the-time bunch of people," he says. "My wife didn't understand that at first. She would be like: Why are you all like that? But all my relatives are female, and that's how everybody was."

What Nelson did not have was a male influence, or any model of a functional marriage. He wanted a marriage for himself that worked, but like many of the Boys of Crenshaw was not able to achieve one—at least not the first time around.

He tried to keep his marriage together, but could not. Two long stints at sea didn't help. The marriage lasted six years. A previous marriage, when he was twenty-seven, ended after seven months.

"We had a nice house in San Diego," he says of his most recent marriage. "I had a son. I would come home at six-thirty P.M., shower, eat, spend time with little Nelson. That's something I definitely didn't have when I was growing up—a mom and a dad, and I really wanted that. To my mind, I tried, but it just wasn't meant to be. My mom didn't understand why I kept at it as long as I did, but when I left, I wanted to be able to say, I've done everything I possibly can to make it work."

Nelson gets back to L.A. about once a month to see his son, although he could not in the immediate aftermath of the September 11 terrorist strikes, when leave from base was suspended. The last time Nelson was with his son, he was reading with him, alternating pages. "He was reading with *expression*," Nelson tells me. "That's what we were working on. I tell him you'll be a better reader if you really feel the meaning of the words."

The Navy offered him a slot in Washington, D.C., teaching classes on how to respond to chemical and biological warfare. He likes to teach; it's like performing. But he declined because it would have taken him too far from his son. He doesn't know what he'll do when he leaves the Navy, but some kind of teaching (along with music, of course) is a possibility.

He has a close friendship, a platonic one, with a woman in the Navy. She was on an aircraft carrier on Valentine's Day, somewhere in the Persian Gulf, and he sent her a care package—"some makeup, candy, other little treats that I knew she would like."

For all the women in his life during his childhood, I got the distinct feeling that women are still something of a puzzle to Nelson—or, at the very least, *relationships* with them are puzzling, and a little scary. He has carefully constructed his life: washing the car on a certain day; spending a set amount and saving the rest; eliminating fast food and sweets, except for the two chocolate chip cookies in the brown bag lunch. But relationships are chancy. They come with unpredictability, sometimes emotional pain, even chaos of a certain sort—all of which Nelson tried to leave behind in L.A.

He is resilient, a survivor of a lot of family pain in childhood. Imagine chasing a promising and beloved sister across several city blocks, letting her go, and then realizing she wasn't coming back any time soon. But resilience always comes with a price. Nelson has built a fortress around himself, an interior tidiness, that will not be easily breached. The routine and discipline of military life have served as an added layer of protection. He wishes now that he had joined straight out of Crenshaw.

When I visited with him, he had been having long phone conversations with a woman back in Southern California, and she was all set to come to see him in Fallon. He was about to buy her a plane ticket, but then thought better of it.

"We were talking one night," he recalls, "and she's crying about something. Crying. And I'm like: Wait a minute. I don't need that. There should be nothing that's got something to do with somebody else, something back home or at work or whatever, that has her crying and yelling at me. When she did that, I'm like: You know what, this won't work. If she disrespects me like that, what's gonna happen if she gets close in to my circle? I said, 'I'm sorry, but you can stay out there.' "

Back in Los Angeles, at Nelson's mother's house, the cycle of his childhood is repeating itself: fatherless babies, and young men and women who keep coming up far short of their vast potential.

His youngest niece—the daughter of his deceased sister—was bright just like her mom. Nelson's mother raised her, along with her disabled sister. She got all that love, all that discipline, all that hovering, and all those high hopes for her success. She got that from Nelson's mother, Emma, and from Nelson, too.

"I helped bring her up just like she was mine," Nelson says. "She's left-handed like me. I taught her how to cook, how to ride a bicycle, and a whole bunch of other things. Before I was married and had a kid, I would walk over to her school and walk her home, then help her do her homework. When she graduated from high school, I gave her money for a car and to help her get going."

But his niece, who had excelled at a Catholic high school, decided not to go to college. "My mom was hot about that. They fell out over it. We were all hot about it. She could have had anything she wanted, been anything she wanted—all she had to do was go to school."

His niece moved out of the house after high school.

At twenty, she came back. With a baby.

Nelson tells me that this new baby is going to get everything that he got. Everything that his sisters got. All the same loving and discipline. All the opportunities.

CHAPTER SEVEN

Called Out
on Strikes

I think that every one of the Boys of Crenshaw used the word *blessed*. They all felt blessed for what they had, even if it wasn't much. They felt blessed for the people who loved them, and blessed just to have survived to this point. They even felt blessed that I had come to visit, that someone would want to know about a piece of their past.

I thought about that word. At first I took it as an expression of religious faith, but in most cases it wasn't that. What I realized over time was that feeling blessed was a way of saying that no matter what, things could be worse. And they all knew that so directly.

Nelson Whiting policed ill-mannered sailors instead of playing drums for a living, but he was acutely aware of what real heartbreak was, of what had befallen his sister and so many others back home. Chris Brown's big-league career had been so disappointing, but he knew that he was still better off than Darryl Strawberry. Every one of the former Crenshaw players could cite numerous examples of family and close friends who were distinctly not blessed.

So even though most of them had not made it in pro baseball and had not cashed their ticket out, they had not, on the other hand, been pulled to the bottom, sucked down to the lowest level of L.A. street life. They knew exactly what that looked like.

* * *

On the surface, the town of Petaluma, California, 400 miles straight up the California coast, would seem to have no connection at all to inner-city L.A. The town and its some 55,000 residents were blessed, too, but in ways utterly foreign to the life experience of the Boys of Crenshaw.

A tradition of deep wealth prevailed in Petaluma; in the first two decades of the twentieth century, it was said that more money was on deposit in Petaluma, per capita, than in any other town on earth. A good bit of that came from the chicken and egg business. The first modern incubator for hatching eggs was invented by a local man, a Canadian who had settled in Petaluma. When egg prices were high, Petaluma flourished. To celebrate the blessings that the poultry business had bestowed, the town held an annual Egg Parade, led by a newly crowned Egg Queen, as well as an Egg Queen Ball and a Chicken Rodeo. For many years, the Chicken Pharmacy—with remedies for sick fowl—was a Main Street landmark. (The pharmacy even earned a mention in *Ripley's Believe It or Not.*)

In addition to its riches, Petaluma benefited from a legacy of extreme good luck. The town was situated just eighteen miles from the epicenter of the 1906 San Francisco earthquake, yet it emerged miraculously unscathed—allowing its impressive mix of Spanish Colonial, Victorian, and Greek Revival architecture to survive.

Over the years, Petaluma became a virtual reflection of America and Americana; its destiny was to be successful and quaint, a place that others looked to in order to feel good about their nation. The movies *American Graffiti*, *Peggy Sue Got Married*, and *The Farmer's Daughter* were filmed in Petaluma. The 1984 presidential campaign of Ronald Reagan used Petaluma's tree-lined streets and Victorian homes as a canvas for his famous "Morning in America" commercials.

But a decade after those campaign commercials, something happened, an unspeakably awful crime that shook the town to its core and focused the attention of an entire nation.

On October 1, 1993, Polly Klaas, twelve, had her two best friends from Petaluma Junior High to her house for a slumber party. The girls played board games. They tried out costumes they might wear later that month for Halloween. They stayed up late. Polly's mother, a single mom (the parents were divorced), fell asleep in an adjacent bedroom. When the girls got sleepy, Polly went to get sleeping bags from a closet in the hall.

At the bedroom door, she was stopped by an intruder with a knife. He bound and gagged all three girls, blindfolded them with pillowcases, then threatened to slit the throat of anyone who made a sound. With the other two girls tied up and paralyzed with fear, he took Polly out through an unlocked back door, the same one that he had used to enter the house.

Local residents were terrified and outraged. They helped police comb every square foot near her home, as well as the hills, canyons, and wilderness areas outside of town. They distributed seven million flyers emblazoned with her picture. The search for Polly dominated CNN.

News stories said that Polly was "apple-cheeked" and "a beautiful girl with warm brown eyes." To *People* magazine, she was "America's Child."

Two months after her abduction, Polly's body was discovered by the side of California Highway 101, under thick brush and about fifty miles from home. She had been strangled and raped.

When a suspect was arrested and his background became known, it only added to the outrage. Richard Allen Davis, forty-two, was a career criminal who had been paroled just five months before he grabbed Polly.

Davis, who would be sentenced to death for Polly's murder, had been arrested at least thirty-six times previously. He had two prior convictions for kidnapping, and had served only half his sixteen-year sentence for the most recent one. As early as 1976, a parole officer filed a report warning of his "accelerating propensity toward violence." Davis had told prison psychiatrists that inner voices made him commit crimes, and that he felt a "glowing" and a release of tension after committing violence.

In short, Davis was a psychopath and a sadist, a vile human being who made a persuasive case that some people are irredeemable and need to be locked up for life with no opportunity for parole and no possibility they will ever cause additional harm.

At the time of Polly's murder, there was just such a bill moving through the California legislative process, one that toughened up sentencing and put more criminals away for keeps. It was called Proposition 184.

After Davis's arrest—and the revelation of his criminal past—Polly Klaas's father, Marc, worked tirelessly in support of Proposition 184. Before Davis even stood trial, voters approved the initiative by a margin of 74 percent to 28 percent.

The new statute, which became law on March 7, 1994, established a "strike" system. After a second felony, or "strike," a criminal faced serious mandatory jail time, normally seven years. A third strike and he was sentenced to life in prison.

Widely copied in other states, the laws became known as "three strikes." This was baseball terminology, of course, and nearly every American instantly understood it.

You start off with the count even—no strikes, no balls.

One strike and you've got to dig in and really keep your eye on the ball.

Two strikes and you're in some trouble. A wise batter steps out of the box, takes stock, makes adjustments. He cannot afford to swing and miss again.

The new law appealed to America's sense of justice and fair play. Three strikes and you're out. Who couldn't abide by that?

*   *   *

The catcher Carl Jones was loved and valued by his teammates, but no one took him for a genius. If Carl didn't make it in baseball, they did not imagine him going to college, getting some kind of white-collar job, and moving up and out of the old neighborhood.

No, if Carl couldn't play ball, he would help out his daddy: drive a truck, lift heavy things, pour concrete, hammer nails. He could still live all dirty and gritty, still chew his tobacco, and he'd grow into someone like Thedo Jones—a good, dependable man. That would be Carl: someone you could count on.

But it didn't play out that way. While most of his high school teammates went off to play pro or college baseball, Carl, ignored in the 1979 amateur draft, drifted. When he had work, it was often good work—$700 a week or more at big construction sites downtown. He poured concrete for the Wells Fargo Bank building and the Crocker Center, prominent features on the L.A. skyline. For a couple of years, Carl drove a Chrysler New Yorker. Off hours, he played baseball and softball.

But there were days he just didn't show up on the job site. He ran the streets, dabbled in drugs. The serious drugs—cocaine, not just reefer— began around 1983, four years after high school. A girlfriend, he says, first turned him on to crack cocaine.

He became an addict, no better and no worse than tens of thousands of other hopeless crackheads in L.A. When he needed money to feed his habit, he stole. Much of what he did, he can't remember. Ten years of his life went down a black hole; Carl can hardly account for any of it.

On October 18, 1989, Carl Quinton Jones was convicted of the burglary of a private home. Less than a year later, July 19, 1990, he was convicted of stealing from another home. The occupants were away from home in each case. No weapon was used, and no one was hurt.

Four years later, on July 23, 1994, after serving jail time for that second burglary, Carl, thirty-four at the time, broke into Crenshaw High in the middle of summer break. No one was inside but a janitor. To this day, he cannot say exactly what drove him back into his old school and what, if anything, he was seeking.

A high school offers plenty of value to steal: audiovisual equipment, athletic equipment, cameras if you know where to look.

What Carl valued about himself, his baseball career and all that it conferred—friendships; a sense of competence; a measure of authority and control ("Punk, throw a fastball!")—had been left inside that building. Crenshaw High was the last place where Carl had felt like a respected man.

He entered near the gymnasium, within sight of the baseball field. He walked down empty school corridors, then let himself into classroom 104. He threw open a couple of cabinets and scattered the contents, mostly paper, on the floor. He yanked the metal shelf under the chalkboard, the little ledge that holds erasers, out of the wall.

It was all nonproductive—pure and senseless vandalism, the behavior of someone who was angry at something, or just strung out beyond the point of reason. A defense lawyer would describe his crime as "an inept and aimless foray into an unoccupied classroom."

A silent alarm alerted school district police. Carl apparently sensed them coming. He crawled out the classroom window and dropped to the ground and into some bushes. He was not armed, and for some reason, he had no shoes on, just socks.

After the officers arrested him, not far from where he had come out the window, they checked all around the bushes to see what he had taken. All they found were Carl's brown cowboy boots. He was in possession of no stolen goods.

Back in the classroom that he had trashed, officers discovered a pair of women's shoes in a school knapsack. With nothing else to go on, prosecutors theorized at trial that Carl, the manly catcher of the Boys of Crenshaw, was planning to make off with a pair of ladies' shoes.

Carl was convicted of second-degree commercial burglary in Los Angeles County Criminal Court. The prosecution successfully argued that he had planned to steal but was interrupted in the act. Intent to steal was enough to make the burglary charge stick.

The home burglary in 1990—no one home; no one hurt—was strike one.

The home burglary a year later—same circumstances—strike two.

This utterly stupid and fruitless break-in at Crenshaw High:

Strike three.

Carl became one of the first defendants sentenced under the new law, the one designed to put away violent psychopaths like Richard Allen Davis. Carl clearly was not that; he was a garden-variety crack addict and a not-too-clever thief.

But the law was the law. The judge imposed the will of the people on Carl, the mandatory three-strikes sentence: Twenty-five years to life in prison. In imposing the sentence, he made no distinction between Carl Jones and someone like Richard Allen Davis.

"The California Legislature spoke to us loud and clear," he said from the bench. "And it said we're tired of crime in California. We're tired of violent and serious felonies being committed. And if someone carries baggage with them of having previously committed a serious and violent felony, that they had better get the message. And that message is they can be a law-abiding citizen and conform with the law of the state of California and thereby remain free from custody. Another alternative is to leave the state of California or go elsewhere. Or the third alternative is to commit crime and be punished in accordance with what the Legislature has decreed."

Carl, by California law, had certainly committed serious crimes, three felonies. Why the judge termed them violent crimes is much less clear. As for the options—stop committing crimes, move out of California, or face life in prison—those had not exactly been laid out for him in advance. In fact, when he had set off on his crime spree (such as it was), the three strikes law was not even in effect.

He was thirty-four years old when he entered prison. His first opportunity for parole will occur in the year 2019; he will be fifty-eight years old.

*   *   *

In the living room where he used to push aside the furniture and assess all the boys' baseball swings, Thedo Jones now sits on a big overstuffed chair and struggles to tell me what caused Carl's downfall.

"Carl had a drug problem, and if I could explain how he got it, I sure would," Thedo says. "He was a good kid. Me and him was like the same thing, you know what I mean? I liked ball, and Carl followed me. Baseball, softball. He loved it just like I did. I did everything a father could do with a sick kid. I talked to Carl. I tried to get him help. But the drugs just got in between us."

Unable to find any other answer, Thedo blames himself. He cannot let go of the notion that if Carl had been able to stay in baseball, his life would have taken a better course. And he fears that he undermined Carl's last chance at playing baseball for money.

Right after Carl's senior season at Crenshaw, he had an opportunity to play in a tournament that would have been heavily scouted. Just that one time, Thedo put something ahead of baseball. He told his son he couldn't play, that he had to go with the rest of the Jones clan to a family reunion down in Texas.

The extended family didn't get together that much. Thedo had come from East Texas, right on the border near Shreveport, Louisiana. He liked his children to see their kin and get a sense of the South.

But this trip in 1979 looms for Thedo Jones as a chance he stole from his son. "I might have played a little part against Carl myself," he says. "This coach really wanted to take him to Florida to play. He called me, and I said Carl can't do that; he's got to come to Texas. I made a mistake. He could have gone down to that tournament and really set it on fire. He did that a lot of times, you know. And then they would have seen him and they would've been all over him scouting him."

I tell Mr. Jones that I don't think one moment like that determines the course of a life. Carl, for whatever reason, had a weakness, a vulnerability—his father preventing him from getting scouted in one last baseball setting could not have turned him into a drug addict. Mr. Jones has heard this before, but he still cannot let it go.

"When one of your children does wrong, you play things back in your head, you know, you ask yourself what could I maybe have done different," he says. "People say, well, you can't think that way. But they're not in your position. You can't help it—you can't *not* think that way."

Carl, in recent years, has been incarcerated hundreds of miles from home. Thedo Jones has never visited him, but it's not the distance that stops him; it's the pain. He fears he could not endure seeing his son behind bars.

"It hurts me too much that he's there, and that they got him for so long on that petty stuff," Thedo says. "I don't want to be face-to-face with it. I know I should visit him, but I just want to stay away from it."

Carl writes to his family and calls collect. They write back and send along little things he needs. Thedo shows me a letter from prison that has just arrived with a request for a new electric Norelco razor, along with a beard and mustache trimmer.

Thedo is going to buy him those items and get them right in the mail. But he can't give Carl everything he asks for. It costs too much. Plus, Thedo still believes you spoil your children if you give them everything they ask for. (Darryl Strawberry, when he was still riding high and making big-league money, used to put money in Carl's prison account. He once sent a money order for $600, but that flow of cash stopped many years ago.)

A lot of Carl's letters and calls home have to do with baseball. He plays on the prison teams. He's still good, still making his family proud. "Even where he is, he gets certificates—first-place team, outstanding player, and so forth," Thedo says. "He sends them to me to keep, and I have them all."

Carl is also still a tough man on the ballfield, and all heart. He was playing shortstop in an all-star game in jail not too long ago. A ground ball hit a rock and popped him in the mouth. (The grooming of prison fields is apparently not the best.) Carl called time-out. His mouth was bleeding, and he had lost a couple of teeth. But all he did was wash his mouth out, trot back out to shortstop, and say, "Let's play ball."

"That's just Carl, the same Carl as always," his sister Tahitha says. "Let's play ball, no matter what."

Tahitha says that Carl is "keeping his skills up." He should have been a big-leaguer. "I will believe that till the day I die," she says.

Carl has told his whole family: When he comes home, he is going to play ball. He doesn't care how old he is.

He has had to transfer prisons several times, often without much warning. They just tell him to pack and be ready, sometimes in the middle of a baseball season. When he gets to a new place, the first thing he does is walk out onto the exercise yard, announce himself as a ballplayer, and try to get on a team. Now that he's a little older, the young guys don't always take him to be a real ballplayer.

A few years back, when he had just arrived at Deuel Vocational Institution in Tracy, California, he went out looking for a team even before his belongings arrived. Even by Carl's loose standards, he looked unkempt. He hadn't shaved or put a comb through his hair. His clothes looked like he had slept in them. His baseball mitt hadn't yet caught up with him.

He saw a team practicing on a diamond and asked to join, but they told him they didn't need anybody. "Can I just play a little and you can decide if you could use me?" he asked. No, the answer came back—this team was the best on the yard and they were all set for players.

Carl went to the next field and got a better welcome. They let him borrow a glove. He was happy; he had himself a team. Next thing he knows, a guy from the first field—the captain of that team, who had been in the restroom—comes running over to talk to Carl. He eagerly shakes Carl's hand.

"You're C.J. from Lancaster, right?" he says.

Lancaster was Carl's old prison, where he had established a reputation as a ballplayer, one that had traveled some through the California state prison system.

Carl says yeah, he's C.J.

"When you told them back there you were C.J. from Lancaster, those guys didn't know about you. But I know who you are. You can come back and practice with us."

But Carl said no thanks, he was content where he was. The team that had just welcomed him seemed like nice guys and good enough players. He'd stay right where he was.

Carl had never played on a ball team that he didn't help win. And this would be no different. That season, not too surprisingly, a new baseball champion was crowned at Deuel Vocational.

The first time I visited with his family, I hadn't yet been to see Carl in prison. But he knew I was going to be in Los Angeles, at his old house on

Ninety-third Street, and made sure to call. Carl and his father talked for a few minutes, then Thedo handed me the phone.

I asked Carl how he was doing. "I'm still knockin' the cover off the ball," he said, laughing. "These young boys in here, they can't believe how good I hit it."

*   *   *

Polly Klaas's father argued for the passage of the three strikes law as "a former liberal who now understands the need to get tough." He wanted habitual violent offenders locked away for life. But after the law passed and was put into practice, Klaas became one of its first and most vocal opponents. He said that he had no idea that the way the law was written, a defendant could get life in prison for breaking into a garage and stealing a stereo.

"I've had my stereo stolen, and I've had my daughter stolen," Klaas said. "I believe I know the difference."

That, to my mind, is about as clear a critique of three strikes as I have heard. But on this issue, clarity and reason have been trumped by fear and politics, as well as by an especially cruel reality of the American economy: One man's life sentence is another's job opportunity.

Earning an hourly wage to guard another human being, to hammer nails into a new penitentiary, to drive the truck that delivers the food to the prison gates, is good and honest work. It can be tough work, especially if you have contact with inmates. And it can pay well.

A lot of people, especially in the rural, struggling communities where new prisons get built, want that work. They see it as a godsend. A blessing.

The equation could not be simpler: The more prisoners there are, the more of these jobs there are. And the harsher the sentencing, the more prisoners there will be.

Of 7,626 defendants serving life on third strikes in California, about 350 are in jail for petty theft. Many others are serving out life terms on drug charges—possession, not dealing.

Several three-strikers have been very young men. In 1998, Andre Wilks, nineteen, of North Hills, California, with two purse snatchings on his rap sheet, smashed a car window and stole a cell phone. That was strike three. He got life in prison. Because of his youth, he has the potential to be a long-term job provider.

Some of the cases have formed the basis for court challenges, and have attracted news coverage: A man sentenced for stealing golf clubs from a pro shop; another for lifting children's videotapes from a Kmart; a third for stealing a pizza. In Alabama, another three strikes state: a Vietnam veteran and father of three, thirteen years from his last brush with the law, caught buying pot from a police informant and sentenced to life in prison.

But in most instances, these sentences do not make any kind of news, not even a community newspaper. Men like Carl Jones, addicts with no money or status, represented by overworked public defenders or court-appointed counsel, are just quietly jailed. They have no advocates on the outside, no resources, no recourse. They settle into their prison cells, petition their loved ones for essentials, find what joy they can, and hope for some kind of a miracle.

California, so often in the vanguard of social trends, pioneered the three strikes concept, and thirty-seven other states have passed some form of it. California's remains the toughest: It allows nonviolent crimes to count as third strikes, and in some cases even elevates crimes from misdemeanors to felonies in order to get a third strike. Three-strikers, nationwide, still make up a relatively small percentage of prison population, but they are the leading edge of a trend toward harsher sentencing.

The sheer numbers of men imprisoned (and they are still mostly men) may be invisible to most white, middle-class Americans, but they are readily apparent in poor black neighborhoods in every corner of America. Ten percent of black men between the ages of twenty-five and twenty-nine were behind bars in 2002; for Hispanic men in that age group, the number was 2.4 percent; and for white men, 1.2 percent. (There is no end to eye-opening statistics: One study says that a black man in America stands a one-in-four chance of being jailed at some point in his life.)

By 2003, the California prison population had reached 162,000—up from 23,000 in 1980. The state has built twenty-one new penitentiaries since 1986, including eight new level four, or maximum security, facilities. California operates the largest penal system in the Western world. The writer Eric Schlosser has pointed out that it jails more people than the nations of France, Great Britain, Germany, Japan, Singapore, and the Netherlands combined.

California's budget for prisons has risen to a staggering $5.3 billion dollars a year—*$5.3 billion.*

Nationwide, more than two million Americans are in prison—double the inmate population of just a decade ago. The prison population increased 2.6 percent in 2002, the last census of the Bureau of Justice Statistics, despite a decline in serious crime over the same period. (The U.S. imprisons an estimated half million more inmates than the more populous and repressive nation of China.)

About one thousand new jails have been built in the last twenty years, but they fill up as soon as they're built—and not because of increased crime. What fills the bunks is the trend toward incarceration for nonviolent offenses. In 1980, half of those entering state prisons were nonviolent offenders; by 2000, that percentage had climbed to two-thirds.

Three-strikes laws and long, mandatory terms for nonviolent crimes have increasingly come into question, and not just from liberals or self-described former liberals like Marc Klaas. The *Los Angeles Times* has editorialized against what it called California's "savage sentencing laws." The conservative *San Diego Times-Union* called for a reassessment of three strikes.

In 1999, *Time* magazine, hardly some left-leaning opinion journal, published a story under the headline "A Get-Tough Policy That Failed." *Time* wrote that three-strikes laws "insult justice."

But the magazine pointed out that the law, rather than being ripe for change, was so "politically untouchable" that (former) Gov. Pete Wilson had vetoed a bill simply to study the law's effects. "Wilson probably knew what the study would conclude: while three-strikes laws sound great to the public, they aren't working. A growing number of states and private groups have scrutinized these and other 'mandatory-minimum laws,' the generic name for statutes forcing judges to impose designated terms. The studies are finding that the laws cost enormous amounts of money, largely to lock up such nonviolent folks as teenage drug couriers, dope-starved addicts and unfortunate offenders like the Iowa man who got 10 years for stealing $30 worth of steaks from a grocery store. . . ."

When I started looking into this issue, I was surprised by the strident language from such mainstream voices. To refer to a law enacted by the legislature and supported by the public as "savage," or to say that it "insults justice," is pretty strong stuff.

What drives voters more than any outrage over these sentences, however, is a fear of crime—often an exaggerated fear. Political pollsters consistently find that crime shows up as a major concern even in communities that are virtually crime-free. And that fear shapes public opinion, much more so than any level of discomfort over America's enormous inmate population.

The U.S. Supreme Court took up the three-strikes issue in 2003, hearing separate appeals involving two California inmates: Gary A. Ewing, whose third strike was the theft of three golf clubs from a pro shop; and Leandro Andrade, dealt a life term after lifting nine videotapes worth $153 from a Kmart.

Andrade was a father of three who had never been convicted of a violent crime. He was thirty-seven years old when the videotape heist earned him a fifty-years-to-life sentence that will leave him eligible for parole at the age of eighty-seven.

In both cases, the Supreme Court split 5–4 in upholding the sentences—and by extension, the constitutionality of California's three-strikes law.

Justice David Souter, in a dissenting opinion, wrote: "If Andrade's sentence is not grossly disproportionate, the principle has no meaning." Another dissenter, Justice Stephen Breyer, noted that if Andrade were sentenced in the federal courts rather than California, he would have received, rather than fifty years to life, twelve to eighteen months.

But Justice Sandra Day O'Connor, writing for the majority, said neither sentence was so grossly disproportionate as to violate the Eighth Amendment's prohibition against cruel and unusual punishment. While allowing that the three-strikes statute may be flawed, she stated that any criticism of the law "is appropriately directed at the legislature."

But in California (and in many other states, too) the legislature and whole political system is in service to what has been called the prison-industrial complex—powerful groups who push for tough sentencing laws because they have a political or economic interest in incarcerating the greatest possible number of human beings, and building ever more penitentiaries.

You can also think of this prison-industrial complex as a triangle. At one point of the triangle is the prison guards union, formally known as the California Correctional Peace Officers Association. The peace officers are huge givers across the California political landscape, and their money helps ensure the continued incarceration of Carl Jones and tens of thousands of others.

In a state full of immense individual and corporate wealth—Hollywood, Silicon Valley, aerospace, agribusiness, timber, oil and gas—the prison guards were the largest single contributor to former California governor Gray Davis. As of June 2003, the peace officers union had contributed $3.4 million to his campaigns. In 2003, the guards blessed Davis with a $251,000 check, his largest single gift ever.

That kind of money buys more than mere access, or a "fair hearing" as political givers like to say. No, $3.4 million from a single interest buys direct influence. It earns the contributor what it wants, and the guards union is clear about what that is.

"California prison guards rank among Sacramento's most powerful interest groups," Charles Mahtesian wrote in *Governing Magazine*, a publication of *Congressional Quarterly*. "They have been able to expand their issues beyond the usual union menu of benefits, wages and work conditions. Their purview now includes prison construction, prison management and sentencing policy."

Mahtesian called the three-strikes law the guards union's "crowning achievement."

Governor Davis, in the midst of a near-bankrupting budget crunch, cut the budget of nearly every state agency in 2003. Fees for college students soared. Indigent amputees lost their state-provided artificial limbs.

But the prison budget was *increased* $40 million—not including a $220 million onetime expense for a new death row at San Quentin. The guards got a raise. They now earn, on average, about $55,000 a year. With overtime, which is plentiful because of the chronically overcrowded penitentiaries, some make better than $100,000.

The peace officers are not partisan in a traditional sense, favoring one party over another; they throw money at whoever is in power. Before cozying up to Democrat Gray Davis, the union was known for its special relationship with his Republican predecessor, Pete Wilson.

"California Governor Pete Wilson is not known for any particular rapport with unions," the *Los Angeles Times* wrote in 1996. "But when the California Correctional Peace Officers Association speaks, the governor listens. Of all the state employees unions, CCPOA is Wilson's favorite."

At the second point of the "prison-industrial" triangle are the hundreds of companies that have an economic stake in high inmate counts. An online directory called the Corrections Yellow Pages ("the #1 place to find people and businesses in corrections") offers up a mind-boggling array of them. A small sampling, by category, would include: bedding, bomb disposal, firearms, food products, inmate phone service, information technology, mattresses, metal detection, padded cells, pepper sprays, riot control, and suicide prevention.

And at the third point of the triangle are the communities that already have a prison, or want one as a form of economic stimulus. At the height of the prison building boom in 1994, Ernie Van Sant, chief of the Correction Division's construction division, explained the allure of prison building in the state's hinterlands. "California towns see a prison as improving their economy or offsetting other losses," he said. "We're not an industrial developer. We don't use a lot of chemicals. We're somewhat recession-proof."

* * *

Carl filed an appeal of his sentence, which went first to a judicial body with an impressive-sounding name: the Court of Appeal of the State of

California, Second Appellate District. Then his case went all the way up to the California Supreme Court. All of this felt hopeful, especially when the state's highest court ruled that the court that originally sentenced Carl should reconsider.

On June 18, 1997, Los Angeles Superior Court convened a new sentencing hearing. The proceeding was nothing lofty like the closely watched three-strikes appeals that would take place in front of the U.S. Supreme Court. Carl's family came downtown to L.A.'s high-rise criminal courts complex and made their way to a small courtroom, where they were given an opportunity to beg for mercy on his behalf.

Carl was incarcerated at Lancaster then—C.J. from Lancaster—and he was transported in on a blue sheriff's bus for the proceeding. Most of his family hadn't seen him for a while, so the brief reunion was a bonus. Carl wore his blue prison jumpsuit, and his legs were shackled. His family had no opportunity to sit and actually visit with him, but they all exchanged smiles and a few brief words over a courtroom railing.

When the hearing started, Carl's sister Tahitha was the first to testify, and she kept it simple: Twenty-five years to life, she said, seemed like a long time to serve for breaking into a building and stealing absolutely nothing.

That had always seemed self-evident to Tahitha, and she had never talked to one person who believed her brother had been sentenced fairly. But she felt it needed to be said, straight out, in court. Tahitha's statement was also consistent with the legal argument made by Carl's lawyer, who urged that Carl's burglary rap be taken down to simple trespassing, which would have liberated Carl after no more than seven years served.

Next to step forward was Joe Jones, a cousin who also happened to be a police officer. He told the judges about his experiences on the street, the hard-won insights he had gained into human nature.

Some people, he said, were just bad. There were more of these dangerous individuals—people who didn't belong back on the streets, ever—than some people realized. When the prison gates got slammed shut on a man who deserved it, Joe Jones testified, he shed no tears. But he said that he could not imagine how Carl could possibly be considered among this group.

His cousin Carl, he said, had committed no violent acts and was not by nature a violent man. He was a junkie who had now accepted his flaws and, given a second chance—"and appropriate drug treatment"—would thrive on the outside.

Joe Jones cut an impressive figure. He was a weight lifter as well as a former baseball and football player. He carried himself with an erect, military bearing, and spoke in a deep baritone. He concluded by pausing, then looking each judge in the eye. "I implore you," he said, speaking slowly and looking from one judge to the other, "to give my cousin another chance. If you do that, I can promise you that he will move forward with his life."

When it was Thedo's turn to speak, he did so, as always, from the heart. He sought to give the judges a context for Carl's behavior—not to *excuse* it, which he knew would not go over well, but at least to try to explain. By necessity, he also sought to explain Carl's behavior during his trial back in 1994, which in its own way was as bizarre as the break-in at Crenshaw High, and just as damaging to his future.

At trial, Carl had raged that the police officers lied in their testimony. He came off as disrespectful to law enforcement, the court, and even to his own counsel.

The whole reason that his case had even gone to trial was that he had rejected a deal that would have resulted in a shorter sentence—albeit, six years in prison for his fruitless break-in. Carl certainly had the right to proclaim his innocence, but doing so had cost him dearly.

The first thing Thedo told the judges was that if he had been fully available to his son back in 1994, Carl would never have shown the court such disrespect. Thedo said he would have personally seen to that, but at the time, Thedo was dealing with another family tragedy. Carl's trial came in the immediate aftermath of the death of Tyrone Jones, Carl's brother—Thedo and Werllean's youngest boy—who succumbed to chronic kidney disease.

"I had just lost my son right before his trial," Thedo Jones told the judges. "My baby boy, I lost him. His kidneys went out on him. He was twenty years old."

Thedo said if he had been more involved, Carl would not have displayed such a "street attitude" at trial. He would not have denied the obvious fact that he had broken into the school, or foolishly imagined that he could beat the rap.

"What I'm asking," Thedo said, "is just for Carl to be given a fair chance to get a new life."

Carl was never the most eloquent person. And he had already hurt himself once by saying all the wrong things in court. So he did not testify.

"A lot of lawyers advise their clients not to testify in these hearings because they can get up and say amazingly unhelpful things. So it wasn't unusual that he let his lawyer and family speak for him," says Barbara Smith, who represented Carl before California's appellate courts, and wrote the briefs that won him the new sentencing hearing.

Smith has been a defense lawyer for twenty-five years, and like most veteran defenders is clear-eyed about her client base. She once gave a client money to copy a sheaf of documents, then learned that the cash was used as seed money for a prison heroin business.

"I represent mostly murderers," Smith tells me. "They are not nice guys. Carl was a nice guy. Maybe he isn't the guy you want living next door to you, I don't know. But he was a minimal offender. He was caught empty-handed outside the school. He had no burglary tools or gloves. Maybe he intended to steal, but he was so messed up he was not competent to do so."

Smith remembers Carl's as the "eraser case" because he had yanked the eraser shelf from the wall. She never told his family to expect a sentence reduction—she didn't want them to be disappointed if it didn't happen—but she was almost sure his life term would be softened.

The higher courts had already cleared away the technical, legal questions. As she saw it, they had empowered, even invited the L.A. Superior Court to give her client a break.

"It was just a mercy thing," she says. "It could have been done on that basis."

But the court found Carl unworthy of mercy. One reason, ironically, was Carl's honesty. Or his stupidity, depending on how you look at it.

Carl was no angel, but being straightforward had been a hallmark of his, a strength. Brooks Hurst, the old Crenshaw coach, always appreciated that Carl "would be direct with you, no matter what the consequences. He wasn't sneaky in any way."

Before his initial sentencing, a probation officer asked Carl (as every defendant is asked) if he had committed other crimes for which he had not been caught. It's a safe assumption that in most cases, the honest answer to this question is *yes*, especially when the defendant is a drug addict who has been desperate for money. Carl answered truthfully, a mistake that would be recalled by a series of judges.

The Superior Court, at his resentencing hearing, noted that "appellant had indicated to the probation officer that he had committed additional crimes for which he was not apprehended and prosecuted." The court said it "had a duty to protect the public" from Carl, who it termed a "proven recidivist" and "career criminal."

Barbara Smith sighs. She has seen detectives and probation officers tell defendants that "confession is good for the soul." But, she says, "The ones who get hammered are the ones who are candid. My clients who do the best are the total hardened assholes who just sit there and don't say a thing."

In the court rulings on Carl, it was clear that he had been issued a virtual *fourth* strike—for behaving poorly at his initial trial. Carl had been a jerk, and the legal system could not forgive him.

In June 1998, Carl's case went back up to the state's highest court. Barbara Smith had found one last avenue of appeal, a thin thread: Carl had not been brought back in to hear the Superior Court issue its ruling, the one declining to shorten his sentence. He had only been informed in writing.

Smith appealed, on the grounds that both the California and U.S. Constitutions guarantee a man the right to stand before a judge and hear his fate. She also noted that Carl's probation report had not been updated, so that all the court had in front of it was a vision of Carl in 1994, the drug addict right off the streets. If four years in jail had taught him anything, the court had no way of knowing.

The State Supreme Court rejected this argument and harked right back to Carl's disrespectful attitude in 1994. "Burglary of a school room is a serious offense, especially when it is considered in light of appellant's

previous record, which includes two previous offenses of residential burglary," the court ruled. "Appellant has an aggravated criminal history. Appellant's attitude toward his own counsel, the police and the criminal
proceedings illustrate he is deeply entrenched in a criminal lifestyle. He
would not accept responsibility for his crimes even in the face of overwhelming evidence of guilt. The only factors in mitigation are that his
family is supportive of him and loves him and that the source of his criminal activity is arguably drug abuse."

The judges seemed particularly incensed that Carl had accused his
arresting officers of lying. It certainly wasn't a smart thing to do. On the
other hand, it is hardly a secret that police officers sometimes do lie under
oath—and that police in L.A. have a particularly uneven relationship
with the truth.

Barbara Smith believes that officers probably did lie in Carl's case.
She doesn't doubt that he was inside Crenshaw High, but she questions
whether any officer actually saw him coming out the window—which is
what put Carl inside the school, rather than just lurking outside.

"They said they saw him coming out the window," she says. "Did
they really?"

But the court made Carl's accusation that the cops lied a central reason for keeping him in prison until at least age fifty-eight. On September
22, 1998, it stated, "Appellant's attitude that the officers lied to secure his
conviction was a clue that appellant's attitude was so bad that he would
not change."

Wouldn't change for the next quarter century? Would never come to
his senses and figure out what to say and what not to say? Would not stop
taking illicit substances and stumbling like a fool into empty high schools?

No, not a chance. The legal system had taken its measure of Carl
Jones, the straight-talking, dirty-uniformed, clutch-hitting catcher of the
1979 Crenshaw High Cougars, the almost champions of the whole damn
city of Los Angeles, from sea to valley.

He was irredeemable, unfit for freedom.

* * *

I went to see Carl in prison straight from my visit with Nelson Whiting in Fallon, Nevada. Just pointed the car west and drove for four hundred miles—through the Donner Pass, with the peaks of the Sierra Nevada above me and the crystalline blue of Lake Tahoe below, and into California, headed for the flat, fertile acres of the San Joaquin Valley.

I felt blessed. Blessed to be alive. Blessed to be free. Blessed to be experiencing the singularly surreal feeling of finding yourself somewhere that you had never quite imagined being.

I was three thousand miles from home, and a long way, too, from the other place that I had been sort of living—the inner-city L.A. of the Boys of Crenshaw. The sense of remove, the natural beauty, the passing of miles on sparsely traveled highways—it was all so quiet that even the radio felt like an intrusion, a violation of some spiritual space.

I thought about Nelson Whiting, whom I had just left behind, and the Spartan life he led at his lonely outpost, one that he had methodically pared down for the sake of his own preservation. He was in exile from everything he knew, maybe from himself.

He had put off his music, his passion, and joined the military so that he could be anywhere but L.A. His self-discipline and sacrifice had become a habit.

The weekend did not begin until the cars were washed. He did not feed even one quarter into the ubiquitous slot machines, because he didn't like games of chance. He canceled his long-distance service because he was spending too much money calling back home. (The pay-as-you-go phone card system cut you right off when you exceeded your budgeted minutes.) And just two cookies in that brown bag lunch, and no sweets after that.

Nelson had not seen much moderation growing up in L.A. There was no model for it. People either abstained, or they fell into the abyss.

This was a defining feature of the poor neighborhoods that all the Boys of Crenshaw had grown up in—the sense of a strong pull from opposing forces. The streets pulled one way. The church and some strong black women, matriarchs like Nelson's mother Emma, pulled the other way. You eventually had to declare yourself in one camp or the other; you couldn't dabble and straddle. What might be construed as "mischief" in a suburban community could all but end your life in South Central.

Nelson was fussy and self-contained, but safe. Carl had been just the opposite. He was sloppy, so lacking in discipline and self-respect that rather than fleeing from trouble, he ran blindly toward it. I spent most of those four hundred miles thinking about Carl—and about the line between personal responsibility and justice.

Whenever I went off on a trip to research this book, my children always wanted to know if I would be seeing Carl or his family. As far as they were concerned, this was his book. Darryl Strawberry? He didn't tug at them like Carl Jones.

My little boy must have asked me a dozen times, "Daddy, isn't there anything you can do to get Carl out of jail?" With a child's sense of moral outrage, he just couldn't accept it when I said I didn't think there was.

I was certainly enraged at the whole simpleminded concept of three strikes. For God's sake, it doesn't even hold up as a baseball metaphor. Three strikes and you're out? Well, yes, but then you get three or four more at bats in the same game. And then hundreds of at bats over a whole spring, summer, and fall of baseball. Some players in the big leagues strike out 150 times a season and get paid very good money to do so.

Baseball is a sport of forgiveness and opportunity. Your turn in the lineup keeps coming back around.

But as angry as I was at the system that jailed him, I was also mad at Carl. He had been screwed by the state of California, but he had given the justice system every opportunity to do just that. Except for his qualities as a ballplayer and teammate, there had been nothing admirable about the way he had lived his life.

Among his other failings, he had fathered three children with three different women—Carl Jr., twenty-four; Kewan, twenty; and Robin, eighteen—all of whom have grown up with a father they have known mainly as a crack addict or prison inmate.

So it was not quite true that Carl's crimes had been victimless. Nonviolent, yes. But he had hurt some people.

Carl had been raised by two parents. His father had stayed close to him and even made him work, which is supposed to be some predictor of stability and future success. By South Central standards, he even had some money in his family.

And he had pissed it all away and brought nothing but sadness on his loved ones. And so, too, had his brother Donald, the talented pitcher who lost his senior season at Crenshaw after attacking the gang member with a baseball bat. Donald was a three-striker, too, jailed for life. Same damn thing: drugs.

At one point, I asked Carl's old teammate George Cook why he thought the Jones boys had fared so badly after growing up in what seemed like such a solid household. His deadpan reply was classic. "I think folks have been studying that kind of thing for a long time, haven't they?"

* * *

From a distance, the low-slung, dull white buildings of Deuel Vocational Institution, set down amid tens of thousands of acres of San Joaquin Valley farmland, appear as a series of little bumps on an otherwise unrelieved agricultural landscape. As I got closer, I could see that the structures, one indistinguishable from the other, were lined up side by side in two long rows for maximum use of space.

It did not take much imagination to see these structures as livestock pens.

Deuel, about one hour east of San Francisco, opened in 1953. It was expanded in 1959, 1981, and 1993. It provides jobs for 1,161 people, including about 800 guards.

The prison's current "designed bed space," or ideal capacity, is 1,725. On the day I was to arrive, the inmate population was more than twice that: 3,885.

Deuel has an annual budget of $89 million.

I had exchanged several letters with Carl, and he was anticipating my visit. I had also been in contact with the media relations staff of the prison and the warden. But I arrived to an unpleasant surprise—Carl Jones was not there.

Two days earlier, he had been transferred. It had nothing to do with my impending visit. In fact, the staff at Deuel had been nothing but professional and cooperative in their dealings with me. But it had just come time for Carl to be transferred, and some other wing of the California Department of Corrections had arranged it.

After my initial shock, my next thought was one of gratitude. Carl's new prison wasn't too far away. (California's a big state; he could have been down on the Mexican border.) He was at Folsom State Prison, about two hours away, the ancient penitentiary memorialized in Johnny Cash's "Folsom Prison Blues." The song is about a much tougher hombre than Carl. "I shot a man in Reno," Cash sings, "just to watch him die."

"Give Carl a big ole hug for me when you see him," his sister Tahitha had said to me. But when I finally got to see him, that wasn't possible. Carl was without certain privileges, although not because he had done anything wrong; as a newcomer to Folsom, he was still on Fish Row, which meant that we could not sit together in the visitor's room.

He was led into a cinder-block cubicle, where he sat on one side of a thick glass window. I sat on the other side. We talked through the telephones bolted onto the walls on each side of the glass.

Carl's face was open and expressive. He looked healthy, although I did notice the missing teeth from where the ball had taken a bad hop on that rocky prison diamond and smashed him in the mouth. He thanked me for coming, and apologized for the uncomfortable way we had to communicate.

"We should be sitting out there," he said, looking behind me, where the wives, children, and parents of inmates were sitting on couches and at small tables, visiting in a more intimate way. "I'm really sorry we have to do it this way."

I told him it was okay, not to worry about it. I was curious about how he spent a typical day in prison. What did he do to occupy himself? What could he possibly do to fill the days until July 23, 2021—his first opportunity for parole?

"I just hang on the yard," he said. "You can be out there from 8:30 to

11:30, then there's lunch, then you go back out there from 12:30 to 3:30. I play my baseball. I play basketball. Sometimes if I'm tired I just talk. I used to lift weights, but that was outlawed because the guards didn't like us getting so muscular."

Some inmates can stay out on the yard all day if they like, even through lunch. But as a lifer, Carl must go back inside twice a day, for count.

In the beginning of his incarceration, he used to get into fights, which he now finds necessary on only the rarest of occasions. "I'm better now at talking my way out of situations," he says. "That's one thing you learn after a while. You give respect; you get respect. But sometimes, in here, you do have to demand respect. So I can still fight if I have to. That's never gonna change in here. You can't be someone who doesn't stand up for yourself if the need arises."

At Deuel Vocational, Carl never had a job, despite the name of the institution, which implies that it trains inmates for some useful vocation on the outside. But the explosion in the inmate population has created unemployment behind bars. Deuel was too crowded to provide job training for everyone, and lifers understandably were given low priority. (The concept of rehabilitation barely exists anymore in America's prisons, and with so many prisoners locked away for such long stretches, there may be less logic to it. Training Carl for some kind of job he won't be able to perform until he is fifty-eight cannot be considered cost-effective.)

At Folsom, which is somewhat less overcrowded, Carl did hope to find work, just to cut the boredom. He was eager, too, to get some time behind him so he could accrue some of the little perks that only come with inmate seniority.

For example, at Folsom he got assigned to a top bunk, which he did not prefer. There was no ladder, so he had to climb up into bed at night and crawl down in the morning.

By the side of his bed, he told me, is a shelf with enough room to keep a fan, his hygiene products, and what he calls "legal mail"—communications from the courts or his lawyer. With his appeals having run their course, the legal mail doesn't pile up like it once did, but Carl still considers keeping that mail one of the shelf's primary functions.

Carl also has a TV in his cell. Inmates watch a lot of TV: sports, mostly, as well as movies piped in on the prison's closed circuit system. When a good game is on, the cell block comes alive. Men up and down the rows whoop it up and shout—*Did you see that play!*—like boys at a sleepover. (The videos are not bad, either. The night before we talked, Carl said he had watched something that featured Jackie Chan and Chris Rock.)

Dinner gets served early, before six P.M., usually cheap cuts of meat— hot dogs or sausages, sometimes burritos—along with plenty of starches. Carl's biggest day-to-day complaint has to do with the food. He gets hungry at night, especially if he has been playing ball during the day. A prison store sells snacks, but if he has no money to buy a bag of potato chips or a candy bar, he goes to bed with his stomach growling and stays hungry till breakfast.

Carl was eager to talk about baseball, Crenshaw, and Darryl Strawberry.

He wants to watch a lot more baseball than most of the other guys on his cell block, so except for the dead of summer he sometimes has to settle for basketball or football. His favorite player is Roberto Alomar, a second baseman of such balletic grace that he seems to float above the diamond.

His affection for Alomar surprises me; I tell Carl that I heard he himself wasn't exactly graceful, that the stories consistently have him caked in dirt by game's end because of his fearless, determined play. "Yeah, that was me," he says. "I like those kind of guys, too; I liked Pete Rose."

Carl understandably feels a kinship with Darryl Strawberry. So many of the others are angry with Darryl, fed up, uncomprehending of how he could squander his great gift. But Carl understands someone having a weakness for drugs.

He remembers Darryl warning him off drugs. "He would say to me, 'Carl, you've got to leave that shit alone.' He would act like he was really mad at me." Now, he wonders if Darryl maybe was trying to convince himself.

"Will you give Darryl my address?" he wanted to know. "I would really like to hear from him."

I told him that I already had, that Darryl had promised to be in touch, and Carl flashed a wide, gap-toothed smile.

*   *   *

The whole time we were talking, Carl's eyes kept darting to the people behind me, the family members sitting in the visiting room with their inmate loved ones. I had seen these people in the parking lot starting at dawn, when we had all arrived at Folsom to line up for our visit.

The women sat in their cars, with the rearview mirrors lowered, and meticulously made themselves up. In nearly every car was a woman working a makeup brush, a tube of lipstick, or an eyeliner pencil. When they were done putting themselves together, they moved on to their children—dabbing cheeks with napkins to remove the residue of breakfast from little boys' faces, straightening collars, combing and recombing the girls' hair.

The idea is to give the illusion, at least, that everything is fine at home: The women are keeping themselves up; the children are clean, well-clothed, and cared for.

In the waiting room, a middle-aged black woman—someone's mother, I guessed—looked like she was on her way to church on Easter Sunday. She wore a tailored black skirt, a smart-looking red blazer, and a wide-brimmed black hat.

Several women pushed strollers. The visitors were a mix of races and, to some extent, classes. Many of them clearly knew each other from years of being together in prison visiting areas. A man in a corduroy jacket and wire-rimmed glasses looked like he could have been a professor. His wife greeted a young black woman, picked up her toddler, and said, "I haven't seen him in so long. He is getting so *big*!"

A form of multiculturalism prevailed here, although not one I've ever seen celebrated. All of these loved ones of inmates—white, black, and Hispanic—were leveled and brought together by a shared sense of sadness and pain.

No matter how many times you have been inside a prison, it is a powerful experience. You are let in, temporarily, to a locked cage. That's what a prison is, regardless of how many acres it sprawls over or how modern its design. They are medieval, remnants of mankind's primitive nature.

Carl, who on the day I visit is in his eighth year of confinement, realizes that he keeps looking past me and into the open room, toward this sea of faces. He apologizes. I glance behind me to see what he's looking at. It's a family: inmate father, his wife, two little girls sitting quietly in matching blue dresses and red ribbons in their hair.

"The thing is, I ain't seen real people in a long time," Carl says.

I'm not sure at first what he means.

"You know, people who aren't inmates or COs [corrections officers]. That's all you see if you don't get any visitors. You don't get to see no normal people."

Carl, not surprisingly, is deeply cynical about the justice system. He believes the purpose of him staying in prison is "so guards can have jobs." He can't see any other interest society would have in keeping him locked up. He copes in prison and stays out of trouble, but the best prison jobs and the most favored treatment go to "the snitches. And I ain't ever gonna be one of them," he says.

(If Carl ever gets on a witness stand again, he will need to be heavily coached. He still blurts out whatever he believes to be the truth.)

He does not have much to say about the series of crimes that landed him here (what *could* he say?) except that he regrets them, and would not repeat his mistakes. "Darryl Strawberry couldn't handle that crack. I couldn't handle it. Nobody can. You think you can when you get into it, but you can't."

He is not one of those inmates who spends time in the prison law library, researching his case and seeking grounds for appeal. "I can't beat this myself," he says. "I don't have the smarts to do the legal stuff."

He prays. Every day. It's all he knows to do. "I pray to God for another chance. I just beg him. I know what I'd do if I got out. I'd pour cement, just like I was doin'. I never minded that, because it was competitive to me. I liked thinking I could become the best person out there at pouring cement.

"The other thing I'd do is get me a little team to coach and give them all the baseball knowledge I have, all that stuff Coach Hurst taught us. Even if they were real young boys, I'd teach them to play proper baseball, the same way we did at Crenshaw."

CHAPTER EIGHT

The Good Stuff

"Where is the good stuff?" asks Darryl Strawberry, who has hit home runs in World Series games, made millions, fathered children.

It is April 14, 1999, and he sits behind the wheel of a gold-colored Ford Expedition. He carries a $20 bill and credit cards in his Louis Vuitton wallet. His left hip pocket is stuffed with a wad of bills, $1,159.

If Crenshaw High was the beginning of the legend and the promise of Darryl Strawberry, Superstar—the first flash of the phenom who would open our eyes to what was possible on the field of play—this is the beginning of the end.

And in between? Let it be said, just for the moment, that Darryl delivered. He truly was epic, larger than life and achingly human. So much so that sometimes you wanted to avert your eyes.

"I am the good stuff," says Kellie Daniel, as she sidles up to the vehicle. Darryl is parked near Cafe Con Trey, which shares a stretch of highway on the outskirts of downtown Tampa, Florida, with a bail bondsman, a liquor store, and a billboard that asks sinners to turn to Jesus. The area is a geographical void, a space, a nowhere land. How does a famous American find his way to such a place? Darryl is drawn here, utterly defenseless against his worst impulses. He suffers from a version of a compromised immune system; he cannot fend off the bad stuff.

Darryl, at this point in 1999, is thirty-seven years old and still a valued member of the world champion New York Yankees. The team has left Florida to begin the regular season. Darryl's wife, Charisse, and their children await him in the family's rented New Jersey home.

The previous October, Darryl had suffered a new setback after it seemed like everything that could happen to him already had: He was diagnosed with colon cancer and underwent surgery to remove the malignancy.

Darryl had started out as a Herculean figure, the strapping young slugger. Now, he is Job. A recovering drug addict (or a lapsed one, depending on the day) with a bad back, gimpy knee, cancer, tax troubles, and serial criminal problems, he lives under the bright lights of Yankee Stadium—and in the startling flash of the mug shot photo.

He has been cleared by his cancer doctors to play baseball again, and has only stayed behind in Tampa to rehabilitate his latest knee injury. The Yankees expect him back in a matter of weeks. When he gets to New York, that will mark the beginning of his third baseball life, or his fourth, or fifth . . . who can keep track?

His agent told him earlier this evening: "You're going to have a great year, Darryl. You're going to be healthy. You're going to put up numbers. You're going to make $2.5 million."

But just two hours after that conversation, he is bantering with Kellie Daniel, Tampa police officer, a decoy in a prostitution sting. "How can I get some good stuff to party with?" Strawberry asks.

From anyone on the street, she says.

He says he wants to "party" with her; she asks what exactly he wants.

"I want it all," he says.

"You mean you want straight sex?"

"Yes," he answers, and when she asks how much he is willing to spend, he says $50.

Officer Daniel gives a hand signal, and her superior officer drives up. Sgt. Marc Hamlin, five years younger than Darryl, grew up in Queens, New York, and cheered him maybe a couple of hundred times from the cheap seats at Shea Stadium. He has seen Darryl at nightspots. He's a huge fan, one of those New Yorkers who invested in the Mets' top draft pick right at the beginning, followed him from the moment he was a callow eighteen-year-old fresh out of Crenshaw High.

"Oh, my God!" the officer says to himself as the spotlight from a nearby squad car illuminates the sad, ashamed face of Darryl Strawberry.

A search turns up half a gram of cocaine in Darryl's wallet, as well as traces on his Automobile Club of Southern California membership card. When Hamlin asks if the residue is crack, Darryl says no, it is "powder"—cocaine in the form that the higher classes prefer it. The officer takes this as an expression of pride: In the midst of this pathetic roadside bust, Darryl wants to make clear that he is no crackhead. He is a higher order of drug abuser.

Darryl is charged, and ultimately pleads no contest to solicitation of prostitution and cocaine possession. Hamlin's report states that Darryl Strawberry "continually apologized and was very remorseful. . . . He asked several times if there was anything that we could do to change the situation because this was going to ruin his career."

Local address?

"One Steinbrenner Drive," he says. The address of the Yankees spring training site.

*   *   *

Darryl had long seen himself on a precipice, weak and wobbly, in constant peril of falling. All the hype and praise that he had internalized did him no good at all; it never metabolized into actual confidence. It didn't give him a Jordanesque arrogance. It was utterly useless.

In his rookie season, he told a writer that he felt the weight of high expectations, but didn't want to put too much pressure on himself. "I don't want to fall down, you know? I want to continue on the uphill."

The 1999 bust in Tampa set into motion a final fall from baseball—and, ultimately, prison time. But not before George Steinbrenner took him back one last time.

The crusty Yankees owner had a soft spot for Darryl, made him a special recipient of his beneficence. Big Daddy Steinbrenner. Years before, he had given a cocaine abuser and talented relief pitcher named Steve Howe countless chances after the rest of baseball wrote Howe off. The former Cleveland shipbuilder, famously tough and demanding, was also forgiving of human frailty. Without Steinbrenner, Darryl might have been out of the game by the mid-1990s.

But employing Darryl (or Howe) was not solely an act of mercy. Steinbrenner reached out to him partly for the same reason the Little League coach plied Darryl with free chicken and sodas: He could get something back in return.

The best of Darryl resided in the left side of the batter's box, waggling that bat, lifting the front foot, uncoiling his powerful frame. Cancer-ridden, drug-addled, in trouble with the law, Darryl still had it. No other player in Steinbrenner's stable could make Yankee Stadium come alive in quite the same way.

Darryl had one more burst of baseball in him. He appeared in twenty-four regular-season games in 1999. He didn't play particularly well, but typically came to life in the postseason, contributing two home runs and helping the Yankees get to yet another World Series.

It was one more unlikely resurrection: a World Series ring, six months after seemingly hitting bottom. But that was the last baseball stat line of his life.

Before the 2000 season, Darryl tested positive for cocaine. Baseball suspended him for one year. Then his cancer recurred, and he had surgery to remove a kidney. The following September, he was arrested for driving while impaired, a violation of his 1999 probation.

The judge sentenced him to two years of "community control," a combination of residential drug treatment and house arrest. What followed were several more violations of probation and numerous threats of prison time, just narrowly averted.

A handful of his friends sat in a small courtroom at a probation hearing in 2000 at which Darryl pleaded for his freedom. Among them was Dwight Gooden, who long ago in 1980s New York shared with Darryl a searing stardom and a sense of youthful invincibility. In the courtroom that morning, Darryl, looking gaunt and dispirited, folded his six-foot-five frame into the witness box. Gooden sat impassively, staring straight ahead, his face betraying nothing but worry.

Darryl and Doc, the Mets' young stars, had owned New York fifteen years ago. But on this day, all of that seemed like fifty years ago. They both looked old, older than they had any right to be.

"I'm not a danger to society," Darryl told Circuit Court Judge Florence Foster. "I've never harmed nobody. I never will. I'd rather go ahead and kill myself, but the reason I haven't killed myself is my five children. It wouldn't be fair to them."

Darryl got the lenience he sought. (Just like he nearly always did.) "If we were to analogize to a nine-inning baseball game, Darryl Strawberry is at bat in the bottom of the ninth with two strikes against him," Judge Foster said, just before announcing that she was declining to impose jail time. "He has proved he is a winner on the field. Now he must prove he is a winner off the field."

But Darryl continued to lapse. The arrest at the seamy Tampa intersection had been just the beginning of a long spiral down.

* * *

"I had a cloudy day today," Darryl tells me one evening. "You know, I woke up, and it was all gray outside. And that's how I felt all day. I was kind of down."

In the spring of 2001, Darryl is at Healthcare Connections in

Tampa, a drug rehabilitation program that Judge Foster sent him to instead of prison. For so many years, as a baseball star, no rules were enforced on him; now, he was living like a teenager sent to his room without privileges.

We have been talking by telephone over several consecutive evenings because contact with the media is one of the many things his addiction counselors want to eliminate from his life. They believe it to be at cross purposes with the therapeutic goal of "ego deflation." A couple of times when we talk, I can hear Motown music—the Supremes, the Four Tops— playing in his room. It reminds me how old Darryl is, how long he has been a part of the landscape.

He has no thought of playing baseball again. It has been more than a year since he even held a bat in his hands, and he has lost a lot of weight; he weighs about what he did in his early years with the Mets. He has been residing in an apartment near the rehab center with three other men. "We have to do for ourselves," he says. "We clean. We cook. We grilled some steaks the other night, and they came out pretty good."

That morning, he says, he participated in group therapy—"process work," he calls it. "It's twelve-step work. It depends what step you're on. Today, we talked about childhood issues."

His free time is spent reading the Bible and various meditations on the subject of recovery. He can watch TV only on weekends. His family visits regularly, and he has been permitted to spend some time with them at the home they rent in nearby Lutz, Florida. He tells me that he is looking forward to a "sleepover pass," an opportunity to spend the night with his wife and children rather than having to return after his day visit. He has worked hard and pushed himself in rehab to earn the privilege.

"You get to certain steps in your recovery, more privileges come along with that," he explains. "You always want things sooner than you can have them, but that's not their agenda here. They don't want to work you back into life too fast."

He has had countless hours of treatment for substance abuse, starting in 1990. I ask if it ever bores him. "I'm not gonna sit here and tell you it doesn't," he says. "I'd be tellin' a tale if I said that. But when it gets boring is when you really have to sit there and hear what has to be said."

There are people like Darryl in every generation—Charlie Parker, Judy Garland, Robert Downey Jr.—artists and entertainers who bring great pleasure to everyone but themselves, stone-cold addicts who can't keep it together. They rarely have insight into their own lives, and never a satisfying answer to the inevitable question: How could you throw it all away? If they did, they wouldn't be in the spot they're in.

Darryl is no different. He doesn't have answers, he has feelings: sadness, faith, fear, regret, love, shame, hope, resignation, gratitude. "I'm not in a disappointment part of my life," he says to me. It is his way of saying that he will not deal in sharp angles or blame, he will do only so much revisiting of fact.

Darryl has contradictory explanations for why he could not fulfill his promise. He loved being so physically gifted but hated the expectations that came with those gifts, the feeling that he could not measure up no matter what. He loved New York and especially New York fans—"God could not have picked a better place for me to play"—but hated the extra attention that comes to New York ballplayers.

"Everybody was amazed at the talent I had," he says. "When I didn't do as well as people thought I should, I felt a lot of tension about that, because people figured I should never have a bad day. But that's impossible. The expectations, they frustrated me more and more inside, as a person, and that's what led to my self-destruction."

Baseball could not raise Darryl Strawberry. It couldn't be his father. It couldn't give him courage or wisdom. Baseball was his ticket out, but he emerged from inner-city L.A. as damaged goods.

Mental health professionals sometimes say that people turn to drugs and alcohol as a "coping mechanism." Darryl could never cope with emotional pain; he had no place to put it and no armor to repel it. He absorbed pain, and it ate away at him. This was equally true of deeply painful events, like his father's leaving, and of much more trivial hurts.

Consider Game 6 of the 1986 World Series. Most baseball fans remember that as the wild night at Shea Stadium when the sure-handed Red Sox first baseman Bill Buckner let a routine ground ball trickle through his legs and the Mets staged an astonishing, back-from-the-dead comeback to set up a seventh-game victory and World Series championship.

But as years passed, what Darryl recalled was his manager, Davey Johnson, removing him late in the game in a "double switch"—a common strategy used by National League managers to avoid having to pinch-hit for a pitcher. The incident came up two different times in my conversations with Darryl. He viewed it as an act of disloyalty, a terrible affront—he even, incredibly, considered it a factor that led him to heavier drinking.

(When I tell Davey Johnson of how Darryl obsessed over this incident, he laughs a little. But it is a sad laugh. "Tell Darryl that I'm sorry about the double switch," he says. "I really am.")

Along with his drug and alcohol counseling, Darryl has spent years finding God, losing Him, and finding Him again. His conversation comes out as a patois of what he has taken from various spiritual advisors and addiction counselors. You can hear him mouthing words and phrases that he remembers, groping to put them together in ways that have some meaning.

"I'm just glad," he tells reporters after returning from one of his drug episodes, "that the Lord spared me the opportunity to live and be able to see the light, because the darkness is still there and you can always fall back into that trap."

And later: "I don't care anymore about being a star in the game of baseball. I care about what my life is really about. And now my life has surrounded me in my church and loving God and that's what I'm going to continue to do. I'm going to wait on the Lord. Whatever he needs me to do, that's what I'll be doing."

In his final days with the Mets, Darryl said his teammates were too reliant on him. Their relationship to him, he said, was one of "codependency."

Lisa Strawberry, Darryl's first wife, told me that her years with Darryl, when he was with the Mets, "were like a magic carpet ride. I don't regret them, because we had some wonderful times. But we were so young. I was twenty years old when I got married. What did I know? But if I knew then what I know now, I would do it differently."

But Darryl probably could not have done it much differently, not without a lot of help. And he was in the wrong place to get that. Baseball is no good at soothing or saving souls. The business of the game, in the crass term of old baseball men, is to put asses in the seats.

There were, for sure, many in baseball who cared deeply for Darryl, among them Frank Cashen, the Mets executive who made Darryl the top draft pick in the nation. A former sportswriter and brewery executive, he counseled him as best he knew how. Right at the beginning, he had promised Ruby Strawberry he would watch over her boy. He meant it, and he believes to this day he kept his word as best he could.

Over time, Darryl left most of his baseball friends bewildered and exhausted. "When he came to the Yankees, we felt like this guy is trying to get his life together," says Willie Randolph. "He was a super guy, a model citizen. He was a guy we wanted to embrace and help. You saw him up on a podium, saying he had found Christ and so forth; you thought everything was cool. And then something would happen, and you felt tricked or duped."

Darryl did not want to trick people. He surely meant what he said at the moment he spoke the words. But he never had an intellectual framework for recovery, or for living. He went about things by rote, trying to match his behavior with key phrases. His spiritual teaching taught him that his life was in God's hands. Exempted from personal responsibility, he cut himself break after break.

When Darryl and I talked, he spoke a lot about the concept of punishment and self-punishment. Counselors told him that the pain he experienced at home as a child, he turned on himself as an adult. He believed he then extended the punishment to those in baseball who expected great things from him—even to the fans.

"The drinking and the drugging, that was a way of punishing myself and the fans, too," he says. "I figured, If you want to get negative on me, you won't get the best out of me. Don't get me wrong, every time I stepped on the field I gave my best effort. But I know if I did not drink and party so much, I would have been better."

When he returned to New York to play for the Yankees, older and already broken, he finally understood how much New Yorkers loved him. He knew, finally, that New York was forgiving of human frailty—that it was as compassionate as it was demanding. And he finally knew that he had cheated his fans. "People cared for me as a person in New York. I will take that to my grave, the feeling that gave me. I received so much love from New York fans. Through everything I've been through, when I would come back with the Yankees, they would give me a standing ovation. I will never forget that, and nothing can ever replace it.

"I wish I was able to give more to those fans who loved me at the time of my career when I had more to give. I'm down in my spirit about that. I didn't give everything I had to offer."

* * *

Baseball players live by statistics, and Darryl still does—although now by an entirely different set of them. His urine, while he was still on probation, was tested three times a week for drugs. "I'm putting together a lot of time clean," he told me once, as if recounting a long hitting streak.

The cancer calls forth more numbers, not good numbers. When colon cancer recurs somewhere else in the abdomen, as it did in Darryl's case, surgeons succeed in removing it all less than 20 percent of the time, according to Dr. Carmen Allegra, a colorectal cancer specialist at the National Cancer Institute in Bethesda, Maryland. Even when they do, the median survival rate is no better than five years. For the majority of patients, those with the less successful surgeries, the median survival rate is between fourteen and sixteen months. Darryl's second surgery, the one in which his left kidney was removed, was August 7, 2000.

Darryl is remarkably sanguine about the statistics. When we talk, he sounds sad and brave at the same time. "I know my odds aren't very good, but that's okay," he says. "I accept that. Each and every one of us will come to a point in our lives where the odds are not in our favor."

Darryl says that he, too, feels "blessed." He doesn't regret all the money that has gone to drugs, lawyers, back taxes, the lavish gifts to family and friends. It's not the end of the world, he says, if he doesn't have millions of dollars.

"God blessed me to be a blessing to others," he says. "And that's all I want to be. There's a day when everyone will move on from life. I have a great idea that I will be going to a better place, even despite my shortcomings. Life is full of shortcomings."

A week after we have this conversation, Darryl flees his court-ordered rehab program, running from the room where I heard the Motown music wafting from the stereo to go back out on the streets. He descends into a cocaine binge, in hotel rooms in Tampa and Orlando, with a female friend and men who he will later claim robbed him at gunpoint of his jewelry.

His flight took place one day before his once-a-week chemotherapy treatment, a highly toxic experimental regimen to treat his virulent colon cancer. The sessions left him violently ill, not just after the treatment but also sometimes before it—from sheer dread. He ran as the Yankees got ready to head north at the end of spring training and leave him behind, a moment when he had fallen into trouble before.

There was one other marker: Darryl took off just one day before he was to receive the "sleepover pass" that he told me he was so looking forward to—that would have allowed him, for the first time in five months, to spend the night at home with his wife and children.

When I talked to Darryl in the days before he took off, he seemed so placid and resigned to whatever his fate would be. He gave no hint that he was about to take off, that he was soon to stun his family and friends and get himself in a load of trouble again.

But then again, Darryl himself almost certainly did not know what he was about to do. Darryl rarely planned; he acted, and only later considered the consequences.

His friends Ron Dock and Ray Negron, both of whom work as drug counselors for big-league teams, spent hours on the street looking for him, approaching dealers in Tampa and pounding on the doors of drug dens. One night they were joined in this grim task by Dwight Gooden, who only the day before had retired after a fine career that was brought up short of its Hall of Fame promise by his own drug detours.

Despite intense media attention to Darryl's escape from rehab, law enforcement did not search particularly hard for him. He was a low-level violator on the lam, nothing more. (Florida has a version of a three-strikes law, but despite Darryl's varied criminal history he was not in danger of running afoul of it.)

"We treated him like any other nonviolent offender," Lt. Rod Reder of the Hillsborough County Sheriffs Department explained. "It was, like, we'll get to it whenever. There was no manhunt."

The police recognized Darryl for what he was at that moment: common. Just another hard-luck but harmless guy on the street. It was almost like Darryl had achieved the wish he shared with his mother two decades before, when he stopped to look at the bum asleep on a street vent and said he wished he could be like him "so nobody would bother me."

Now nobody was bothering him, save for two of the last friends he had left.

Darryl finally called from Daytona Beach. Negron and Dock drove immediately to get him, picking him up at a Chevron station where he was sitting out in the hot sun, waiting. "We didn't ask him what he did for four days," Negron says. "When you're dealing with addicts, there is no new story. We knew what had gone on."

But what made him run?

"You can't ask that," Negron says. "He's a junkie. There's never a rational explanation."

For most of the two-and-a-half-hour trip back to Tampa, Darryl cried. At one point, Negron says, they stopped so that he could get some fresh air and compose himself. When the drive resumed, the great Darryl Strawberry stayed focused on the same two questions.

"Do you think I'm in trouble?" he kept asking. And: "What do you think will happen next?"

*   *   *

229

The last remnant of the Strawberry largesse in California is a house in the San Gabriel Valley about one hour east of downtown Los Angeles, a four-bedroom split-level with mountain views that Darryl built for Ruby, who died of breast cancer in 1996.

Nine people are living there on the day I visit: Darryl's sister Michelle and her daughter; his sister Regina, her husband and their four children; and Anthony Strawberry, Ruby's nineteen-year-old adopted son. The house is pleasant but shows signs of wear and tear. The roof appears to need work. A green shag carpet in the living room is tired-looking.

There's a little Darryl shrine around a fireplace, pictures of him at various stages of his career. In one, a young Darryl is posed in a Mets uniform with his arm around his mother. They're standing in front of a new Buick Riviera, the first car he bought after he signed out of high school.

When I knock on the door, I am told by Anthony that no one else is home, but a few minutes later Michelle, thirty-six, Darryl's youngest sister, comes to greet me. She is broad-shouldered and skinny and has the same expressive face and openness of her famous brother.

When I ask Michelle who the owner of this house is, she says: "Basically, us. We are. The house is free and clear. There were too many things attached to him," which I take to mean that this house is beyond the reach of anyone who might like to seize it. "This is the foundation right here. It's not going anywhere. This is where all the grandkids grew up. This is where they all still come. You know, this place is for everybody. This is the rock."

Darryl calls every week or so, she says. "He always asks, 'Are you guys okay?' That's what he wants to know. Even with everything he's been through, his addictions and everything, we don't feel he's let us down."

Ruby wanted her children to have togetherness, and they do. When Darryl has been free to travel, this is where he comes to relax, where he plops himself in a chair in her living room, stretches his long legs and sits for hours watching televised sports while the women lavish him with home-cooked food.

It is easy to see why Darryl would feel at home here, where he is measured by his devotion to family rather than by his lifetime home run total. Here, an alternate reality is observed: Darryl didn't blow a Hall of Fame career; he just had too much to handle. He was blinded by New York, buried by sports-page hype. Darryl was more a bystander than an actor in his own life. He was awesomely powerful from the left side of the batter's box, powerless everywhere else. Things happened to him.

"Darryl is a passive person," Michelle says. "The Strawberrys are all passive people."

Darryl's pain, his sister says, has rippled through the whole Strawberry clan. "We've been very quiet, but we've been the backbone to Darryl. Everything he's felt, we've felt."

In one way, for sure, it is hard to be a Strawberry. It's an uncommon name, and every time a family member shows an ID or writes a check, they are asked about their famous relative. They have grown weary of it over the years and do not go out of their way to be found by the press. Darryl's father, Henry, now lives in San Diego. One of his brothers, Ronnie, has been in and out of jail over the years. Michael Strawberry, the oldest, is a former minor league ballplayer and ex-L.A. cop who left the force in the mid-nineties to come out on the road to try to shield Darryl from drugs and temptation. But he has fallen on hard times himself in recent years; on the day I visited with Michelle, Michael Strawberry was in Los Angeles County Central Jail, awaiting trial on forgery charges. (Later he would plead guilty and be sentenced to probation.)

Michelle confirms that the family believed Darryl's success diminished their employment prospects. "Because of Darryl's fame, you know what I'm saying? The escalation of his fame. People would say, you don't need to work. They figured we had all this money."

"We didn't really require a lot of him," Michelle says of the money that flowed over the years. "We just asked him to do whatever he wanted to do. You know, we really didn't care. People were against it. They thought we weren't his responsibility, and he didn't owe us anything. But we never thought he did. Whatever Darryl did, he did from the heart."

I ask how many cars Darryl gave to family. "I don't know," Michelle says. "One, two, three, four, five . . . it was quite a few. I really can't remember. They were always good cars—Mercedes, Jaguars, Porsches. You know, maybe that was the problem. Maybe there were just too many of us. If he got tired of something, he would just give it away. One time he didn't want a house anymore, so he just gave it to my brother Michael. That's just how he was."

Michelle Strawberry is in the music business. Over the last decade, she tells me, she has been the producer on three singles and has high hopes now for a group called MAS-1, which is soon to release the album *Armed and Dangerous*, which includes the cuts "Ballin" and "It Ain't Your Money."

Michelle dreams of bringing the family saga full circle. Soon, maybe, she will lavish riches on Darryl. She says, "If my label blows up"—makes a lot of money—"I will be there for him."

The habit of leveraging a famous family member's name is hard to break. As I leave, Michelle Strawberry hands me a press release. "Darryl Strawberry, former New York Yankee," the release says, "has launched back into the market with his siblings, Michelle, Michael and Ronnie Strawberry, with the new imprint, 'Strawberry Entertainment Group.'"

* * *

Darryl's run from rehab finally exhausted his chances, and a judge sent him to Gainesville Correctional Institution for what was technically his fifth violation of the terms of his probation. He had broken several rules at the rehab center, among them smoking cigarettes, signing autographs, and, as Darryl puts it, "messing with girls."

He served eleven months.

On April 29, 2003, he accepted the $100 that Florida gives inmates upon their release, declined the new suit of clothes, and walked out a free man. His wife Charisse met him at the gate, and the two of them drove home in a silver Lincoln Navigator.

Not long after that, I visited him at his home in Lutz, Florida, east of Tampa. The picture with Darryl is always changing. He looked happy. He looked healthy. He laughed a lot.

His head was shaved, as it had been through most of the latter part of his baseball days. With a big smile, he patted his newly thick midsection and told me that he weighed 240 pounds, more than he ever had. Somehow, after all that he had been through—drugs, cancer, jail—the beginnings of this little belly suited him.

Darryl was home alone when we talked. Charisse was out doing errands. The kids were in California with her mother. He was padding around in a T-shirt, shorts, and leather sandals. The TV was on; he had been watching CNN.

The house itself is classic high-end Florida—a one-level, peach-colored stucco structure inside a gated golf-course community; five bedrooms, big modern kitchen, and a small pool out back, ringed by an impressive collection of children's inflatable pool toys.

Darryl tells me that he and Charisse own this house, then amends it and says they are "in the process" of buying it. He says that he has no money worries, that between his baseball pension and the income he can bring in signing autographs at card shows—along with whatever he'll make when he accepts George Steinbrenner's standing offer of employment—he will never want for money.

"God," he says, "showed me a long time ago that money is never going to be a major worry for me."

But Darryl's finances will probably always remain complicated. Public records show that the government in December 2002 filed a lien against him for unpaid federal taxes of $472,086.

Unlike the vast majority of big-time athletes and famous people I have talked to, Darryl gives the impression of actually listening. He wants to know, of course, about all his old Crenshaw teammates. As I tell him, he keeps his gaze fixed on me, interjecting with an occasional "right," or "okay," to show he is following along.

One reason he attracted so many mentors over the years is that Darryl hooks into people. He pays attention. He asks questions. "Nelson's in the Navy?" he says. "Did you get to see him?" "Carl's at Folsom? That's a pretty rough place, isn't it?"

His ability to be an engaged listener is also the source of much of the frustration with him. The financial advisors who begged him to stop giving away so much money, the team executives who warned him against his unsavory associations, the pastors who believed they had reached him on some spiritual level all thought they were making an impact. But then he quickly forgot or disregarded their guidance, or simply would not or could not follow it.

But at the time, he seemed for sure to be listening. To be *agreeing*.

As Darryl and I talk, his cell phone rings numerous times. Each time, he looks at the number of the incoming call and ignores it. But when a call comes in from Charisse's mother's house in California, he answers. It is Jade, his eight-year-old, who is crying as her grandmother attempts to take out her braids.

"Now, Jade, c'mon, sweetie," Darryl says. "Your nana is not trying to hurt you. Let her take your braids out. No, listen to what I said. Your nana is not being too rough. That's just the way it feels."

Darryl listens for a moment. He tries to break in but Jade is still crying. Then he says, "Jade, stop for a minute. Listen to me. You are just a little tender-headed. You know you are tender-headed. Your nana is doing the best she can."

Listening to this, you would never know that Darryl has been away a long time. Nearly three years. I am impressed by his patience, and impressed that his children still count on him for comfort.

*   *   *

It dawns on me, in the course of talking to Darryl, that he did not mind that much being in jail. He spent his adult life becoming less than he should have been. Squandering this unimaginable baseball talent. Sullying himself in various ways.

Prison is about as low as a man can get. But unkind as it may be to say, prison for Darryl was the crowning achievement of his life's work.

He did anything but hard time. Darryl had a prison job, sort of; he was supposed to be part of the crew that cut the grass outside the prison gates and tended the grounds. But the guards quickly let him know he didn't really have to push a mower or pick up trash. Even in prison, after all, he was still Darryl Strawberry.

"They were like, a guy like you, you don't belong in here," Darryl says. "So I just sort of hung out, and they were okay with that."

Darryl had essentially volunteered for prison. Endless months of rehab were wearing on him. There were so many rules, and some of them—specifically the ones designed to deflate ego—were especially difficult on a former superstar athlete. Even a humbled one like Darryl.

His lawyer finally told the judge, "Mr. Strawberry would like to serve out the rest of his time in state prison."

As Darryl recalls it, "Everybody was like, 'What? He wants to do time? Okay. Sure.' "

He describes the day he walked out of Gainesville Correctional and back into the demands of real life—making his marriage work; being a father; staying clean—with a surprising lack of emotion or even enthusiasm. Prison was a place of low expectations. No pressure.

"Yeah, it was a happy day," he says of the day of his release. "I mean, I knew that day would come. I knew I wasn't there forever. It wasn't like I had any major strikes against me and the judge could lock me up forever.

"You know, what I did was gravy, compared to the sentences some people catch, those ten-year deals, or the twenty-five years to life. Between rehab and Gainesville, it was just about three years, but it wasn't that bad."

Darryl, like many people of a certain kind of faith, believes that everything happens for a reason. It is all God's intention, God's will. Darryl's role, as he sees it, is to divine what God's plan is for him and to follow along and be a witness, a vehicle, of God's love.

"Nothing happens by mistake," he says. "Life is life. There's different journeys. God did not call me for the game. It was not the purpose of my life; it was just a platform where I was used."

I challenge Darryl on this. By his theology, God made him screw up, or let him screw up, so he could be a testimony to others. (Of what, I'm not entirely sure.)

But what if God is a baseball fan? I figure He must be. Why else would we even *have* baseball? And for what purpose would Darryl have been gifted with his magnificent ballplayer's body and his *God-given talent?* Why was he put in a neighborhood with baseball in its blood, together with Carl Jones and the McNealy twins, Chris Brown and Marvin and

George and all the other Boys of Crenshaw? And why was he brought together with Brooks Hurst, a man in need of redemption himself, a good
but flawed man looking for some fine young athletes to make into a real
ball team?

If everything happens for a reason, what was the reason for all of
that?

I say to Darryl, "Don't you think God might be a little angry with
you? He gave you this Hall of Fame physique and skill, and you could not
find your way to the promised land of Cooperstown."

Darryl is a very good sport about this, but he stays on message.

His God is not a big fan of striving, of pushing for excellence in one's
chosen field. Darryl believes that dedicating himself to hitting, say, five
hundred career home runs would have required an abundance of arrogance and pride on his part, "but God cannot use an arrogant, prideful
person as testimony."

All of this gets tangled up with Darryl's other theme, the unfairness
of the expectations that were heaped upon him and the crushing impact
of feeling that he could never fully live up to them.

He tells me that his old teammate Chris Brown was a lucky man. He
got to play in San Francisco and San Diego, baseball backwaters compared to New York. The fans in those cities were not as passionate, the
sportswriters not as demanding and critical. Baseball mattered less, and
Darryl would have liked that.

"C'mon man, think about what Chris had to deal with compared to
me. He had it made. There wasn't no pressure out there. They weren't expecting him to hit thirty a year and drive in one hundred like they were
me. If he didn't want to play one night and sat out, it was no big deal. But
me, it was a big story if that happened."

Darryl now realizes that in some ways he was not cut out for baseball,
or at least not for stardom. "I was a sensitive person. I didn't like the idea
of being important." (He was, like his daughter, a little tender-headed.)

All these years down the road, all the thousands of hours of drug
rehab sessions and Narcotics Anonymous and Alcoholics Anonymous
meetings, and Darryl Strawberry still reserves a lot of the blame for his

troubles for the New York Mets, who drafted him out of Crenshaw High School and put him on the big, scary New York stage.

"All the drugs and drinking, that opens up to a person who feels like he is giving his all and not being appreciated, and I did feel like I was giving my all to the Mets," he says. "Let's be real. The team was built around me. Whatever anybody else did was a bonus. I hit thirty-nine home runs that season. Okay, I didn't hit forty. I missed by one. Big deal. But they made it a big deal. I reached the point, I said, The hell with them. I'm going to go out drinking and partying every night."

Darryl does not deny that these high times could be fun, and some of them he remembers fondly. "The whole world of women," he says, "was open to me."

Like many pro athletes, he had a fondness for airline stewardesses. He had one-nighters with women who worked the Mets charter flights, and with those who served on commercial flights.

"All the girls were real pretty. On the charter or regular flights."

* * *

While Darryl was in Gainesville Correctional Institution, a new spiritual advisor came into his life, the Rev. Randy White, who leads the fast-growing Church Without Walls with his televangelist wife, the Rev. Paula White.

The blond-haired, telegenic Whites are controversial figures. They do good works in Tampa—job training for welfare recipients, food banks, outreach to children in public housing projects. They are also extremely flamboyant, and not at all shy about flaunting their wealth.

According to a 2002 story in the *Tampa Tribune*, Paula White drives a Mercedes sedan, while Randy White drives a Cadillac Escalade emblazoned on the side with the words *Big Daddy*, the nickname that he is supposedly called by the poor children of Tampa who view him as a benefactor.

Darryl Strawberry may not care about money, but he is attached now to pastors who clearly do. The Whites live in an 8,000-square-foot, $2.1 million home. A *Tampa Tribune* reporter, Michelle Bearden, attended a Sunday church service at which Randy White gave a PowerPoint presentation of the home's interior and of other lavish homes the couple has owned.

"The decision to live in poverty or prosperity is yours," Reverend White told his congregation after the PowerPoint tour. "God has already cast His vote. He wants you to be prosperous."

Darryl has always attracted people of varying agendas. The kindly Richie Bry, his first agent. The stranger who walked into the sandwich shop near Crenshaw High and wanted his phone number. George Steinbrenner, the Yankees boss, who extended Darryl's playing career when no one else would. The bloodsuckers who called themselves friends but just wanted to be near him to catch the surplus cocaine and women.

Darryl welcomed them all. He has never been able to make distinctions.

So what do the Whites want with him? Their Church Without Walls courts celebrities and athletes, and counts several members of the Tampa Bay Buccaneers among its 15,000 members. The former NFL star Deion Sanders participates in ministries with the Whites.

Randy White first paid a visit to Charisse Strawberry, whom Darryl married in 1994 and who has stuck with him through times harder than many women would endure. (People marvel at how Hillary Clinton endured the humiliation of her husband's misbehavior, but she has nothing on Charisse Strawberry.)

Reverend White spent time counseling and praying with Charisse, then arranged to visit Darryl in prison. Darryl sees only love coming from the Whites. They are the latest people who have come on the scene to save him—from himself, from his worst instincts, from the devil, from whatever it is that leads him astray.

"The first time I met Reverend Randy," Darryl says, "he just started by telling me how much he loved me and my family. He never wanted nothing. He just wanted me to see his ministry and give me an opportunity to see what God would do in my life. And how God would use me and change my life and how I could be a testimony to other people.

"And I believed that from the time I was incarcerated till the time I got out, and I've been with him ever since."

Darryl has been speaking at church functions. He attends staff meetings at the church. He went to Atlanta for a men's ministry with Randy White and Deion Sanders. He is learning all he can from the Whites, and may one day become the Rev. Darryl Strawberry.

His health is good, he says. The cancer has been in remission for three years. At this very moment, he tells me in the summer of 2003, "I am in a physical and mental state of mind where it looks like life is going to be pretty good, after all."

* * *

To the other Boys of Crenshaw, Darryl once embodied the dream. But now he is the dream in some mutated form, with all its genetic coding scrambled—a grotesque manifestation of what they had all hoped to become.

They were sad about Darryl. Angry at him. Sometimes, just tired of him. But they couldn't get away from him.

Darryl was this lifelong looming figure, a ghost they once knew, whom they *still* knew, or at least recognized, in all of his incarnations: the glorious athlete loping on the rich green outfield grass of Yankee Stadium; the frightened, chagrined figure in the police photos; the repentant sinner, promising to do better if only he could have just one more chance.

Yeah, they knew all of those Darryl Strawberrys. Wasn't one of them that looked the least bit unfamiliar.

For sure, they still loved him. The Boys of Crenshaw were a family, and Darryl's place within it was well established. He was the little brother who could not live up to his glorious potential, the one who could not stay out of trouble, who kept letting them down. But to outsiders, they defended the hell out of him.

"Darryl is like entertainment to people," Marvin McWhorter says. "I have people come up to me, like my supervisor, and want to talk about him. He'll say, 'Did you hear what your boy did now?' It's like he wants to know if I'm gonna stick up for Darryl, or talk Darryl down. Well, I'm not gonna talk Darryl down.

"Someone else will say to me, 'He belongs in prison for a long time. He should learn his lesson, don't you think?' Like I'm supposed to agree with that. Tell me something, what the hell is jail gonna do for someone like Darryl?"

But Marvin, who loved baseball so deeply himself, who read and reread Ted Williams's *The Science of Hitting* even as Darryl was being compared to Ted Williams without having any idea who he was, does allow himself this judgment: "Baseball wanted Darryl more than Darryl wanted baseball. That was the problem right there."

For Fernando Becker, the shortstop who spent most of his adult life away from L.A., Darryl was a constant connection to home. Every time Fernando picked up a newspaper or turned on a news telecast, there was his old buddy hitting some dramatic home run—or flagrantly screwing up. He celebrated Darryl's exploits, and suffered over his transgressions in a deeply personal way. Every time Darryl fell, Fernando felt like he had been kicked in the gut.

"I love Darryl. I will always love Darryl," he says. "I've cried about Darryl, literally cried. But I'm disappointed in him. More was given to him than to any of us. And Darryl done messed it all up. I forgive him, but it's hard, because he shouldn't have done all that. He let a lot of us down."

CHAPTER NINE

Family

Every one of the Boys of Crenshaw measured themselves against Darryl Strawberry's reflection. It was unavoidable. Here was this person they came up with, whom they considered a peer, who had so much more of everything—more notoriety, more money, more troubles. They felt small in comparison—or lucky, depending on what was up with Darryl.

No one had a harder time separating from Darryl than Chris Brown, who on the face of it lived such a parallel life. Chris and Darryl were the two huge talents, the two who made it all the way up. But they were natural rivals at Crenshaw, and in some ways were even more so afterward.

When Darryl left the Mets and signed with the Dodgers, it was a civic moment in L.A.—the homecoming of a local hero, even though everyone already knew that Darryl, in some regards, was returning broken. But maybe coming home would set him right. At least that was the hope.

Crenshaw High School staged an elaborate "Salute to Darryl Strawberry." The color guard and choir performed. State senators and U.S. congressmen attended. Mayor Tom Bradley read a proclamation. The legendary Dodger announcer Vin Scully served as master of ceremonies. At the end, Darryl's jersey—he wore number 8 at Crenshaw—was retired.

All of this annoyed Chris Brown to no end, and it gnaws him still. He believes, and rightly so, that he had a more distinguished high school career than Darryl. Maybe Darryl was the more promising pro—and without a doubt, Darryl had a more significant big-league career—but Chris was the more dominant player at Crenshaw. No one who knows the facts could disagree with that.

Some people could have let that anger go, especially considering how things have gone for Darryl. But not Chris. The next time he saw Brooks Hurst, he let him have it. "If you are retiring his number for what he did here," he remembers saying, "then there's a number of guys who should come first. Darryl wasn't better than me. He wasn't better than Reggie Dymally. He wasn't better than Cordie." He concluded, "Don't you ever try to retire my jersey after you done stepped on me like that."

And they haven't. Nearly every year at Crenshaw High, someone wears Chris's old number 32.

Chris sets himself in opposition to Darryl partly out of a sense of competition, but even more out of a clash of styles. Chris is prickly, not easy like Darryl. He won't tell people what they want to hear just for the sake of peace. He doesn't just go along; if he doesn't want to do something, no amount of cajoling can make him. If he has a beef with you, you'll know it. He is honest and direct, too much so for his own good.

On the other hand, he is dependable, a man of his word. When I was researching this book, I sometimes joked that when I was in Los Angeles, I lived on BPT. That's an expression I knew from friends that stands for Black People's Time. What it means is that if you have a two P.M. appointment, it may not occur until three P.M. Or four. Or, in extreme cases, not until the following day. (I've also heard of Jewish Standard Time. Same idea, but not quite as late.)

Chris Brown no longer lives in Los Angeles, but he said he would fly in to meet me. (His wife's job as a flight attendant allows him to fly for free.) At the appointed time he was right there, waiting for me just like he promised.

Chris cannot fathom Darryl's irresponsibility, and how richly he was rewarded in spite of it. Money, not surprisingly, is partly at the root of what rankles Chris. He never made better than $300,000 in any baseball season—a good salary for sure, but nothing compared to what ballplayers now are making, and a fraction of what Darryl made in his best years.

"Darryl's drinking and doping, that's an illness," Chris says. "The cancer, that's an illness. But for a man to make $20 or $30 million in his career and have none of it left, I have no sympathy for that. You could not spend that much on dope.

"I would tell that to Darryl to his face. I have no respect for him. As a ballplayer, yes—but as a man, no."

Chris told me that he had been trying to get in touch with Darryl for several years. He had written him letters, tried to call, passed word through friends and family. Wherever Darryl was—home in Florida, in jail, in rehab—Chris reached out to him, but always without success. Why, Chris wanted to know, was his old friend ducking him? He figured Darryl must have suspected he wanted something from him, as so many people have over the years.

"But I don't want nothin' from Darryl," Chris says. "I just want to reach out to him, to talk with him."

When Chris said what he wanted to share with Darryl, I understood why Darryl might not be eager to be in touch. "All I've been wanting to tell Darryl is what it's like to wake up sober every morning," Chris says. "That's something I thought he would want to hear. I'm the only one of us from Crenshaw, at least that I know of, that has never drank or smoked. There's not been one morning in my forty-two years that I have gotten up that I was drunk or doped up.

"That's the perspective that I want to give to Darryl, but he's out there, doin' whatever, and I guess he doesn't want to hear it."

*   *   *

Chris lives in Missouri City, Texas, a suburb of Houston, with his wife, Lisa, and their two children. The former can't-miss prospect and 1986 National League All-Star rises each weekday morning at 4:30 A.M. and, about an hour later, arrives at his job at a power plant, where he makes good money operating one of the largest cranes in the world. (It rises to as high as eighteen stories.) One year, he made $83,000, and that was working only ten months.

He often does not return home until six P.M. No matter how tired he is, he changes, then takes a one-mile walk around the neighborhood with his twelve-year-old son and eight-year-old daughter. Someone at his church suggested that would be a good thing to do, and Chris found that he likes it. He tries not to say too much on these walks; he lets his kids tell him about their day.

Chris is fastidious, like Nelson Whiting. He is very much his mother's son, the product of the woman I saw in L.A. bustling around her house in rubber gloves, touching up surfaces that to my eye already looked awfully clean. To Chris, there are certain ways things should be done, and other ways in which they cannot be done.

When he gives his children their weekly allowance, he says, each time: The first ten percent goes to the Lord. They hand him some of the money back, and he puts it away to give to their church.

He has been teaching his son to cut the grass, and they have extensive lessons in the backyard: Neat cutting rows. Proper trimming around trees. His son wants to move on to the front yard, but that is the part of the property which the Brown family shows to the outside world. Chris tells him, You can mess up in the backyard all you want, but I mow the front until we're sure you know what you're doing.

Baseball, the game itself—its orderliness, its rules—suited him. He always liked it when he heard baseball compared to chess, enjoyed that it wasn't a game you could just physically overwhelm. You had to *think* the game as well as play it. Even Michael Jordan, he points out, could not convert his extraordinary athleticism into success as a baseball player.

But the whole scene around baseball was sloppy. Nights stretching into early morning. The whole anything-goes aspect. The milieu was as messy as the game was tidy. And that's the part that Chris seemed to rebel against, the aspect that made him shut down.

Of course, the notion that Chris Brown has some kind of beef with baseball would make no sense to many who knew him as a big leaguer. To everyone else, it was Chris who seemed like the irresponsible party, the undisciplined kid who wouldn't take the field with aches and pains. He came off as some kind of rebel, a bad-ass from South Central.

But that most definitely is not his perception. In Chris's mind, he was always going against the flow, standing in opposition to the lax and lenient standards that he found in the game.

He met his future wife on a roadtrip to Houston when he was playing with the Padres. The next time he was in town, they talked by phone, then he sent a limousine to pick her up where she was staying, about twenty miles from the team hotel. They talked for three hours. Then, as she was leaving, he gave her a little kiss on the cheek. There was no sex, and no suggestion of it.

You can get drummed out of big-league baseball for that sort of behavior.

"If we would have had sex, I would have never respected her," he says. "I admit, I had done that kind of sex when I was playing. But if she had did that with me, I would figure she would do that with any guy. After that, we saw each other, but we didn't do anything sexually for like maybe four or five months."

For two years after baseball, Chris was the primary caretaker of his daughter, Paris, while his wife flew for Continental. "I was there from day one," he says. "I changed the diapers. I cared for her when she was sick. She never had a day when she woke up and I was not there. She's my princess. She calmed me down.

"But I'll tell you something, it made me respect women even more. Because when it came time for me to go back to work, I was ready. It's hell raising a child."

The scout George Genovese believed Chris had Hall of Fame talent, but the life he leads now suits him far better than big-league ball ever did.

It turns out he is much better at getting up at dawn, earning an hourly wage, and being a family man than he ever was at traveling the National League circuit and playing baseball.

He operates his crane from ground level, inside a cab that is a little computerized control room. All day long, he looks up. (He keeps a pillow behind his head to ward off stiff necks.) He takes direction from a supervisor, whom he hears through earphones.

It is easily as stressful as standing in against big-league pitching. The crane itself costs about $7 million. He lifts loads that weigh as much as half a million pounds. If the wind blows, the whole thing gets even more difficult. If it gusts to twenty-five miles per hour or more, he has to quickly shut everything down.

He tries to get to work early, so he can sit inside the cab of the crane before his shift starts and just relax and get prepared. He puts his feet up and leafs through the sports section of the *Houston Chronicle*. His head has to be clear; he can't take any family problems to work with him, no distractions whatsoever. He thinks of it like being in the batter's box; the blanker his mind is, the better he can react to what comes his way.

Lately, a woman coworker has been coming around asking to borrow the section with the horoscopes. She asked him one day what his sign was. That was more of an encroachment in his zone of concentration and privacy than he could allow. "You can borrow part of my paper," he told her, "but as far as what my sign is, that's none of your business. That is not something you need to know."

On the job, Chris is no more one of the boys than he was in the baseball clubhouse. Friends at work wanted him to play softball at a company picnic, but he said no. He couldn't imagine just playing for fun. Plus, he was afraid he might hit the ball up the middle and hurt somebody. "If I did that, I'd feel bad. But it's just not possible for me to go out there and play halfway. I can't do that."

He would rather go bowling or ride bicycles with his kids, or play tennis with his wife or with friends in the neighborhood.

His baseball glove is up in his attic, in a bag emblazoned with the logo of the Detroit Tigers, his last team. He doesn't use the glove anymore, but he knows right where it is and still considers it, as he says, a *prized possession.*

Some of his coworkers also wanted him to go hunting with them on weekends—either to shoot deer with bows and arrows, or to hunt wild boar. But he had to decline that, too. He said: "Thanks but no thanks. You guys have fun, but you are not gettin' me to run around the woods chasing wild pigs."

Not too long ago, a guy at work asked him to stand in for him in one of the random drug tests given on the job, and Chris did not decline in nearly such good humor. "Are you crazy?" he said. "I ain't pissin' in no bottle for you." Chris told him if somebody got hurt because he had helped a guy keep working while on drugs, he would feel bad. "You go piss in the bottle yourself. You get fired, that's your problem."

There might have been a gentler way to say no, but that would not be Chris's style.

Chris has a funny way of speaking. He'll be talking about someone, and then he'll all of a sudden turn it around as if he is addressing that person directly. For example, he says that he cannot believe that Barry Bonds, who for the first part of his career was a good but not historic slugger, started hitting huge numbers of home runs after he turned thirty. Many people have wondered if Bonds began taking dietary supplements to build muscle, or perhaps even steroids.

Chris has the same question. As he puts it, "Barry, I understand you are a strong guy. But don't take me for no fool, Barry. All the sudden you hit seventy-three home runs? C'mon, Barry, I mean, really."

Chris still follows baseball, and occasionally goes to a game. One moment he'll say, "I don't give a damn about baseball," but then he'll tell you who is leading the league in hitting and which teams are in the pennant race. Like a lot of pro athletes who just missed out on the big money, the huge salaries bother him.

He brings up former NFL quarterback Ryan Leaf, a college star who walked away with millions in bonus money after he quickly washed out in the pros and gave the distinct impression that he did not care. Chris says, "Ryan, I can't believe you, man. C'mon Ryan, what is up with you? Were you even trying?"

He does not see his own career as a failure. He could have been a league leader in runs batted in or in batting average or even as a Most Valuable Player once or twice, but all he ever led the National League in was in the category of being hit by pitches. (Eleven times in 1985.)

But Chris was blessed with a hard shell. The expectations that were so difficult for Darryl Strawberry had no impact whatsoever on him. He never gave a damn what anybody thought—not his Crenshaw coach, Brooks Hurst; not the Giants' GM, Al Rosen; not all the sportswriters and fans who dogged him. He got to the big leagues. He was a starting player and an All-Star. How many guys can say that?

"There's things that happened that I regret, but overall, I'd say I had a good career."

Chris's son plays a little baseball, but Chris doesn't push him into the sport. His favorite thing is tinkering. He can fix anything—clocks, vacuum cleaners. His daughter is interested in sports, but Chris would prefer she not play something like basketball, which he considers too "mannish" for girls to play. (Gender roles in Chris's mind are fixed. He does not believe in male flight attendants, because "it just doesn't look right for a man to be carrying something to you on a tray.")

Chris can draw on his big-league pension at age forty-five, but plans to wait until he is fifty-five. He figures he'll retire from his other job at the same time and take his Teamsters pension. His wife will stop flying.

"I'll see the world with her," he says. "We've already been to London and Madrid. I want to take our kids around, too. I want my kids to get some culture in them. Different languages, different people."

Even without having made millions in baseball, Chris Brown has a strong sense of having made it out of inner-city L.A. He has the money he needs.

"Growing up," he says, "my mother put a roof over our heads, food on the table, and clothes on my back. And those were the only three things I ever needed. But looking back on it, we were in poverty, and I don't plan on going back down there."

* * *

For the Boys of Crenshaw, catching up on family can be bittersweet. Drugs have swept through their lives like some kind of virus—and not a rare virus, but a real common one. Darryl Strawberry may be famous for his drug problems, but among the people he comes from he is no aberration. Even those who have risen up out of the inner city never fully escape it thanks to family members in need.

"I don't know if you know anything about women's sizes," Chris Brown says to Reggie Dymally one day when we are all sitting together. "Well, you remember my baby sister, right? She is like five-foot-ten, and she was wearing a size zero."

Reggie is nodding, following along. He knows exactly where this is going. "She finally got detoxed after a couple of tries. She got herself cleaned up. But before that, it was touch and go. She was out on the street. Her daughter was staying with my mother. I told her, 'Please don't let that happen to you again. I don't ever want to see you like that again.' "

Chris estimates that he has spent, over the years, $75,000 to put various relatives through rehab.

"Same thing with me," Reggie says. He has not had as much money, of course, not having played big-league ball, but he has given to his financial limit. "With one relative," Reggie says, "I gave my last twenty dollars once to keep her in rehab. I gave my last everything. It didn't help. They have to be ready. Later on, she was, thank God."

I have known people from middle-class, white upbringings who ultimately give up on close family members who can't get off drugs or keep themselves on the right side of the law. They give them a certain number of chances, then write them off and get on with their own lives. It's like a family three-strikes system.

Where Reggie and Chris come from, there is an absence of such harsh judgment. (Chris reserves his harshness for Darryl Strawberry.) Family members are never written off; they never run out of chances and you never stop loving them.

To my surprise, neither Chris nor Reggie, straight arrows both, was particularly judgmental about the drug dealers in their midst. They express a kind of moral neutrality on the subject; to them, drug dealing is just part of the inner city's ecosystem, a naturally occurring phenomenon.

"I knew Crips. I still know drug dealers," Reggie says. "I could say, 'Can you loan me $20,000 to help my catering business?' and they'd say, 'Is that all you need, Reggie?' But I'm not into that. I don't want them bringing no drugs around me. But if they want to come in my house and eat, fine. If they want to talk to me, fine. I can still know them. They can still be my friends. But I tell them, 'You want to smoke your crack, you want to sell it, you've got to do it outside.'"

Chris says he has an old childhood buddy who is now a dope dealer. The guy once showed him a briefcase with stacks of money in it. He said it contained a million dollars. Chris didn't believe him, but it was clearly a lot. "I could have counted it," he says. "All I said was, 'That's a lot of money.'

"I know a lot a drug dealers. They have respect for me. They don't push it on me. They got their thing, I got mine."

*   *   *

I was struck by the hole that baseball left in so many of the former Crenshaw players. Chris Brown filled it with family, faith, and his seemingly indestructible self-esteem. Reggie Dymally had his cooking, which was really his first love. Nelson Whiting had the military, his music, and all those rules and routines he has set out for himself.

The twins drifted, and are still drifting. Carl Jones never recovered from losing baseball, and holds on to it still, playing it on the prison yard to fill up the days between now and twenty-five years to life.

Cordie Dillard was the "original varsity player." That is what he called himself. He used the term several times in our conversations. I had no idea what it meant, but I loved the sound of it. *The original varsity player.* Like the first guy who ever earned a letter. I guess it is Cordie's way of reminding himself that he was once the Big Man on Campus, which he was.

Back at Crenshaw, Cordie had a clever way of speaking, a good "rap," as it used to be said before rap was a style of music. He had the lowrider car, a little money in his pocket, and all of that extreme self-regard, off the field and on it—the audacity to shout "curve!" as a breaking ball was coming in, just before taking a whack at it.

"In terms of personality, I was sort of the dominant guy," Cordie says. "I took the lead."

No one, at the age of eighteen years old, could have been more comfortable with himself than Cordie Dillard. And he still is, in his own way.

We are sitting in the living room of his pleasant house in a middle-class neighborhood not far from Crenshaw High. Cordie's wife De-leanna, who is a caterer, serves us a dish of chicken and vegetables, which she puts on little TV trays near where we are sitting. I accept her offer of a beer. She doesn't ask Cordie what he wants to drink; she just sets down a glass of ice water.

In the backyard of this home is a typical inner-city L.A. slice of par-adise—fig trees, apricot trees, orange trees, apple trees. The neighbor-hood catches good breezes. Cordie says it never gets too chilly or too hot. They never need air-conditioning. On rare occasions in the winter, they warm themselves by sitting near one of the home's several fireplaces.

Cordie has six children from two marriages. The oldest played base-ball for Brooks Hurst at Crenshaw High, although he was not the athlete his father was. He was studying computer science at Mississippi State. His youngest, an eleven-year-old girl, is an actress who has appeared in Mc-Donald's commercials and episodes of *Moesha*.

Cordie mentions that his brother talks of moving to Hancock Park, an upscale neighborhood not far from Beverly Hills. He has his eye on a mansion, something like twenty rooms. But Cordie is a creature of habit. He knows some people who are "jumpers," always jumping from one place to the next, looking for something better. Not Cordie. He plans to stay right where he is.

He puts his feet up, leans back. "Let me ask you something," he says to me. "And answer this honestly. If you did not already know it, you would never guess that I'm a plumber, would you?"

It is important for Cordie to feel that he's thriving. That he has status, control over a situation, money. He can't be the original varsity player any longer, but he likes to hold his head high.

As a plumber, he gets around town a lot. Everyone knows about Darryl Strawberry's situation, of course, but Cordie was also up to date on Carl Jones and the McNealy twins. "It's unfortunate," he says, "that a lot of my brothers are not doing too good for themselves."

Cordie's truck, inscribed with the name of the family business, Speed Rooter, is parked out on the street. It is all racked up with his tools—his drain snakes and pumps and pipe wrenches and so forth—in all the exact places they have been for years.

He could afford a new truck, but that, too, would be a form of jumping. This one drives just right: not too fast, not too slow. And he could go half-blind and still find whatever he needed.

"We get calls from people who say someone else was out on the job and they couldn't fix it," Cordie says. "And that's where I get competitive. It gets like a sport to me. They call me the Michael Jordan, the Magic Johnson of plumbing. That's because I can always get the job done, no matter what. It even amazes me sometimes. But I got that heart from sports. I hate to fail. I love the challenge."

The Dillards' plumbing business puts sixteen trucks out on the street and employs about twenty-five people, about a dozen of them family. Cordie learned the old-fashioned way, on the job from his older relatives, and never attended a day of plumbing school. "A lot of those book-taught plumbers," he says, "they can't fix a damn thing. Those are the ones I'm comin' in behind."

On a good day he can earn $500 repairing or installing fixtures in homes and businesses, and in a good year—"if I feel like working hard"—$100,000 or more.

He started working as a plumber immediately after being sent home from minor league ball in Great Falls, Montana, following the credit card theft. The transition was not entirely smooth. Before he could become the Michael Jordan and Magic Johnson of plumbing, Cordie had some issues to work through, some rough patches to overcome.

As he begins to tell me about this, his tone abruptly changes. No more easy patter. No more pretending that it has always been a lark to be Cordie Dillard.

"I had a cocaine problem for a number of years, at least ten," he says. "It started when I was about twenty-four. The problem had to do with me being frustrated with myself, because, you know, I let something get away from me in life that I really wanted. I was frustrated with myself. The thing in Great Falls, it should have never, never happened. It's something I should have known better.

"But it happened so fast, and it was sort of devastating. One day, you know, I was a baseball player, and I was pretty sure I had a legitimate future in that. And the next thing you know, I'm sittin' back here in L.A., and I'm a plumber. It was just automatic when I came back that I would deal with my family and get into this business. But I wasn't prepared for it, you know, emotionally."

"I admit that I could not handle the reality of the situation, and that's where I let the drugs enter in."

Cordie did not go into rehab. Over time, he says, he cut back, then just quit. He thinks he was lucky not to have the kind of cash that was available to Darryl Strawberry. "I was just a brother who was working and having a drug problem," he says. "I didn't have all the money in the world to be spending on the drugs. That's the difference.

"I had kids. I had a wife. I had car payments and a house payment and electricity to keep on. I was taught that no matter what, you keep a roof over your head, and I managed to do that. But of course at the same time, I was hurting my family and my kids. But with me, it was private. It was behind closed doors. I didn't have to have the whole world watching me mess up my life."

Cordie feels sure he has it all back together. He told me about some fairly regular and exotic wagers he makes on NBA basketball with his "man" (his bookie), including one year when he bet that his favorite team, the Lakers, would not lose a playoff game. If the wager would have paid off, Cordie would have won $100,000—but the Lakers lost one game, so he was out $1,000.

"That's all right," Cordie says. "If you bet within your means and you have a sensible system, you'll come out ahead."

Cordie looks to be in good physical shape, and plays basketball a couple of times a week. He has lost several steps with age, but he can always compensate for that.

"Even if the guys are a little younger than me and faster," he says, "I'm always gonna be the smartest one on the court. That's not gonna change."

*   *   *

Fernando Becker, the accidental shortstop, never stopped being amazed that he was a part of the great 1979 team. And he never quite got past making those two key errors in the championship game at Dodger Stadium.

The onus for that heartbreaking loss did not fall on just one player, of course. The stars—Darryl Strawberry, Chris Brown, Cordie Dillard, Carl Jones—should have delivered. They should have done enough great things to make up for whatever mistakes the lesser players committed. That's how it is on every level of sport. The game should not have turned on the performance of a role player.

But Fernando felt responsible. He was an outsider to begin with, a Panamanian kid, the lone Hispanic on an otherwise all-black team. And he was no playground star, not one of the hotshots who came to Crenshaw carrying a reputation.

Brooks Hurst wanted to turn him into a catcher, thought he'd make a decent backup to Carl Jones. Then, after Donald Jones got kicked out of school for the brawl on the playground, and after a couple of other prospective infielders got themselves tripped up in various kinds of trouble, Fernando became the starting shortstop. He was striving to make a name for himself, trying to get noticed. He recognized the starting role as a gift, an unanticipated opportunity to earn his own ticket out.

"All those guys, after high school, they got drafted," Fernando says. "Chris Brown, Cordie, Reggie, the twins, Darryl. Then Marvin and George. Dino (Lee Mays, a pitcher), he got drafted. My whole infield got drafted but me. You know, I would have liked that. It's what I was hoping for. Every kid has that aspiration."

The error that sticks with Fernando occurred on what should have been a routine ground ball. Granada Hills had runners on first and second, with one out. Fernando was already shaded toward second base, hoping for a double play. The ball was hit to his left. All he had to do was field it and flip it to Cordie Dillard, who would have pivoted and fired to first base for a rally-killing double play.

But Fernando committed the fundamental mistake of not staying down on a ground ball—not getting his glove to dirt level and keeping it there. The ball ticked off his mitt and rolled into the outfield. One run scored. John Elway, the next batter, lashed a double, scoring two more. Crenshaw had fallen way behind and never recovered.

The play really never left Fernando. A decade later, during eight months of living in the desert while serving in a tank company for the U.S. Army in the first Persian Gulf War, he would close his eyes at night and try to summon that championship game in Dodger Stadium. Except for the brief days of combat, Desert Storm was numbingly boring. Dodger Stadium wasn't boring. It was the most exciting thing he had ever been involved in, a moment of great promise when everything seemed possible. But every time he conjured it in memory—the lights, the crowd, his teammates, his grandfather in the stands—the error popped into the picture.

"What I always tried to remember is that my teammates supported me," he says. "I do believe they did."

Fernando has used that night in Dodger Stadium as a lesson. "That game tore me up," he says. "It still does if I think too hard on it. But it made me stronger. You realize, whatever it is, you pick yourself up and keep on going."

Fernando lives in a pleasant hillside neighborhood on the outskirts of San Diego. You take your shoes off just inside the front door before walking onto the plush carpets; that's the rule laid down by his fiancée, Roxane, who owns a string of successful nail salons.

"She's my queen," Fernando says. "She's my backbone. She runs the house. I'm not ashamed to admit it."

After high school, Fernando attended junior college for a brief time, but mainly to continue playing ball and give the scouts another shot at seeing him. He was an advanced student, but he didn't have the money to pursue college seriously. He played one summer of semipro ball. Then he enlisted in the military. That had always been his plan: pro baseball or the Army.

He lost touch with all his old Crenshaw teammates, and tried to find them on the sports pages. He would buy a newspaper, turn to the big page of baseball boxscores, and run his finger down the columns looking for them. Fernando would find Darryl Strawberry, of course, and for a stretch Chris Brown, but where were the others?

"The twins were ones I was always thinking I'd see," he says. "I thought they could make it to the big leagues. And Cordie, and Reggie Dymally. I was always surprised I couldn't find them."

Fernando got married for the first time before he was twenty-one. He quickly became a father, then set off with his wife and new daughter on the typical far-flung travels of a military man: Missouri, Virginia, Colorado, Germany, Texas, and, for four years, Fairbanks, Alaska.

He liked Alaska the best. The northern lights. Catching more fish than he could possibly eat. He didn't even mind the cold. He figured he would take that over the sense of danger he felt back home in L.A.

His unit continued with P.T.—physical training—as long as it didn't get any colder than twenty degrees below zero. "I hated that at the time," he says. "But you realize, it's an experience you'll have all your life. You can train in that, you're pretty good."

Fernando's marriage faltered. "It wasn't her fault; it was mine," he says. "I would say I was going to stay on the true and narrow, but I would still be doing wrong"—by which he means he dallied with other women. (When Fernando received my letter and saw the return address, his first thought was, "I've never been stationed in Maryland, so it can't be about no issues with women.")

When he met his current fiancée, Fernando's first marriage had just ended and he was scuffling. He'd left the military with no particular plan for the future. His personal finances were a wreck, even though one of his

Army jobs was to run a $3 million budget as the supply sergeant for a tank company.

He credits Roxane with virtually rescuing him from the scrap heap. I have never heard a man express such heartfelt gratitude to his mate. (Many no doubt should; they just don't.)

"I have worked so hard to improve myself, because when she met me I really didn't have too much," Fernando says. "She believed in me. I was having a hard time—no drugs or substances, I just lacked confidence in my abilities. I had stopped striving. I was too happy with little mediocre jobs."

No one could say now that Fernando does not strive for advancement and self-improvement. His main job, but not his only one, is working maintenance at scenic San Diego State. "I'm blessed," he says. "I get to work and look at the ocean at the same time. How many people can say that?"

At night and on most weekends, he drives a limousine. One weekend a month, he fulfills his commitment to the Army National Guard. In addition, he is taking courses toward earning his B.A. degree.

He lives on five hours of sleep a night. That's all he has time for between his jobs and his studies and keeping up his house and his relationship. His stepfather (whom he refers to as his father) was a hard worker, and Fernando has dedicated himself to following that example.

"I lost some years through lack of ambition and I want to get them back. I really do. I want to make something of myself."

Fernando desperately wanted to go to his ten-year Crenshaw reunion. The perpetual outsider, he wanted to feel connected to his old teammates. And he admits that maybe, on some level, he wanted to be assured that they still loved him. Even after Dodger Stadium.

"I was thinking, I'm going to go back, looking all nice, dressed in the finest threads I can find. But on the night of the reunion, I was in the desert, looking up at the stars during Desert Storm. I was frustrated, because I missed out on something that really meant something to me. I wanted to see the guys I had grown up with and make sure everybody was doing okay."

He did make it to the twentieth reunion. But his classmates—the juniors on the 1979 team—were not there. No George. No Marvin. No Dar-ryl Strawberry. None of them could make it.

Fernando wants to make an even deeper commitment to Crenshaw. "My dream is to get my degree and go back to Crenshaw and teach and coach the baseball team. And I'm going to do it. Somebody from our team should coach there. I believe that. One of us should take what we learned from Brooks and apply it. We should bring that tradition back to life."

*   *   *

George Cook and Marvin McWhorter are solid. Shoulders squared, feet firmly on the ground. In the face of whatever other turmoil might have been swirling around them, they had each other.

They were best friends at Crenshaw, the two who sat side by side on Saturday mornings and watched *This Week in Baseball*. Marvin waited pa-tiently for his chance to play, then in his senior year came out swinging for the fences. George was the nimble second baseman who whispered strat-egy suggestions to Brooks Hurst, which the coach pretended to ignore but sometimes put to use.

After high school, Marvin and George played a season together at Los Angeles City College, which they remember as a fairly dicey atmo-sphere. Guys they knew there from the neighborhood were involved in drugs, gambling, breaking into lockers.

They stuck together, as always. In certain situations, one of them would give the other a little look, a silent "let's go," and they would be off in Marvin's old Mercury Cougar—to get a sandwich somewhere, or throw some quarters into the batting cage. They were each living on $300 Pell Grants that came twice a semester; they didn't feel like they had a lot of room to screw up.

"That's a big thing in life right there," George says. "You need to have someone who wants to do the same things you want to do—and doesn't want to do the same things you *don't* want to do. Marvin and me, we were that person for each other."

I am sitting in a restaurant with George. He works overnight for the city, so his shift has not yet begun.

"I'm a traffic officer. I guess I'm what you would call a meter maid," he says. "But it's not so much a ticket thing as a service thing. You come home, your driveway is blocked, you call us, and we get on it."

We are waiting for Marvin, who will take an extended lunch hour with us. Soon enough, he comes striding in. He is a big, barrel-chested man dressed for his job as a shift supervisor at a juvenile detention home. He wears brown pants, a short-sleeved white shirt, and a brown patterned tie. His head is shaved, and he has a small stud earring in his left ear. I imagine that back at the detention center, he gets the boys' attention when he needs to.

Marvin and George were best man at each other's weddings. They talk about renting a boat and going fishing together, but they've been talking about that for years. Life gets busy. Marvin works and lives way out in the Valley, and George works those night hours. They still consider themselves best friends. They talk on the phone, but have not actually been together in at least two years.

"Two years?" Marvin says. "It can't have been two years."

"Two years," says George. "I'm sure of it."

Soon enough, they are laughing and reminiscing over long-ago events. "Marvin," George says. "Do you remember our coach at LACC? He would violate your personal space big-time. He'd be talkin' to you, and just when he made the point he wanted to make, he'd reach over and pinch you on your cheek!"

George remembers. The coach was Phil Pote, the big-league scout who was Brooks Hurst's old friend.

"Yeah," George says. "And Phil would throw that slow-motion batting practice to us. He'd be like, 'See if you can hit that!' And you couldn't hit it 'cause it was so slow."

George is the only one of the Boys of Crenshaw still married to his first wife. Marvin is the only one to earn a degree from a four-year college. Life has never been exactly effortless for either one of them, but it has unfolded on a little smoother course than for some of the others.

Their opinion on why a couple of their teammates fell on hard times surprises me. They identify the problem in certain cases as money—too much of it. In the calculus of inner-city L.A., the Joneses and Cordie Dillard came from wealth.

"In our neighborhood, those families were well-to-do," George says.

Marvin still remembers what Carl Jones made on weekends working on construction sites with his dad: $11.57 an hour. In 1979, or even now, that was pretty good money for a high school senior.

"But the ones who had some money," Marvin says, "they got focused on it. And they were crybabies when something went wrong. They couldn't handle adversity. You know, they would whine about it instead of getting up on their own two feet."

George laughs. I can tell he has heard this from his good friend many times before.

"Marvin doesn't like crybabies," he explains to me. "He came up pretty tough."

George has another thought on what derailed some of the Boys of Crenshaw. Maybe it was partly money, he says, but more so it was baseball. Losing baseball.

"You know what I think it is? We were all going so hard at that one thing, and then we had to deal with it in some way when it was over. Some of us could survive without it, even if it was difficult. But some guys, they could not afford to lose that piece of themselves, if you know what I mean?

"They didn't have that good a foundation to begin with. And baseball was that one thing holding them together."

* * *

The first time I got together with George Cook, we met at his house, which lies one block off Crenshaw Boulevard on a little street of Spanish-style cottages. The homes have manicured lawns, well-tended flower beds, and vibrantly colored rosebushes.

When I drove up, George was out front holding a hose over one of his flower beds. His hair was styled in short braids, and he wore baggy jeans and a loose-fitting sweatshirt. It was sort of an aging hip-hop look overlaid on an old-school guy who really likes to keep up his property.

George has taken a big step up from the house some forty blocks to the east where he was raised, the cramped dwelling he shared with ten siblings. "Where I used to live, some people would call South Central," he says. "But we never did. That's a term that came into being after the Rodney King riots. When we were growing up, it was just called L.A. Only the rich neighborhoods had names."

Where he lives now is not even technically L.A.; it is just over the line, in Inglewood. He estimates his house is worth about $225,000. "But a lot of people who don't know any better would probably call *this* South Central," he says. "People make assumptions. They don't realize that this exists, that right in the inner city here, you can live on a nice street like this."

George was far more curious than most of the others about what I was doing. He wanted to know, What made me want to write about his old high school baseball team? What did I think so far? How would I make it all into a book? Did I have to pay for my own travel to L.A.? (Yes.) Who would transcribe all these tapes I was making? (I would.)

When I mentioned that I was reading the crime novels of Walter Mosley, who I thought was awfully smart about L.A., he wanted to know, "Did you read *Devil in a Blue Dress*? That's his best one."

As a journalist whose job it is to ask questions, I'm always a little surprised that I don't get more of them in return. George's inquisitiveness seemed perfectly natural to me, the mark of an engaged mind.

After being drafted out of high school, and spurning the paltry bonus offer from the Baltimore Orioles, George played for two years at Los Angeles City College, then accepted a baseball scholarship at the University of Arizona. It all seemed sensible at the time. He was a smart kid. He put education first.

But then he hurt his shoulder. He did not fit in at Arizona, which like nearly all college baseball programs had few black players. He soured on school and left after just one semester.

Just as it did for nearly all of the Boys of Crenshaw, baseball ended more suddenly than he had ever imagined it could. "It was a pretty rough adjustment," he says. "You put all this time in since you were eight years old—like twelve, thirteen, fourteen years of your life—and nobody comes and warns you it's about to be over. It just is. Then you have to find something else you halfway like to do, because at that point, there's nothing you really like to do but play ball.

"It's a shock to you. You run away from it. You take a long time to explain to yourself what happened. Whatever your part was in it, you don't want to admit for a long time. And then there's all these other people in your life who saw you as this up-and-coming baseball player. And they're like, 'Why ain't you playing ball no more?' And you have to keep explaining to other people, but you don't even really know yourself what happened."

George has a good, steady job, but I wonder if he could have done better than working in parking enforcement. He thinks the same thing.

But he and his wife, Acquinette, have two teenage boys. Both do well in school. Between his salary and the money his wife makes as a fifth-grade teacher at a fine arts magnet school, they have what they need—although not a lot more.

They certainly don't have the money to buy the sprawling horse ranch that George once dreamed of, the big property that baseball was going to deliver. George laughs when I remind him of the ranch that was going to stretch halfway across South Central.

"I've got a good family," he says. "That's good enough. Maybe we can all go ride horses some day."

*   *   *

"For a long time," Big Marvin McWhorter says, "I was kind of bitter with baseball, to tell you the truth. I didn't watch games. I didn't go to games.

I just couldn't deal with it. I had wanted to play so bad. I just couldn't cope with how it all came out."

Marvin had played that one season of college baseball at Pomona, where he spent weeks of preseason practice being made to take little half-swings in order to make contact, rather than his beloved home run cuts. He had endured rude, racist jokes in a setting that was nearly all white. Then he got a brief opportunity with the independent minor league team in Florida.

"The whole college baseball thing, it wasn't a welcoming environment," he says. "If I would have felt more accepted, it might have been different. Then, the pro thing, if they don't put money into you, you better prove to them real fast you can play. That's what it boils down to."

Just like it had for his friend George Cook, baseball for Marvin came to a jarring halt. He was moving forward toward his dream, setting records in junior college, getting drafted, then he wasn't moving at all. He felt like he ran into a brick wall at full speed. It was not a feeling you quickly recover from.

"Sometimes in life, things are not meant to be," he says. "You make the best of who you are and what you're doing, and you move on. But it was *years* before I could tell myself that and really believe it."

Marvin can still talk about hitting. And talk. And talk.

"When you had a good pitcher on the mound, and he could bring heat"—a good fastball—"and you knew he was gonna bring heat, that was the competitive spark. The ultimate pump-up. Man to man. Your best fastball against my best swing.

"Now when I watch on TV, even pitchers with good fastballs, they don't want to challenge a hitter. I get frustrated. I yell at the TV. I'm like, 'Challenge that man. See what he's got!' I guess I'm just old school."

There was no way that Marvin was going to just stop swinging a baseball bat cold turkey. He has played many years of high-level competitive softball, basically semipro ball. Sponsors cover travel and hotel charges, uniforms, bats, and spikes. Some pay cash bonuses for winning tournaments.

When I talked to him last, he was playing for a team called the Piedmont Boys. The year before, he had been with the One West Warriors, which won a California championship and traveled to a national tournament in Detroit.

Slow-pitch softball is a brute-strength game. Marvin goes to the gym three or four times a week. He drinks protein shakes. He is one of the older guys still playing. His value, besides being able to still hit the hell out of the ball, is in helping to recruit other players and in keeping a team in focus and on an even emotional keel.

"I'm sort of like the elder statesman now."

In nearly any setting, Marvin is what he calls the "go-to guy," the person counted on to solve problems. It started out at a young age, when as the oldest of a very large family he helped raise younger brothers, sisters, and cousins. At work, he mentors younger staff members at the juvenile detention home. He makes about $65,000 a year.

"I've got this teaching thing inside me," he says. "I thought I would teach in a school setting and coach. But the way it comes out is at work with people under me. New staff comes in and I take them aside and say: 'There's a right way to do things, and a wrong way. Don't be afraid to do it the right way.' "

When Marvin's marriage was breaking up, he says that a marriage counselor asked both him and his wife to take a look at each other and express what they saw. His former wife, Marvin recalls, said, "I see this great big guy who can handle any problem that comes up."

"Sometimes you don't want to be that go-to guy," he says. "But that's your role in life. There's nothing you can do about it, even if at times you get tired of it."

Marvin's ethos of doing things the right way—of standing up and speaking out when he sees things that are wrong—extends in many directions. He had a close friend who he saw hit his very young baby. "Why did you do that?" Marvin asked. His friend replied that it was his house, his son, and he could do what he wanted.

That was pretty much the end of that friendship.

"I had a hard time accepting what I had just seen. I'm the kind of person who is very loyal, but if you commit some kind of act like that and don't understand how wrong it is, I don't want anything to do with you. I will forgive you in my heart, but we don't have to be close."

Only once has Marvin lapsed from being a go-to guy—a problem solver, someone who carries the load and does the right and expected thing. Near the end of his marriage, he had an affair. "I ended up having a child out of wedlock. I was really disappointed in myself. It was a case of going through something later in life that I should have gone through earlier and didn't. That was no time to be carrying on like that."

At the juvenile detention center where he works, the residents include drug dealers, armed robbers, and a handful of murderers. Very few, Marvin says, have had "any male authority at home to guide them."

Marvin had a father. The man with three jobs who worked mornings, nights, and weekends—who threw the ball to him so hard during their ritual Friday-evening catches that he made Marvin wince. His father was a drinker, and a man with no understanding of his son's passion for baseball. (Until Marvin got drafted and it looked more like a job.)

"In some ways, okay, I didn't have the best father," Marvin says. "But I could learn some things from him about how to be a father and how *not* to be a father. And I had uncles and other family members I could emulate. So I try to carry myself in a fashion that some kid could emulate. That's like a goal of mine."

*   *   *

None of the Boys of Crenshaw have been able to pass baseball on to their sons. They've tried. Just can't do it.

D.J. Strawberry, Darryl's son by his first marriage, established a reputation as a promising outfielder in Southern California. But he gave up the game in his mid-teens to concentrate on basketball, and in 2003 accepted a scholarship to play guard for the University of Maryland.

Darryl lately has been playing catch and pitching batting practice to his nine-year-old son Jordan. They go to a nearby park. Darryl uses his old glove, the one that last saw use at Yankee Stadium.

"He's a natural. He's really good," Darryl says of young Jordan

Strawberry, as if any son of his would be anything but. "If he ever really got into it, my goodness."

But he's not into it. "Jordan just wants to play basketball," Darryl says. "Maybe he'll develop a love of baseball. Charisse says you have to try to instill that in him, but it doesn't work that way."

Both George Cook and Marvin McWhorter had also hoped their sons would be baseball players, wanted them to love it like they did. And, secondarily, if their boys ever had a dream of making a mark in sports— or a living at it—baseball seemed to make the most sense.

Ironically, the fewer black kids who play baseball, the greater the need is—and the bigger the opportunity—for that rare gifted black athlete who chooses to dedicate himself to baseball. The ticket out, or the lure of it, still looms.

Between 1995 and 2002, the percentage of American-born black players in the big leagues fell from 19 percent to 10 percent, a precipitous decline and one that will not soon be reversed.

The figures, released by the Institute for Diversity and Ethics in Sport at the University of Central Florida, showed that big-league teams had few black players in the pipeline. The Dodgers, Jackie Robinson's franchise, had only six on the team's forty-man big-league roster. The other L.A.-area team, the Anaheim Angels, had just three—and in the most recent amateur draft, just two of the Angels' fifty selections were American-born blacks.

"I don't want this to come out wrong," George says, "but you have a typical black kid from the inner city, he can run a little bit. He's probably strong and a little fearless. In basketball, he might be an okay athlete. But in baseball, he's closer to the top, athletically speaking, because there's not the same pool of kids playing that sport."

But George did not want to do "that father thing" and try to impose a sport on his boys. They knew he was a good baseball player, but he never spoke of it that much. "I didn't go into detail" is the way he says it.

George still prefers watching baseball to basketball because of its slower, less intense pace. But it's too slow for his kids. When he watches baseball, they leave the room.

He played catch with his sons. Ahmaad, the youngest, never got the baseball bug at all; he plays strictly basketball. The oldest, Ashanti, played a year of Little League, and he was good, but basketball captured him, too.

In 2002, Ashanti Cook played point guard for the state championship team at Westchester High in L.A. He is just down the road from D.J. Strawberry, playing basketball for Georgetown University in Washington, D.C.

That is a high level of play. But Ashanti is six-foot-three, wiry strong and lightning quick. There are many basketball players who fit that basic description. "If he had made baseball his main thing," his father says, "I don't think he would have had any trouble getting the scouts' attention."

Marvin coached his son's baseball teams for years, beginning when Marvin Jr. was about eight. But his son recently informed him he was through with baseball. "He said to me, 'Dad, the only reason I played baseball was because you like it,'" Marvin says. "At first, he kind of looked at me like he didn't want to tell me. I said, 'Okay, no problem. As long as you're doing something, and it's something you love.'

"But truthfully, it did hurt a little bit. To me, baseball is still the greatest game ever invented and I really wanted him to enjoy it like I did. But the funny thing is, after the season started, he said that maybe he should have signed up. He missed it a little. So I think maybe he'll pick it back up, but, you know, I don't want to push him."

*   *   *

On a Sunday afternoon in September 2003, most of the Boys of Crenshaw, men now, gathered at a Mexican restaurant near the beach for a reunion. It has been nearly twenty-five years since they were all together.

Reggie Dymally, dependable Reggie, is the first to arrive. He comes with his new wife, Joy, and with news of a new job: He is cooking kosher food at the Kabbalah Center in Beverly Hills, which offers a trendy mix of Judaism and New Age self-help tools. Reggie is the executive chef. A couple of times, he has cooked Friday night Shabbat dinner for Madonna.

Brooks Hurst, the old coach, put this event together. He stepped down as Crenshaw's coach in 1982, then got out of teaching altogether. He worked in restaurants, worked as a carpenter, sold vegetables. He had his own period of drifting. Now he is back teaching again, and would like nothing better than to return to Crenshaw or some other city high school and run all his drills again and make some group of eager, strong boys into real ballplayers.

Cordie Dillard, the original varsity player, pulls up in the parking lot in a purple Camaro convertible. The room begins to fill up, and it's as if everyone is playing their old roles. They have organized themselves as I imagine they did a quarter century ago at the Record Shop, the joint across from Crenshaw where they ate sandwiches after practice.

Reggie Dymally is standing quietly off to the side, taking in the whole scene. Marvin and George are yakking at each other. Cordie, the coach's pet, is locked in a long conversation with Brooks Hurst.

The twins, Darryl and Derwin McNealy, are among the last to show. They come walking into the room in fine-looking, matching black suits over hip black T-shirts. They have on black spats, shined so hard you can almost see your reflection in them. All eyes turn to the twins, who have nearly glided to the middle of the small room.

I ask Marvin if he can tell them apart. Does he know which one is Darryl, and which is Derwin? "Nope," he says. "Not yet. Let me go over and talk to them and see if I can figure it out."

The twins have sort of made it back to the West Coast, sort of not. Sometimes they stay with an older brother in Anaheim, and sometimes back with their parents in Las Vegas. Their mother has not succeeded in reopening her hair salon, and Napoleon hasn't gotten that janitorial service going. But they're reachable by phone now; Derwin has a cell phone.

The twins sit down to eat with their old buddy Nelson Whiting, their surrogate big brother, who has flown here from his barren outpost in Fallon, Nevada. I see them telling him stories, and Nelson is throwing his head back and laughing.

Fernando Becker, the skinny Panamanian shortstop who was so sad about missing his class reunion while he served in Desert Storm, is taking a lot of ribbing because he's put on about seventy-five pounds. A couple of the guys go over and run their hands over his belly.

Fernando spots a video camera that someone is carrying around the room, and talks loudly into it. "I'm Fernando Becker," he says. "I was the shortstop. I could not hit. Okay, I admit it," he says, as several of the others laugh. "But I could field. I was a fielding fool!"

And Fernando could field, except on that one night. No one, though, says anything about the errors at Dodger Stadium.

Chris Brown has not flown in from Houston, and Darryl Strawberry, after saying he would be here, decided to stay in Tampa.

Carl Jones, of course, is the other one who's missing—he is at Folsom State Prison. Unless the law changes or some lawyer finds a way to spring him, Carl won't be together with the Boys of Crenshaw for their forty-year reunion, either.

But Carl's father, Thedo Jones, is here, mixing with the boys whose swings he corrected in his living room, who all bunked together during those long, joyous weekends at his house on Ninety-third Street, the unofficial clubhouse of the Boys of Crenshaw.

Mr. Jones walks slowly around the room, talking with "his boys," as he calls them. He thanks Brooks Hurst for inviting him. But he doesn't stay for long. "I've got two boys of my own who should be here with their teammates," he says to me, his voice cracking. "It was hard for me to come here today."

*   *   *

They are still playing baseball at the old diamond on Sixth Avenue and Fifty-second Street, just off Crenshaw Boulevard. The field is not groomed to quite the same loving perfection that Brooks Hurst's team maintained, but it is hard enough these days to convince a boy to play baseball let alone to tell him he must first get on his hands and knees and mine for pebbles.

It is crisp and clear, a little cooler than normal, but all around a perfect Southern California afternoon. The Crenshaw boys run out to their positions, looking like a ball team in their white uniforms with green trim, their baseball stirrup socks pulled up real high to accentuate young, strong legs.

About fifty Crenshaw students nearly fill a small set of bleachers. They are eating big sloppy burritos from a joint across the street. Someone has a big box of a CD player that blasts hip-hop music between innings. The whole atmosphere is fun and festive and more alive than I anticipated, considering what everyone acknowledges is the sad state of baseball in the inner city.

The Whitney Young building, one of the batting practice targets for the Boys of Crenshaw, is still sitting out there beyond the center-field fence. Over the right-field fence is a block of houses, including the third one up the street—the one where there ought to be some kind of monument, right on the spot in the front yard that a young Darryl Strawberry bombed with a home run ball.

No one is going to put a baseball there today. No one, ever again, is going to do that. It wasn't possible on the day the great Darryl Strawberry hit that monumental blast. And it's still not possible.

Brooks Hurst is standing along the third-base line, looking on. The old coach is watching this game with Cordie Dillard. They are focused on the Crenshaw shortstop, a kid named Daniel Nelson who moves with an evident comfort on the ballfield, a baseball knowingness that is missing in most of the others. He is the best player on one of the better Crenshaw teams in years, one that has an outside chance at making the playoffs. There has even been some talk of "getting back to Dodger Stadium," although no realistic chance of that exists.

"You think any of these kids could have played for us back in '79?" Cordie says to Brooks Hurst.

"The shortstop," Brooks answers. "He could have played for our team."

"You sure?"

"Yeah, I think so, but not as a starter."

I am looking at two other kids. One of them is the first baseman, a broad-shouldered, intense-looking senior who wears his baseball socks down around his shoe tops, retro style.

His name is Keaundre "Kiki" Moore. He is the son of Ernest Moore and Tahitha Jones Moore, the grandson of Thedo Jones, and the nephew of Carl Jones.

Like all the descendants of the Jones clan, Kiki Moore has baseball in his blood.

When Crenshaw is up to bat, he pulls a folding chair right up against the backstop, to be as close as possible to the action. His mitt is stuffed under his waistband, right up against the small of his back.

"Would you look at that?" Tahitha says to me. "That is just how Carl did with his glove. I don't even know how Kiki knows to do that."

Carl Jones was the team's truth-telling taskmaster, the one who would march to the mound, rip off his mask, and demand: "Punk, throw a fast-ball!"

But Carl, behind bars, has never seen his nephews play.

Now Kiki Moore is rising up out of that folding chair in anger at a teammate who has just failed to run hard enough to first base. When he gets fully to his feet, he shouts in a voice loud enough to be heard out on Crenshaw Boulevard:

"You ought to run harder than that!" he says. "You ain't got no will, you mutt!"

* * *

One other Jones boy plays for this Crenshaw team, Kiki's younger brother Anthony, who is called just "Ant."

Ant is smaller in frame than his big brother, but fast and talented. Just a sophomore, he starts at second base for this team and was a star running back on the varsity football team. Everyone has the highest hopes for Ant's future.

He comes up to bat in the first inning and lines a ball just foul down the right-field line. "You a little tardy on that swing, baby," Tahitha shouts. "Just get that bat out there a little faster."

Next pitch, Ant is quicker to get the bat around and lashes a line drive to right-center field. His father, Ernest, a classmate of the Boys of Crenshaw but never quite good enough to make the baseball team, beams as his son coasts into second base with a standup double.

Ernest turns to me. "You see that boy out there?" he says. "He the one gonna get me out of the ghetto."

Afterword

Whether writing nonfiction or fiction, an author dwells with his characters over the course of months and years. They are there when he rises, sometimes springing awake before he does, and they stay with him all day, through the evening, and right up until the last moments before sleep—when they can be counted on to be especially active and attention-demanding, like babies kicking in utero. All in all, they take up an extraordinary amount of psychic space, and after the last word of a book has been written, the author is often quite happy to say good-bye.

I didn't feel that way when I finished writing *The Ticket Out*. Not in the months afterward, and not now. The men I wrote about had been, back in the day, like family to each other—a band of ball-playing brothers, loving and competitive and quarrelsome, bonded by baseball and a shared set of hopes and fears. But over time, mostly they had drifted apart. My research put them back in touch with one another and, in some sense, with memories they could not easily summon on their own.

"How do you know about Crenshaw?" Derwin McNealy asked me after I had found him and his twin brother, Darryl, in a seedy corner of Las Vegas where they lived in a cramped apartment with their parents. He kept repeating variations of the same question. For the McNealy twins, my interest was proof that they had been involved in something worthy of documentation—that their flash of greatness would not pass without history having taken proper notice.

I moved from player to player—Nelson Whiting at his Navy base in what I came to think of as Nowhere, Nevada (in actuality, the town of Fallon, given to spooky moonscapes and fierce sandstorms); Darryl Strawberry, outside Tampa, Florida; Carl Jones, stuck inside Folsom State Prison; most of the rest in Los Angeles, in varying states of struggle and success.

I don't know what I hoped for at first—mostly, I guess, that I'd be able to find most of the guys, and that they would have good stories to share—but I quickly came to understand that I had hit a kind of jackpot. Simply put, I found more than I could have wished for: men filled with decency and humanity, and layered with complexity. George Cook: watering the flowers in front of his neatly kept stucco cottage the first time I encountered him, dreadlocked, handsome as a movie star, as smart and thoughtful as a college professor. Nelson Whiting: as disciplined as a monk in that little town of Nowhere so as to not fall into any L.A.-style trouble, counting the fat content in his brown-bag lunch, and still writing music bought by hip-hop artists. Darryl Strawberry: poor Darryl, attached to another church and another flashy preacher, hoping this time the word of God would finally take hold and beat back his demons. All of them: decent, deep, unforgettable, hardly the types you want to say good-bye to when you move on to the next thing.

Not long after this book was first published in April 2004, I was privileged to sign copies and give a little talk about it at Eso Won, a landmark African American bookstore in Los Angeles. As I stood at the podium, several of the men I had written about, along with many of their family members, sat in the rows directly in front of me. It was, truth be told, a bit disconcerting. I had chronicled their lives and made the kinds of educated guesses that writers do—why they had responded in certain ways or had made particular choices at various junctures of their lives—and here they were, George and Marvin, Cordie and Reggie, Coach Brooks Hurst, listening to me talk about them.

But they had all told me they liked the book—that it had faithfully told their stories and had hit the right emotional chords (of not just those at the reading, but all the Boys of Crenshaw). George Cook, unsurprisingly, had an observation, a point he wanted to raise: He told me that he believed the narrative leaned too heavily on their desperation, the desire to use baseball as a ticket out of L.A., and did not fully reflect their love of the game. I don't think too many others have read it that way, but for George, and anyone else who may have a doubt, let me say it without equivocation: The Boys of Crenshaw loved, cherished, and brought great honor to the game of baseball—without a deep and abiding passion, there is no way they could have played it so well.

Two stories bear updating.

Not long after the book was published, Chris Brown, who had been living a settled life outside of Houston with his wife and two children, lost his crane-operating job. The local economy slowed and the men lowest down on the seniority list, Chris among them, got laid off.

I already knew that Chris had a profound respect for money, which came from the days when he didn't have any. Sitting in the bleachers one afternoon at the old ball field at Crenshaw, he said to me: "I been in poverty, and I ain't ever going back." He had a competitive, tangled relationship with Darryl Strawberry and genuine sympathy for Darryl's travails, but with all that Darryl went through, the thing that seemed to rankle Chris the most was that his old teammate had blown through career earnings of close to $30 million.

I had been trying to reach him for a couple of weeks in the summer of 2004, without success. His wife, Lisa, promised she would have him call me when he was able to get to a phone, but she would not say where he was. "He'll tell you when he calls," she said. Finally, the phone rang in my office late one afternoon and there was Chris, talking very loud, almost yelling in the way people do when they're calling from someplace that feels especially far away.

"Where are you?" I asked immediately.

"I'm in Iraq," he said.

"You're where?" I said, thinking I had not heard correctly.

"Iraq, man."

Chris Brown, whom so many in baseball had considered too "soft," not a man's man, had an old-fashioned view of himself as a provider, as someone who must support his family by whatever legal means necessary. A neighbor of his in Missouri City, Texas, also out of work, had seen a newspaper ad placed by the contractor Halliburton seeking truck drivers in Iraq. He showed it to Chris and they both went to the address listed in the ad and signed up.

Chris knew how to drive a truck but the conditions of driving one in Iraq were, obviously, entirely new to him. He told me that just a few days before, he had been driving his 18-wheeler, hauling diesel fuel from a depot to a military base, when his long fuel convoy drove into a sandstorm. When the sand lifted, Chris was alone, separated from the convoy. He spotted a man in a face mask off to the side of the road pointing an AK-47 at him and swerved; a bullet pierced his windshield. Somehow he was able to get the truck back on the road and out of danger. Another time, he was just a mile behind a convoy that was ambushed—seven Halliburton drivers and security guards died in that attack.

I already knew that Chris was not the person so many in baseball thought they knew. If this book proved anything to me, it was that the qualities most valued in sports often have little to do with what matters in the rest of life. Chris certainly hadn't done everything right in his years in baseball, but he had been impugned by lesser men—like his former manager in San Diego, the odious Larry Bowa, who made a habit of blaming others for his own shortcomings. (Bowa was the one who reported Chris's conjunctivitis to the press by saying "he slept on his eye wrong.") In baseball, it's hard to outrun a bad reputation—a "label," as they call it in the game—and Chris had established his early as someone who was not up to the task. A person who shut down when the going got tough. And now here he was, driving a fuel truck through gunfire.

Chris said that a few of his coworkers in Iraq know he played pro baseball, that he hit a double in the 1986 All-Star Game, but he never talks about it unless asked. "I'm not ashamed of it," he told me, "but if I were to raise it, I would look at it as bragging on myself."

I wondered if, based on his reputation in baseball, going to Iraq was in some way an effort to prove something to others, or to himself, but Chris would have none of that. "I know who I am," he said. "I would never do nothing to prove myself to anybody." Deeply religious, as always, he said he was not frightened. "The Lord has my back. I just have to try to not do anything to make him mad at me."

Conditions in Iraq became ever more dangerous in the months after he signed up with Halliburton, with the insurgency gaining strength and targeting both U.S. military forces and private contractors, as well as Iraqi civilians. The roads were laced with IEDs (improvised explosive devices), and fuel trucks were a large and gratifying target. Waves and waves of new truck drivers signed up stateside, reported for duty in Iraq, then quickly headed home. But Chris kept on hauling fuel. When he made it back to base, he watched videos, played basketball, and read his Bible. He ate well at the Halliburton mess hall: steak, shrimp, just about anything he wanted. Every day, he called home, and he looked for the e-mails that Lisa sent with digital pictures of the kids.

Chris made several visits home. But he went back each time, hugging everyone good-bye and returning to his job in Iraq. As I write this, he is still there, earning his paycheck.

* * *

Not long after I heard from Chris Brown, I got a letter in the mail from Carl Jones, postmarked, as usual, from Folsom State and stamped with his prisoner number: E-66555. But this letter was different because it included a new sentiment: hope. At long last, California was taking a serious look at its harsh three-strikes statute, which had put Carl and other nonviolent criminals in jail for life. "I hope to see you and your family when I get out," Carl wrote. "I'm hoping that they will change the three strikes law in November."

Early polls showed a large majority, nearly two-thirds of the electorate, poised to vote in favor of Proposition 66, which would have kept the most violent offenders locked up while freeing Carl and others. Californians had read newspaper accounts of men put away for life for such offenses as stealing a set of golf clubs. The *Los Angeles Times* published a column I wrote specifically about Carl's case—the "eraser case," as his lawyer called it, because the only result of his entry into an unoccupied classroom was that the ledge under the blackboard, the shelf that holds erasers, was ripped from the wall. Many voters, a majority it seemed, felt that life sentences for crimes like these defied common sense and basic fairness.

But as the election drew nearer, Governor Arnold Schwarzenegger and the powerful prison guards union fell back on what drove enactment of the law in the first place: raw, primitive fear. The governor said that Proposition 66 would "flood our streets with thousands of dangerous felons, including rapists, child molesters and murderers" and that it would lead to the release of 26,000 convicted criminals—a figure more than seven times greater than the number of inmates that other estimates said could even have their sentences reconsidered.

Fear, though, is a powerful force in any election, and Schwarzenegger's graphic predictions of prison gates swinging open and murderers and rapists pouring out onto the streets turned the tide. The vote took place in November 2004, the same day that voters reelected George Bush. The change in the law was voted down resoundingly, by about the same margin that polls had once predicted it would pass.

Carl was crushed. His letters no longer mentioned his baseball-playing, which had been his passion and his only pleasure inside prison walls. In fact, he said he no longer even liked leaving his cell to go outside to the yard.

He wrote me late in the summer of 2005:

> *May this letter find you in strong mind, body and spirits. I pray that you and your family are experiencing the best that life has to offer. I was so glad to hear your voice over the phone it made my day to hear a familiar voice thank you mike. MIKE, like I was telling you on the phone that we just got off lock down. I just hope that we're not right back on lock down because as you well know it only take one of these young fools to kick it off and everybody must drop to the ground face down until they sort through the wounded. I won't be going to the yard that much during the summer I ain't going to lie on nobody hot cement this last time we were on the ground for 4 hours and it was hot.*
>
> *MIKE, I'm trying to hang in there but form me to you, it gets real ruff sometime and it's a constant test of faith. I thank God for walking by my side each and every step of the way. Between me and you I've been real depressed although I try my hardest never to let them see me sweat but it's really starting to sink in that I might have to give them 15 more years because I don't see the law chang- ing anytime soon. I think of my life in 15 more years and they let me out. What the heck am I to do at age 59 with no income and no place to go. I mean sure I will still be living but what will I be doing at that age?*

I wrote Carl back, but I can't say I had any good answers for him. There aren't any. I talk to him when he calls and if my kids are around, I put one of them on because I know it makes him happy. But every time I think of his case, it makes me sad, angry, and ashamed that I live in a na- tion that would lock a man up for life rather than treat his drug addiction. My fondest hope is that when I update some future edition of this book, some legislative or electoral justice will have occurred and I can report Carl's release from prison.

* * *

After my reading at Eso Won, we all drove the few blocks over to the home of Reggie Dymally, where Chef Reggie laid out a fine meal of pasta and salad and warm bread. My wife Ann was with me, thrilled to finally meet the men who animated the pages of my book and my thoughts. They gave her great big hugs, as if they had known her for years. We drank red wine and talked late into the night. It felt like, well, family.

Bethesda, Maryland
September 2005

Acknowledgments

I spent months in inner-city Los Angeles researching this book, away from my own family, with people who welcomed me into their homes and lives and nourished me with food and friendship. When I would return home to my own comfortable surroundings, people would sometimes say to me, with some alarm: You go into South Central L.A.? Indeed I did, and it was a pleasure, an honor, and a privilege. The warmth I felt was overwhelming.

My deepest gratitude goes to the men who a quarter-century ago were the Boys of Crenshaw. To Carl Jones, Darryl and Derwin McNealy, Marvin McWhorter, Cordie Dillard, George Cook, Fernando Becker, Chris Brown, Nelson Whiting, Reggie Dymally, and Darryl Strawberry, and also to Coach Brooks Hurst: Thank you for your time, your generosity of spirit, and your trust. I hope that I have repaid it by telling your story with integrity and heart. My thanks, as well, to the extended Jones clan—Thedo, Werrlean, Tracy, Tahitha, and Joe.

I trace the evolution of this book to the fall of 2000, when my wife, Ann Gerhart, all but insisted that I leave a secure and very good job at *The Philadelphia Inquirer* to seek out the greater career challenges she knew I craved. About ten minutes later, the economy tanked. Not to worry, she assured, and as usual, she was right.

Kyle Crichton gave me a golden opportunity—story assignments at

The New York Times Magazine—and along the way became a mentor and friend. Adam Moss, Gerald Marzorati, and Katherine Bouton made the magazine a home for me by bringing me on as a contributing writer. Joel Lovell and Dean Robinson have been wise and valued story editors.

David Rosenthal at Simon & Schuster read my profile of Darryl Strawberry in *The New York Times Magazine* and saw it as a book—specifically, this book, meaning not a biography but instead a sprawling, searching story in which Darryl would be just one among many characters. Jeff Neuman helped shape the narrative and edited the manuscript, and was even smarter than when we teamed up a decade ago.

Heather Schroder at International Creative Management was a good reader, thinker, advocate, and everything else a writer would want an agent to be.

Kevin Merida and Ben Yagoda read parts of this book and offered invaluable guidance, as did Avery Rome, who as my editor for many years in Philadelphia made everything I wrote better.

Sally Jenkins and Nicole Bengiveno offered a haven to write in at a critical moment when progress and sanity seemed most elusive.

Sara, Sofia, and Bill hung in there as not just one, but both parents hurtled toward book deadlines. (Admit it, guys, it wasn't that bad, right—didn't we get dinner on the table at least *most* of the time?)

Finally, my thanks to my fabulous wife for urging me forward toward everything that has ever been worth doing.

A Note on Sources

This book was researched, primarily, through my interviews with the men who form the basis of the story—the members of the 1979 Crenshaw High baseball team and their coach, Brooks Hurst. Over the course of two years of research, I also conducted dozens of other interviews with people who helped give context to their lives: their family members; former teachers and administrators at Crenshaw High; baseball coaches and scouts; numerous longtime Angelenos who helped educate me about the life and history of their city. In nearly all cases, the interviews are attributed in the text.

I relied on numerous books and articles as well, particularly for the first two chapters of the book, which deal with the black migration to Los Angeles and the history of Jim Crow–like discrimination. Several books were particularly helpful in these early chapters. They were Kevin Starr's authoritative histories of California: *Americans and the California Dream* (New York: Oxford University Press, 1973), *Inventing the Dream* (1985), *Material Dreams* (1990), *Endangered Dreams* (1996), and *The Dream Endures* (1997).

Arnold Rampersad's 1979 biography of Jackie Robinson helped me understand not just Robinson but much about the black experience in Southern California. Mike Davis's *City of Quartz* (London: Verso, 1990) and his essay in the collection *Metropolis in the Making* (Berkeley: University of California Press, 2001) were enormously helpful. Walter Mosley's fiction, including *Devil in a Blue Dress* (New York: Simon & Schuster, 1990), enhanced my understanding of the whole inner-city L.A. experience.

OTHER SOURCES

Collins, Keith E. *Black Los Angeles: The Maturing of the Ghetto, 1940–1950*. Saratoga, Calif.: Century 21 Publishing.

Corwin, Miles. *And Still We Rise: The Trials and Triumphs of Twelve Gifted Inner-City High School Students*. New York: William Morrow, 2000.

Klapisch, Bob. *High and Tight: The Rise and Fall of Dwight Gooden and Darryl Strawberry*. New York: Villard, 1996.

McWilliams, Carey. *Southern California: An Island on the Land*. Salt Lake City: Gibbs Smith, 1946 and (republished in) 1973.

Medved, Michael, and David Wallechinsky. *What Really Happened to the Class of '65*. New York: Random House, 1976.

Robinson, Jackie, *I Never Had It Made*. New York: Putnam, 1972.

Strawberry, Charisse, and Darryl Strawberry. *Recovering Life*. Farmington, Pa.: Plough Publishing, 1999.

Strawberry, Darryl, with Art Rust Jr. *Darryl*. New York: Bantam, 1992.

Timberg, Scott, and Dana Gioia. *The Misread City: New Literary Los Angeles*. Los Angeles: Red Hen Press, 2003.

Vivian, Octavia B. *The Story of the Negro in Los Angeles County* (Compiled by the Federal Writers Project of the Works Progress Administration).

ARTICLES

Aubry, Erin J. "Legacy of the Eastside Boys." *Los Angeles Times Magazine*, July 20, 1997.

Bearden, Michelle. "Power Pastors Give, Get a Lot." *Tampa Tribune*, April 14, 2002.

Berkow, Ira. "Strawberry's Other Side." *New York Times*, July 19, 1987.

Broder, John M. "No Hard Time for Prison Budgets." *New York Times*, January 19, 2003.

Butterfield, Fox. "Political Gains by Prison Guards." *New York Times*, November 7, 1995.

Cloud, John. "A Get-Tough Policy That Failed." *Time*, February 1, 1999.

Crouse, Karen. "The Souring of Darryl Strawberry." *Orange County Register*, April 16, 1994.

Dodd, Mike. "Strawberry Savors Return to World Series." *USA Today*, October 14, 1996.

Greenhouse, Linda. "Justices Uphold Long Sentences in Repeat Cases." *New York Times*, March 6, 2003.

Howard, Johnette. "Strawberry's Latest Strikeout May Be Last." *Washington Post*, April 14, 1994.

Jares, Joe. "Next Pick: Strawberry." *Sports Illustrated*, April 7, 1980.

Kriegel, Mark. "Long Shot Is All Straw." (New York) *Daily News*, October 14, 1996.

Mahtesian, Charles. "The Uprising of the Prison Guards." *Governing Magazine*, August 1996.

Morain, Dan. "Davis Gets More Money from Prison Guards." *Los Angeles Times*, March 30, 2002.

Morain, Dan (and other *Los Angeles Times* staff writers). "The Price of Punishment." *Los Angeles Times*, October 16–19, 1994.

Moran, Malcom. "Strawberry Handles Pressure." *New York Times*, October 16, 1986.

Nack, William. "The Perils of Darryl." *Sports Illustrated*, April 23, 1984.

Pertman, Adam. "A Children's Crusade: Father of Slain Kidnap Victim Lobbies for Tougher Laws." *Boston Globe*, August 17, 1994.

Ross, Corey. "Strawberry's Bat Still Shows Pop." *Omaha World-Herald*, June 19, 1996.

Schlosser, Eric. "The Prison-Industrial Complex." *The Atlantic Monthly*, December 1998.

Sherer, Michael. "Brandy's Dandy." *Beverage Dynamics*, November/December, 2001.

Vecsey, George. "Picking Up the Strawberry Trail." *New York Times*, July 29, 1980.

Warren, Jennifer. "Friends Recall Polly's Abduction." *Los Angeles Times*, May 11, 1994.

Wiley, Ralph. "Doc and Darryl." *Sports Illustrated*, July 11, 1988.

Wood, Terry. "Granada Hills Enjoys a Perfect Finish." *Valley News*, June 8, 1979.

Index

About the Author

Michael Sokolove is a contributing writer for *The New York Times Magazine* and the author of *Hustle: The Myth, Life, and Lies of Pete Rose*. He lives in Bethesda, Maryland, with his wife and their three children.

Also from Michael Sokolove

Who was Pete Rose? The all-American kid ballplayer or the bloated ex-athlete and gambler? Should he be allowed into the Baseball Hall of Fame? With a new, updated introduction and revealing interviews with Rose's family, teammates, sportswriters, and police investigators, Michael Sokolove's *Hustle* delves into the mystery that is Pete Rose.

"Anyone interested in the true story should read Michael Sokolove's . . . book on Rose."
—Bob Ryan, *The Boston Globe*

"This is a book for all seasons, not just summer."
—*The New York Times Book Review*